Pre-Intermediate
Matters

GILLIE CUNNINGHAM
with JAN BELL
and ROGER GOWER

Pearson Education Limited
Edinburgh Gate, Harlow
Essex CM20 2JE, England
and Associated Companies throughout the world.

First published 1995
Fifth impression 2000

Set in Adobe ITC Garamond Light 10/12 pt
and Frutiger Light 8.5/10pt
Printed in Malaysia, GPS
ISBN 0 582 25338 1

Photocopying

Authors' Acknowledgements

We would like to thank the following people.
- Our close advisors for their constructive support, in particular: Marc
  Beeby, Gillie Cunningham, Olivia Date, Sara Humphreys.
- Those people who reported on and/or piloted the material, in
  particular: Jacqueline Donohoe, Rebecca Fong, Teresa Pego, Jacqui
  Robinson, Sarah Stratford, Liz Waters.
- Our publisher, Kate Goldrick; our Senior Developmental Editor, Sue
  Ullstein; our editor, Carol Hadwen; our designers, Marnie
  Searchwell, Amanda Easter and Jennifer Coles; as well as Pat Dutch
  (permissions editor), Susan Cooper (secretary) Alma Gray (audio
  producer), Lisa Bondesio and Cathy May (project managers), Donna
  Wright (production controller), Diane May (art editor) – all at
  Longman ELT.
- The staffs of Bell School , Old House, in particular, Maria Heron, and
  Bell School, Saffron Walden for their support and advice.

> We are grateful to Annie Roberts who wrote the tests for this
> Teacher's Book.

Illustrated by

1–11 Line Art, Kathy Baxendale, Mark Roberts, Sharon Scotland,
Kevin White, Celia Witchard.

Cover illustration by Zap Art.

Photo Acknowledgements

We are grateful to the following for permission to reproduce copyright
photographs:
Colorific!/Nick Barrington for page 143(left); Robert Harding Picture
Library for page 143(middle); Popperfoto Ltd for page 143(right).

Text Acknowledgements

We are grateful to the following for permission to reproduce copyright
material:
Dick James Music Ltd for full and gapped version of lyrics from 'Your
Song' written by Elton John and Bernie Taupin © 1969 Dick James
Music Ltd; MPL Communications Ltd for the lyrics from 'Baby it's cold
outside' written by Frank Loessner © 1948 renewed Frank Music Corp.

Contents

Contents chart (Students' Book)

Grammar	Vocabulary	Dictation and Pronunciation (See Workbook)
Question forms with the Present Simple, *be* and *have got* Question words Short answers	Countries, nationalities and languages	Dates and times Word stress
Present Continuous and Present Simple Adverbs of frequency	Buying clothes	Sound and spelling: /ə/ Clothes
Past Simple and Past Continuous	Personality types	Weak and contracted forms Giving personal information
Modals: obligation (*don't*) *have to*, *should(n't)*, *must(n't)*; possibility *can('t)*	At the doctor's	Sound and spelling: /iː/
The future: plans, decisions and arrangements (*will*, *going to* and the Present Continuous)	Transport	Pronunciation: /ðeə/ *they're, their, there*
Quantity expressions: *a, some, any, a few, a little, a lot, much, many*	Food and drink	Sound and spelling: /ɔː/ Contractions and weak forms
Present Perfect Simple or Past Simple? Time expressions: *just, ever, never, yet*	Feelings and opinions (*-ing* and *-ed* adjectives)	Questions and pronunciation
Verbs followed by *-ing* or *to*	Jobs	Sound and spelling: *o* An application form: names, dates, numbers and countries
Opinions: *will, won't, might, may* First Conditional	Rooms and furniture	Word stress Contracted forms
REVISION Question forms Obligation Mixed verb forms Quantity	REVISION Non-idiomatic phrasal verbs Idiomatic phrasal verbs	Sound and spelling: *c*

Grammar	Vocabulary	Dictation and Pronunciation (See Workbook)
Comparative and superlative adjectives *as ... as*	Hobbies	Spelling and the alphabet
Second Conditional	Crime	Grammar and pronunciation Sound and spelling: /v/ and /w/
Defining relative clauses: *who, which, that, where* Adjective word order *We use a ... for ...-ing*	Describing people Relationships	Rhyming words Vocabulary
Used to Question tags	Entertainment	Sound and spelling: *a*
Quantity words: *some-, any-, no-, every-* *too* and *very* *too much* and *too many*	Education	Vocabulary and word stress
The passive (Present and Past Simple)	News stories	The passive
The unfinished past: Present Perfect Continuous and Present Perfect Simple *For* and *since*	Having a party	Contrastive stress
Sentence patterns (1): verb + person + *to* + base form of the verb Sentence patterns (2): reported sentences *say* and *tell*	Doing things in the house *Do* or *make* ?	Sentence completion Sound and spelling: *u*
Verb patterns (1): *if, when, as soon as, unless* Verb patterns (2): verb and 2 objects (*Give it to him. Give him the present.*)	Sports	Rhythm and sentence stress
REVISION Mixed practice Second Conditional Making comparisons Question tags	REVISION Phrasal verbs Mixed words	Sound and spelling: *g*

Word list PAGE 133   Tapescripts PAGE 137

Introduction

Who is *Pre-Intermediate Matters* for?

Pre-Intermediate Matters is part of the Matters series for adult and young adult learners of English. It precedes *Intermediate Matters* and *Upper Intermediate Matters* and aims to meet the needs of students who have completed a beginner or elementary course or who are returning to English having studied it in the past.

The course contains twenty units and provides approximately 90-120 hours of classroom material. It can be used by students studying in Britain or in their own countries. The flexible structure of the course makes it suitable for students on intensive courses as well as those on part-time courses for an academic year.

Components

1 Students' Book and Class Cassettes

The Students' Book has twenty units, each providing approximately six hours of classroom work. The *Contents chart* at the beginning of the Students' Book (see also Teacher's Book, pages 4 and 5) gives a breakdown of the language areas covered in each unit. Note that Units 10 and 20 are Revision Units.

Each unit consists of the following sections:

USE YOUR ENGLISH, which encourages students to use the English they already know in everyday situations;

SKILLS, which develops Reading, Listening, Vocabulary and Writing skills;

GRAMMAR, which presents and practises areas of grammar and provides opportunities for students to use them in communicative situations;

VOCABULARY, which presents vocabulary related to a topic and provides activities for students to use it communicatively;

USE AND REVIEW, which revises the language of the previous unit, e.g., Unit 2 USE AND REVIEW revises Unit 1 etc. (note that in Unit 1 this section focuses on language taught at elementary level and on language learning experiences, and in Units 10 and 20 the section revises the USE YOUR ENGLISH and Writing sections of the previous nine units);

Language reference, which provides an easy-to-understand summary of the main grammar areas covered in the unit (note that in Units 10 and 20 there is no *Language reference* section; instead there is a *Learning review* section which focuses on learning skills).

Speaking skills and pronunciation work are integrated throughout the Students' Book. There is also extra listening practice in the USE YOUR ENGLISH and GRAMMAR sections.

Support material at the back of the Students' Book consists of a Word list of the most useful new words in each unit, a Pronunciation chart, an Irregular verbs list and Tapescripts of the recordings used in the Students' Book, if they are not already printed in the relevant unit.

The two Class Cassettes contain all the recordings used in the Students' Book.

2 Workbook and Workbook Cassette

The Workbook consolidates the language practised in the Students' Book. It can be used for homework, for further practice in class, or as material to be worked on in a self-access centre.

Each Workbook unit contains a GRAMMAR section and a VOCABULARY section, which revise the work done in the Students' Book; a READING or a LISTENING section; a DICTATION, which revises language areas in the Students' Book and practises sound-spelling relationships; and a WRITING section, which gives controlled practice of some important areas of written English, including linking expressions and letter formats.

There is a *Contents chart* at the front of the Workbook so that teachers and students can quickly locate what they want to practise. The Workbook is available with or without a key to the exercises.

The Workbook Cassette contains all the recorded material needed for the Listening and Dictation exercises in the Workbook. It allows students to listen to material in their own time, using their own cassette recorders.

3 Teacher's Book

Each unit of the Teacher's Book opens with a summary of the material covered in the Students' Book and Workbook. This opening section helps teachers to prepare their teaching and homework programme. It also shows the theme and topic of each unit and the main focus of each section. The Teacher's Book then goes on to provide support for each section in the following areas:

 - the Aims of the section

 - useful notes on the Language areas covered

 - useful methodological support for many of the exercises in the Students' Book

 - ideas for visual presentations on the board

 - the Tapescripts of any Listening material

 - an Answer Key

Extra material and ideas

At the end of the Teacher's Book there are photocopiable materials for further practice and these are signalled **P** in the relevant exercise.

There are also Tests for every five units of the Students' Book covering mainly grammar, vocabulary and the mechanics of writing.

Guiding principles

1 Use

A guiding principle of *Pre-Intermediate Matters* is 'use it or lose it'. We have assumed that students have learned quite a lot of language before they get to this level but are not very good at using it. The USE YOUR ENGLISH sections are intended to re-activate this language.

We believe that students should not only be presented with new areas of grammar and vocabulary and given controlled practice of it; they must also be given opportunities to use this language in a less controlled way in communicative activities. The *Use your grammar, Use your vocabulary* and USE AND REVIEW sections all give opportunities for

students to use the language that has been presented to them.

Learning how to use language in a restricted but not totally controlled environment is vital if students are to develop their full communicative potential in real-life situations. It will also help them retain their knowledge of the language.

2 Confidence-building

In our experience, pre-intermediate level students find it difficult to use with confidence the language they know. We believe that building up confidence, by giving students opportunities to use language in the classroom through tasks which they can succeed in, is a key part of teaching at this level. In practice, this usually means restricting tasks and giving students the tools they need to perform those tasks satisfactorily. The principle of developing confidence by providing support applies to all areas of the course.

GRAMMAR

In grammar presentations, for example, paradigms are given where possible to illustrate structural patterns. This is often done through a blue Grammar box for students to look at before they practise the language presented.

At the end of each unit there is a *Language reference* section which summarises the main grammar points of the unit and often provides timelines to support the concept behind verb forms.

LISTENING AND READING

To increase confidence at this level, we believe Listening and Reading texts are better adapted from authentic material rather than being fully authentic. Although texts need to be natural, they also need to be accessible and to provide comprehensible input. The tasks students are then expected to accomplish are restricted and vocabulary support is given where appropriate. Tapescripts have been provided in the Students' Book for additional support.

WRITING

Writing tasks too should be realistic and achievable for the level. Students should not be expected to write whole texts unless they want to, and then it should be for communicative reasons and without fear of being corrected. Students' communicative written work should only be corrected if they ask for it to be. In *Pre-*

Intermediate Matters the tasks in the Writing sections are both restricted and controlled. There are also different writing tasks, like dialogue writing and short poems, in other sections, which allow for more creativity.

SPEAKING

Speaking tasks should also not be too open or unrealistic. Obviously students should be encouraged to express themselves naturally in the course of a lesson if they can, but it is better if specific classroom activities to develop speaking skills are of the semi-controlled communicative type, linked to the areas of language to be practised. In *Pre-Intermediate Matters* speaking tasks are integrated with other tasks.

The overall message to students of *Pre-Intermediate Matters* is 'You can do it!'

3 Integration

In order to build up students' confidence at this level we believe it is useful to integrate skills work into many activities. So in *Pre-Intermediate Matters,* Listening and Vocabulary are integrated into the USE YOUR ENGLISH section and Pronunciation is integrated into the USE YOUR ENGLISH, GRAMMAR and VOCABULARY sections. Speaking is integrated into every section.

The principle behind this is 'a little and often', so that rather than giving students major tasks which focus exclusively on one skill area (which can be overwhelming at this level) they are given integrated tasks which contain small amounts of practice of a number of skills. This helps develop the skills in parallel and gives students confidence to work with them.

We also believe in the need for learner development activities, such as dictionary skills work and deducing meaning from context. In our view it is more profitable to integrate this kind of work throughout a course rather than do it only at the beginning. In *Pre-Intermediate Matters,* learner development activities are most often included in the SKILLS sections. There are also *Learning review* sections in Revision Units 10 and 20, which ask students to reflect on their experiences of learning English.

4 Review

It is necessary at pre-intermediate level constantly to activate previous knowledge. This is why each unit of *Pre-Intermediate Matters* begins with a USE YOUR ENGLISH section. It recycles functional language in everyday situations, activating grammar previously practised, and does not necessarily link to the main topic of the unit.

At any level it is all too easy for students to forget the language they have learned. At pre-intermediate level, we believe that not only should language be covertly recycled in subsequent units, in the USE YOUR ENGLISH section or in texts and practice activities, it should also be overtly revised. For this reason each unit contains a USE AND REVIEW section which gives students the opportunity to go back and revise both grammar and vocabulary through a 'fun' activity.

Teaching with *Pre-Intermediate Matters*

1 Unit organisation

As already stated, there are six sections in each unit. There are five sections of activities followed by the *Language reference*.

The sections can obviously be worked through in the order that they appear. Each unit begins with a USE YOUR ENGLISH section and ends with a USE AND REVIEW section. However, either of these sections could be taught at other stages. For example, you could begin with USE AND REVIEW and go on to USE YOUR ENGLISH in the same or a different lesson. The other three sections (SKILLS, GRAMMAR, VOCABULARY) can also be done in any order. For example, there is no reason why you should not begin with the GRAMMAR section.

Note that the GRAMMAR and SKILLS sections are longer than the others, and you may prefer to break them up. In fact, this may be necessary if your lessons are less than an hour. For example, the *Use your grammar* part of the GRAMMAR section might work well at the beginning of the next lesson, and the Writing part of the SKILLS section could also be done in the next lesson or for homework.

In summary, the units have been designed so that sections can either be worked through in the order that they appear or be switched around to meet the needs of your particular situation. Even parts of a section (such as *Use*

your grammar, Use your vocabulary and Writing)
could be left to another lesson.

2 The different sections

USE YOUR ENGLISH

The USE YOUR ENGLISH section is based around
an everyday topic or situation and aims to be
fairly light in terms of language input, to give
students a feeling of achievement that they can
use the English they already know.

The section has two main aims for students:

1 To revise and extend language (grammar,
   functions, vocabulary) already met at
   elementary level, usually including work on
   polite intonation and informal language. The
   language is often introduced through short,
   accessible listening extracts from everyday
   situations.
2 To use this language input in a
   communicative speaking and/or writing
   activity, often as pairwork.

Because of the confidence-building nature of the
opening section, it is obviously important not to
embark on detailed grammatical explanations or
to correct students too much when they are
speaking or writing. However, you may want to
make notes and feed back later on gaps and
errors, or just use the activity as a diagnostic
exercise to identify where students need more
revision.

SKILLS

The aim of this section is to develop confidence
in reading and listening to English and to
practise vocabulary and writing skills. The
Vocabulary and Writing activities are usually
linked in some way to the text.

READING and LISTENING

Each section begins with either a reading or a
listening text (usually in alternate units). The
topics are sometimes, but not always, linked to
the USE YOUR ENGLISH topic. Where there is a
link, it is often a loose link because we feel that
at this level it is difficult to sustain students'
interest in one topic throughout a unit.

The reading texts have been shortened and
simplified from their original sources in order
not to destroy students' confidence. For the same
reasons, the listening texts have been scripted,
although great effort has been made to ensure
they retain the features of natural connected

speech. Note that there is also a reading or
listening text in every unit in the Workbook.

Before students read or listen to a text there is
often an activity which gets them to relate to the
text personally and provides an opportunity for
them to speak in a less controlled way. Where
there has not been space for this in the Students'
Book, there is often a suggestion in the
Teacher's Book. By doing this, and by focusing
on some of the key vocabulary which comes up
in the text we hope to make the process of
listening or reading easier for students.

With Listening you might like to provide even
more support by playing the cassette as often as
you feel is necessary (without becoming
boring!), pausing the cassette at regular intervals,
and accepting answers to comprehension
questions in the first language if necessary. The
tasks themselves are graded from easier, more
global activities to more detailed tasks. This
means that if students find the text difficult, you
can stop after the first exercise and provide
more support.

The tapescripts are at the back of the Students'
Book as well as in the Teacher's Book. As a final
activity students can often benefit from reading
the tapescript at the same time as they listen to
the cassette. If students have not had much
listening practice this could, of course, also be
done as a first stage. Some teachers might find it
helpful to make use of the tapescript in the
class, for example by blanking key words out for
a gap-fill exercise, or jumbling the text for
students to put in order while they listen.

It should not be forgotten that the teacher can
be an important resource as listening input, not
only in general classroom language like
instructions. For example, some teachers might
like to read texts aloud or act out dialogues to
give students extra listening practice. The teacher
is usually less threatening than a cassette of
disembodied voices!

VOCABULARY

We believe that vocabulary is very important and
motivating at this level and we have therefore
given it a high priority in *Pre-Intermediate
Matters*. The main aim of this sub-section of
SKILLS is to focus on developing vocabulary
skills. It is therefore different from the
VOCABULARY section on the fifth page of each
unit, which introduces and practises specific
lexical areas.

The main aims of this section are to help
students :

1 To deduce the meaning of words in context.
To do this, we suggest that you encourage
students to make intelligent guesses and
defend these guesses in pairs or groups. It is
important to remember that you are teaching
a skill, not testing it, and that the process is
as important as the answer. For this reason, if
necessary, students could give their guesses in
their own language.

2 To learn to use monolingual dictionaries
efficiently and confidently. There are extracts
from monolingual dictionaries and practice
exercises in *Pre-Intermediate Matters*. If
possible, recommend a specific dictionary that
all students can work from, or take in class
sets. We also feel that it is also very useful at
this level for students to use a good bilingual
dictionary.

When new words come up in the lesson write
them on the board and mark the stressed
syllable. Make sure you give students plenty of
practice in the correct pronunciation. Although
we use the symbol (') which is usually found in
dictionaries, you may prefer to use a different
method. Show students the phonemic chart on
page 132 of the Students' Book and, if possible,
put one up in your classroom. Refer to it
regularly so that students gain confidence in
being able to work out the pronunciation of new
words for themselves. Show students how to
find the pronunciation and stressed syllables of
words in the dictionary.

It is useful for you to keep a record of new
vocabulary as it comes up, perhaps on one side
of the board, so that students can easily see it
and copy it down. Some teachers like to transfer
this new vocabulary to paper or card at the end
of each lesson and keep it in a box or bag in
the classroom. This is useful for future recycling
activities and games, as well as testing.

We also recommend that you encourage
students to keep vocabulary notebooks. It is
useful if you can help with ways of organising
them. For example, by putting the words into
topic groups, by using spidergrams (see pages
58 and 83 of the Students' Book), by adding in
definitions, translations, drawings and so on.
Give students time to update their vocabulary
records regularly, and perhaps collect them in to
look at from time to time, so that students realise
how important they are. Students should be
encouraged to add any words/expressions at any

time, from their own reading and listening,
grouping them, if relevant, under a topic area.

At the end the book, there is a Word list, which
includes the most useful words from each unit.
You may like to go over this with students at the
end of each unit, or give it for homework,
perhaps getting students to add a translation and
an example sentence. It is useful for students to
look at the lists regularly and try to use the
words. They could also add them to their
personal vocabulary notebooks and try to group
them according to topic.

WRITING

For the reasons given earlier, the writing tasks in
this section and the GRAMMAR section are fairly
controlled and achievable. The kind of activities
we ask students to do are mainly on linguistic
and organisational aspects of writing at sentence
and paragraph level (in particular, linking words,
reference words and punctuation), although
there are also some simple creative poems and
dialogues.

We suggest that the marking of students' work
should focus on what they have been asked to
practise and that they should be encouraged to
monitor their own work, or each other's work,
before handing it in.

If you ask students to do more creative and
'fun' writing tasks, we suggest that correction
symbols are agreed on with the class (for
example: G = a grammar mistake; WO = word
order; V = vocabulary; VF = verb form and so
on). This helps you to indicate the type of error
and encourages the student to correct his/her
own work.

If you ask students do any creative writing, it is
very motivating if this can be displayed on the
classroom walls or circulated to the rest of the
class.

There is more writing in the Workbook -
including dictations focusing on sound-spelling
relationships, which you may want to integrate
into your lessons. You will also find Workbook
exercises on the layout of formal and informal
letters.

GRAMMAR

Students have many different learning styles and
we believe that teachers should cater for these
by varying the presentation and practice of
grammar.

The Students' Book has a variety of approaches
and the Teacher's Book gives suggestions for
alternatives. Sometimes the rules for a
grammatical area are given to students and

sometimes we ask students to work out the rules from examples or a text. A lot of students benefit from visual highlighting, so we have included visual support in the form of blue paradigm boxes and timelines. The Teacher's Book gives lots of ideas for highlighting form on the board and provides easy-to-copy visuals, signalled ✎ Making the form and rules clear to students allows them to concentrate on when and how the language is used.

It is important to encourage students to refer to and use the *Language reference* at the end of each unit. For example, they could try a practice activity, guess the grammatical rules and then check their guesses.

Many students also find it useful to keep their own personal grammar notes based on these pages, perhaps comparing and contrasting the use and form with their own language.

After each grammar presentation there is oral and written controlled practice, including relevant pronunciation work. Obviously, students at this level benefit from repeating examples and gaining confidence in manipulating the form, including the pronunciation. Extra ideas are given in the Teacher's Book and there are further exercises in the Workbook, either for homework, or for extra practice in the classroom.

It is useful for students to work on controlled practice activities in pairs, or to compare their answers. However, in the *Use your grammar* section we also included oral communicative activities. We recommend that teachers monitor these activities and give feedback at the end of the lesson, both on accuracy of form, including pronunciation, and on the communicative success of the activity. Note that the grammar is revised in the USE AND REVIEW section of the following unit, and in Revision Units 10 and 20.

VOCABULARY

In contrast to the Vocabulary section in SKILLS, the main VOCABULARY section focuses on a particular topic. However, much of what we said in the notes under SKILLS (see page 11), applies here. For example, although students are very motivated when it comes to learning vocabulary, they need to be encouraged to take responsibility for recording the vocabulary they learn, including the stress and pronunciation. It is also important to get them to fix this vocabulary in their memory by revising it and using it.

You should monitor the *Use your vocabulary*

activities and correct students' pronunciation, as well as encourage them to use it if they try to avoid it. Note that some of this vocabulary is recycled at the end of each following unit in the USE AND REVIEW section.

You may want to refer students to the unit by unit Word list at the end of the Students' Book (page 133), give further practice and test them, using games and activities.

USE AND REVIEW

This section revises areas of grammar and vocabulary which came up in the previous unit. In general, they are interactive activities, which can then lead on to further revision if necessary.

3 Speaking

Speaking is integrated throughout *Pre-Intermediate Matters,* and the most desirable outcome of the course would be for students to be able to express themselves with confidence and reasonable accuracy. Great care has been given to provide lots of opportunities for speaking practice.

Here are ten classroom management hints when organising speaking activities in the classroom at this level.

1 Try to predict the language the students will use during the activity, the time the activity is likely to take and the problems students might have. Adapt the task accordingly and provide support if necessary.

2 Give students clear instructions to make sure they know what they are doing before the activity begins and check they have understood your instructions. It helps to work out your instructions in advance.

3 Give a time limit so that students know when to stop talking and to prevent them from wasting time. Time limits can always be extended if necessary.

4 Decide how you want to divide students up during pair or group work. For example, will you put all the strong students together or will you mix them with the weak students to provide support? Will you let students work with their preferred partners – since students often get more out of an activity if they do? Or will you want students to work with a different partner each lesson? There are many different tasks for pairing students at random. For example, deal students a card with a word on it and they have to find their partner (so *salt* would find

pepper and *hot* would find *cold* etc.).

5 If you are planning a jigsaw activity involving grouping and regrouping, plan the grouping before the lesson. Thinking it through on the spot can sometimes lead to confusion.

6 Decide what you will do if you have an uneven number of students. Don't forget it can be very motivating if the teacher joins in sometimes.

7 Make sure students are sitting in the best way for the activity. For example, in an information gap activity using the book, make sure they can't see each other's picture. This arrangement is known as 'tango seating'.

8 Decide on your correction policy beforehand and make it clear to students. So in a fluency-based lesson in the USE YOUR ENGLISH section it is probably better not to give on-the-spot correction but take notes and give feedback later. In lessons where the language is tightly controlled it is often best to correct during the activity.

9 When monitoring the activity, watch the pace even if you have given a time limit. Don't let the activity drag on and remember to leave time for feedback. On the other hand, make sure students have enough time to do the task you have set.

10 Give students encouragement on how well they are communicating and get them to acknowledge they are making progress.

Abbreviations

L   Language
T   Teacher
SS   Students
SB   Students' Book
WB   Workbook
TB   Teacher's Book
GW   Group work
PW   Pair work
OHT Overhead projector transparency

Do you remember me?

Students' Book

General theme: memory.
Unit topic: finding out information about people.

USE YOUR ENGLISH: starting a conversation.
SKILLS: reading and speaking (memory); vocabulary (dictionary work; parts of speech - noun, verb, adjective, adverb); writing (punctuation).
GRAMMAR: questions and answers with the Present Simple, *be* and *have got;* question words.
VOCABULARY: countries, nationalities and languages.
USE AND REVIEW: pronouns and possessive adjectives.

Workbook

GRAMMAR: questions and answers; subject and object questions; questions with *whose*.
VOCABULARY: nationalities and countries.
SKILLS: listening (first meetings); writing (punctuation).
DICTATION/PRONUNCIATION: dates and times; word stress.

USE YOUR ENGLISH
Starting a conversation

• The intention is to see how much of the language SS can use. Don't analyse the grammar in detail, revision of this comes later in the unit.

• There is a difference in register between *Do you want to dance?* and *Would you like to dance? Do you ...?* seems quite direct for a first meeting and could be considered less formal. However, it's not impolite.

• Accepting an invitation. It's possible to reply with *I'd love to.* or *I'd love to dance*. However, it isn't possible to say **I'd love.*

• It's common to refuse with *I'd love to, but ...*

• Pronunciation. When accepting an invitation a high fall is often used with *I'd love to.* This signals enthusiasm.

Students' Book (page 6)

Exercise 1a) It's a good rule of thumb to go from the known to the unknown so begin by asking SS about their own situations. Ask *Where can you go to meet people?* Possibilities could include *a disco, night club, a rave, night school, a sports club, a bar/pub, a library.* Ask SS to look at the pictures and give suggestions. If any of their ideas are possible in English write them on the board. This gives an added incentive to listen to the cassette.

Exercise 1b) [1.1]
1 A: Excuse me, is this seat free?
  B: No, I'm sorry. Someone's sitting here.
2 A: Haven't I met you somewhere before?
  B: No, I'm afraid not.
3 A: Would you like to dance?
  B: Yes, I'd love to.

Picture a) 3, Picture b) 1, Picture c) 2

Exercise 1c) If any SS are confident enough, get them to work at the board. This becomes an efficient checking technique as you only have to ask the others if they agree or disagree and correct accordingly.

Exercise 1e)
1 No, I'm sorry ...
  No, I'm afraid not.
2 Yes, I'd love to.
3 Would you like to (dance)?

Exercise 2a) You could ask two or three pairs to work at the board.

2 f)   3 d)   4 e)   5 a)   6 c)

Exercise 3 Information about Britain
Although customs are changing, it's not yet common to kiss a person when you meet for the first time. When male and female friends meet and female and female friends meet, it's becoming more common to kiss on the cheek. However, it's not yet common for male friends to kiss when they meet. People often shake hands in more formal situations, e.g., in a business setting. In less formal situations people tend to nod the head slightly, smile and say *Hello* or *Nice/Pleased to meet you.* It's generally considered rude to ask *How much do you earn?* Some adults would be offended if you asked *How old are you?* It could be misconstrued if you ask *Are you married?* !

Extra material and ideas

1 If you can, find a clip from a video (feature film if possible) where two people are meeting for the first time. Turn the sound down and ask SS *What's happening? What are they saying?*

2 An alternative lead in to Exercise 1 would be to write these sentences on the board with the words jumbled up.

| seat me excuse is free this ? | to would you dance like ? | met I you haven't before somewhere ? |

Ask SS to make three questions with the words in the boxes. Then ask SS *Where are you when you ask these questions?* Finally get SS to practise these using a rising intonation which will sound polite.

SKILLS

- Reading and speaking: prediction, reading for gist and detail.
- Vocabulary: using a monolingual dictionary; identifying parts of speech.
- Writing: punctuation.

Reading and speaking

L These words may be unfamiliar:
'memory, to re'member, to be'lieve, mind,
'crossword puzzle, goal, to for'get, board,
to 'rub something 'out.

Students' Book (page 7)

Exercise 1 Preteach vocabulary (see L) and write the words on the left hand side of the board with visual clues wherever possible. Leave the words on the board while the SS read so they can refer to them. Join in the discussion by telling SS about your memory, things you forget etc.

Exercise 2a)
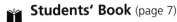
Paragraph A 2   Paragraph B 3   Paragraph C 1

Exercise 2b) SS may think the list in paragraph three is the answer. Highlight that the question asks for the best way not ways.

He says you should connect new information with what you know already.

Exercise 2c) You could let SS work in pairs and make different pairs responsible for giving feedback on one T/F statement. They should work on the one you set them before doing others. Although the SS may fully understand why the statement is T or F, don't expect them to have sufficient language to explain why. However, they could give the number of the line where the information can be found or give feedback, in the L1 (in a monolingual situation).

1 F   2 F   3 T   4 T   5 F

Extra material and ideas

You could begin the lesson by playing some memory games. SS will need to understand the words *remember* and *memory*.

1 Kim's game Put about 12 objects on a tray (e.g. a hat, a cup, a tomato, a pen, a toy cat, a spoon, a pair of scissors, a shoe, a flower, a watch etc.) for SS to look at for 20-30 seconds. Then remove it or cover it with a cloth. Ask SS to write down as many of the objects as they can remember. If they don't know the word, they can draw it. SS then exchange lists with a partner. Put the tray back or uncover it. They then check their partners' papers.

2 The magic number 7 plus and minus 2 George Miller, a Harvard University Professor, had a theory that most people can remember between 5 and 9 items on a list, the average being 7. You can test the theory with the SS by doing this activity.

Read the following list to SS once only.

> dog pen breakfast flower computer umbrella homework

They shouldn't write while you give the list. When you have finished they write as many as they can remember. Write the words up and SS check. You can expect between 5 and 7 to be recalled accurately.
Then read the following list once only.

> table man station coffee sky bicycle teacher bank hat children bed cinema

They write the ones they can recall. Then you write the words on the board for the SS to check. You can expect them to recall the same number of words or even fewer. When you present a larger number some people seem to give up and therefore recall fewer. If any of the words are unfamiliar to the SS replace them with words you think they'll know. However, don't choose words which can be related in any way as this helps the memory.

3 Association Remembering names can be helped by association. When SS give their names to each other you could try the following:
- **Name and adjective** SS give an adjective that begins with the first letter of their name. The T can provide adjectives if necessary.
This is Angelo, he's angry.
This is Coletta, she's cold. etc.
It will help if they mime the adjective for the class as this adds a visual clue.
- **Name and profession** This is similar but ask the SS to visualise the person and the job, as the S gives the name.
I'm Benita, I'm a banker.
I'm Daniel, I'm a doctor. etc.

Vocabulary

L The parts of speech are: nouns, verbs, adjectives and adverbs.

Students' Book (page 7)

Exercise 1 Make sure the SS have some idea of what the parts of speech are. You could write **noun, verb, adjective** and **adverb** on one side of the board and **table big run quickly** on the other side. Point to noun and tell SS that this is the name of something. Then ask them which of the words on the other side of the board is a noun. Tell them a verb is a doing word/an action, then ask SS to find the verb. Then tell them an adjective tells us more about the noun and ask them to find the adjective. Finally tell them an adverb tells us more about the verb and ask them to find the adverb. Then go to the exercise in the SB.

1 elderly = adjective,   often = adverb,   lose = verb, memory = noun

Exercise 2a) adj= adjective

Exercise 2b) If your SS found Exercise 1 very

difficult or they aren't analytically minded, just explain they can find this information in a dictionary and don't do b).

Exercise 3 Try not to make this exercise too heavy. (See *Extra material and ideas* below). If you don't want to do the whole chart at once, limit the introduction of symbols to the ones needed for the exercise.

consonants /d/, /l/
vowels /e/, /ə/, /ɪ/

Point out the dictionary has this information which means they can always find out how to pronounce a word.

Exercise 3b) Point out how the dictionary shows where the stress is and highlight its importance. Highlight how important word stress is. If you use a different system from the dictionary, make this clear for the SS.

The first syllable. The ' symbol tells you which syllable is stressed.

Extra material and ideas

1 How do you remember new words in English? Discuss the various ways of recording new vocabulary with your SS and put the following on the board for them: 1 word trees 2 pictures
3 translations 4 example sentences and synonyms.

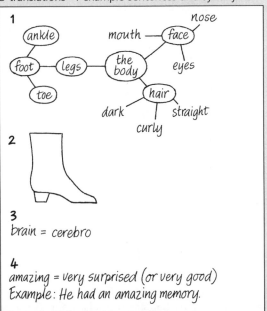

1
ankle — foot — legs — the body — mouth — face — nose
foot — toe
the body — eyes
hair — dark — curly — straight

2

3
brain = cerebro

4
amazing = very surprised (or very good)
Example: He had an amazing memory.

---

2 To practise phonemics, hand out simple words for SS to write in phonemics. They then pass their phonemes to a partner, who transcribes the word back into normal script. Or SS could write the phonemic transcriptions on the board and others write the normal script underneath. Although SS may not need to write phonemics, it's often by producing them that we learn to recognise them, which is a very useful skill in language learning.

Writing

Capital letters, question marks, full stops and commas.

Students' Book (page 8)

Write the words and the symbols on the board before doing the exercise, e.g., comma = , . Then let SS read the grammar box. Meanwhile write these on the board:

is mary at school today
i bought some bread butter and tea
ian is from russia

Check SS have understood the explanations by asking them to punctuate the sentences on the board. Have copies of the punctuated paragraphs around the room so the SS can go and check their own work when they have finished. Point out that the use of the comma in English is often idiosyncratic, since it is used as the written equivalent of a pause when speaking (there could be a comma after *country* in 2.)

1 Dominic O'Brien, the memory man, lives near Cambridge. When he is not trying to remember things, he spends his time playing the piano, gardening and cycling. He eats a lot of bananas, apples and oranges, which help his brain.
2 My family live in Switzerland and we speak German. From Monday to Friday I work in an office in the centre of Geneva. I live in the country with my parents, two sisters, my dog and rabbit.

Extra material and ideas

1 WB page 6, Writing, Exercise 10.
2 You could divide SS into two groups. Each group has one paragraph to punctuate. They then give their papers to a person from the opposite group who checks to see if they think it's correct and then checks it against a correct version you have placed somewhere in the room.
3 S to S Dictations page 126, 1.1. PW. Give each S a different part of the paragraph to dictate to his/her partner. SS can check their own work because between them they have the complete paragraph. Remind SS they have to include the punctuation words in the dictation. It's a good idea to write the following on the board and encourage SS to use them:
How do you spell _____?
Can you repeat that please?
What does _____ mean?
You could do short dictation activities at the beginning or end of the following few lessons. The dictations could include revision of something the class had done the previous day.

GRAMMAR

Revision of the verb *to be, have/has got,* Present Simple, question words and short answers.

Questions and answers

L SS will probably have a working knowledge of all the verb forms in the unit but they will not be accurate in producing the form, and the meaning may need highlighting.

• Question forms are likely to cause problems because of difficulties with word order: *to be* = subject and verb inversion; *has/have got* = inversion of subject and *has/have*; Present Simple = auxiliary *do/does* + subject + base form.

• Pronunciation: weak forms in questions; *does* /dəz/ *do you* /djʊ/ *have* /həv/ *has* /həz/; Strong forms in short answers: *does* /dʌz/ *do* /duː/ *have* /hæv/ *has* /hæz/. Rising intonation is common with inverted questions. Falling intonation is common with questions beginning with question words, *What/Why* etc.

📖 Students' Book (page 8)

Exercise 1a) Elicit some of SS' questions and write them on the board as a focus point when SS are listening so they are not only checking against their suggestions but the suggestions of other SS. Correct any mistakes and highlight important features using boxes, colour, underlining etc. (see L).

🔑
1 Does he like spaghetti?
2 Do you come here often?
3 Are you Spanish?
4 Have you got the time?

📼 Exercise 1b) [1.3]
1 A: Does he like spaghetti?
   B: Yes, he does.
2 A: Do you come here often?
   B: No, I don't.
3 A: Are you Spanish?
   B: No, I'm not. I'm Mexican.
4 A: Have you got the time?
   B: Yes, I have. It's nearly three o'clock.

Exercise 2a) Before SS begin, ask them to read the grammar boxes on page 8. Ask some confident SS to work at the board. Ask other SS if they agree with what is written and correct where necessary. Focus attention on intonation used with inverted questions (see L).

🔑
1 Are we going?
2 Do they drink a lot of coffee?
3 Are they over there?
4 Is this seat free?
5 Have they got the tickets?
6 Has she got a blue car?
7 Am I ready?
8 Can he swim?
9 Do you know her?

Exercise 2b)

1 Do they drink a lot of coffee?
  Do you know her?
2 Are we going?
  Are they over there?
  Is this seat free?

Have they got the tickets?
Has she got a blue car?
Am I ready?
Can he swim?

Exercise 2c)
2 Yes, they do.
3 Yes, they are.
4 Yes, it is.
5 Yes, they have.
6 No, she hasn't.
7 No, I'm not.
8 No, he can't.
9 No, I don't.

After checking both the questions and short answers SS could practise these in pairs.

Question words

Exercise a) Do an example before beginning the exercise. Write on the board:
When ...? Where ...?
1) *24 Blinker Street.*
2) *At 7 am.*
Ask SS which question word goes with which answer.

🔑 1 what 2 when 3 why 4 who 5 where 6 whose
7 how 8 how many 9 which

Exercise b) Focus attention on intonation (see L). Examples:

🔑
1 What do you do?
2 When do you go to bed?
3 Why are you learning English?
4 Who is your favourite singer?
5 Where do you come from?
6 Whose is that car?
7 How do you get to work?
8 How many brothers have you got?
9 Which one do you want?

Exercise c) You could get SS to compare the intonation patterns of: *Where does he live? Does he live in London?*

Exercise d) SS may appreciate the opportunity to move around. In which case this could be a mingle activity. SS are either A or B. For the first few minutes As ask the questions as they mingle around and Bs answer. Then they change roles.

Using your grammar

Exercise 1a) Monitor SS as they prepare questions for the interview. If you find problems common to many SS, stop the class and do some quick remedial work at the board. Ask them to look at the questions they have done so far and correct if necessary. Check the questions before playing the cassette.

🔑
1 How old are you?
2 Are you married?
3 Are you engaged?
4 Have you got a family?
5 Have you got any children?

6 What is your nationality?/What nationality are you?
7 Where do you live?
8 What are you doing at the moment?
9 What music do you like?
10 What clothes do you like?

Exercise 1b) Make sure SS realise that they shouldn't write complete sentences, only facts.

[1.5]

INTERVIEWER: Hi, I hope it's OK if I record what you're saying on my tape-recorder, then I can write it up for the magazine later

ACTOR: That's fine. What do you want to ask me?

I: Well, all the newspapers are talking about your new film *Family Trouble*. Tell us something about it.

A: Well, it's a comedy about a man who gets married too young and then has to make a choice between his family and his career.

I: And ... um are you married?

A: No, I'm too young to be married , don't you think?

I: How old are you? 22?

A: Yes, that's right.

I: But you do have a girlfriend at the moment.

A: Her name is Isabelle. She plays my fiancée in *Family Trouble*. We have no plans to get married.

I: Do you live with her?

A: No, I live with my family in Los Angeles - my mum and dad and three sisters.

I: You are American, then?

A: Yes, I was born here in Britain but I am an American citizen.

I: What kind of music do you like to?

A: Oh, all kinds. Classical, rock, rap. Jazz is my favourite, I guess.

I: I notice you always seem to wear black clothes. Is this your favourite colour?

A: No, not really. I mean I wear blue jeans and white T-shirts a lot. I don't like bright colours like red and yellow - that's true.

I: And, very important - your next film. Is it true that you're in a horror movie?

A: Yeah, *A Night with Frankenstein* ... it's about this guy...

1 22   2 No   3 No   4 Yes, my parents and 3 sisters
5 No   6 American   7 Los Angeles   8 Making a film called *A night with Frankenstein*   9 All kinds
10 Blue jeans, white T-shirts

Extra material and ideas

1 WB pages 4 and 5, Grammar, Exercises 1-30

2 WB page 5, Grammar, Exercise 5 is on questions with *whose* and subject and object questions. If your SS are struggling with basic forms, then leave subject and object questions for some future lesson. Note that with subject questions it's better not to tell SS that we never use the auxiliary, as it is frequently used with the negative question e.g., *Who doesn't take sugar in tea?* It's better to say the auxiliary is *usually* not used in subject questions.

3 Questions and answers Write on the board:
 ME and MY SISTER (or any relation)
Explain they have 4 minutes to get as much information about you and your relation but you will only answer questions which are grammatically correct. You may want to write some cues on the board to help SS:
How old? Where/live? Married? Work? Free time? Favourite drink/clothes/colour? etc.
If you use this activity at the end of the lesson, or during some future lesson, it will help you ascertain how much remedial work is still necessary. You could

---

use it at the beginning of GRAMMAR for diagnosis purposes.
The same idea could be used in group work. SS have 2 minutes to find out about a S in the group and his/her relative. When the time is up, they move to another member of the group and so on. Ask if they discovered anything interesting about other SS or their relatives.

4 To begin the *Question words* exercise, write on the board; hwo (x2) hnwe hewre ywh ahwt iwhhc. SS compete to be the first to unscramble the letters to form question words. who, how, when, where, why, what, which.

VOCABULARY
Countries and nationalities

L • The main difficulties will be L1 interference and remembering which word refers to the country and which to the nationality.

• Pronunciation: there may be a lot of L1 interference with the pronunciation of countries and nationalities. There's sometimes a stress shift between the country and the nationality e.g., 'Italy → I'talian, 'China → Chi'nese, Ja'pan → Japa'nese, Tai'wan → Taiwa'nese 'Portugal → Portu'guese, 'Canada → Ca'nadian 'Norway → Nor'wegian, 'Egypt → Egyp'tian.

Students' Book (page 10)

Exercise 1 You could begin by asking what countries SS would like to live in. This will give you some idea of what they already know.

a) 1 Belgiúm   2 Poland   3 Spain   4 Scotland
5 Portugal   6 Turkey   7 The Netherlands   8 Japan

b) 1 China   2 Saudi Arabia   3 Greece   4 The United States of America   5 Italy   6 England/Britain

c) a France   b Germany   c England/Britain   d Australia
e Russia

d) 1 Spanish   2 Austrian   3 English   4 Indian   5 American
6 Russian   7 Brazilian   8 French

e) 1 Portuguese   2 English   3 Spanish   4 Japanese   5 Dutch
6 French   7 German   8 Arabic

Exercise 2a)
COUNTRIES: 'Belgium, 'Poland, Spain, 'Scotland, 'Portugal, 'Turkey, the 'Netherlands, Ja'pan, 'China, 'Saudi 'Arabia, Greece, the U'nited 'States of A'merica, 'Italy, France, 'Germany, 'Russia, Au'stralia, Bri'tain

NATIONALITIES: 'Spanish, 'Austrian, 'English, 'Indian, A'merican, 'Russian, Bra'zilian, French, 'Belgian, 'Polish etc.

LANGUAGES: Portu'guese, 'English, 'Spanish, Japa'nese, Dutch, French, 'German, 'Arabic, Greek, I'talian, Chi'nese etc.

Exercise 2b) Highlight the possibility of a stress change (see L).

Exercise 2c) Focus on the /ə/ sound. There is a listening exercise in the WB page 10 you could use to help SS with recognition and pronunciation of the sound /ə/.

Using your vocabulary

Note that SS are revising question forms as well as vocabulary.

Exercise a) Give examples, e.g., *Where is Edinburgh? What language do people speak in Scotland? Is London in Scotland? What nationality was Robbie Burns?*

Exercise b) As SS ask the questions, make a note of any mistakes with vocabulary and question forms. This could form the basis of a correct the mistakes exercise in the following lesson. Note the pronunciation mistakes in phonemics so you don't forget how the mistake was pronounced.

Extra material and ideas

1 WB page 5, Vocabulary and pronunciation, Exercises 6 and 7.

2 Wordsearch page 126, 1.2. Give SS photocopies of the puzzle and ask them to find 10 words for countries and nationalities/languages, across, down or diagonally up or down.

3 Countries and continents page 127, 1.3. Hand out the map of the world (country boundaries are included). Ask SS to name as many continents and countries as they can.

USE AND REVIEW

- Pronouns and possessive adjectives.
- Raising awareness of language learning.
- Possessive adjectives, unlike genitives (John's) don't have apostrophes and they all end in *-s* except *mine*.

Students' Book (page 11)

Exercise 1 Highlight the difference between the first person subject and object pronouns and the possessive adjectives, *I, me, my, mine*. Then write the following sentences on the board. Ask SS to complete them.

That book is _____.

There's _____ book.

Give the book to _____.

_____ want that book.

Then write the following chart on the board. Ask SS to complete it:

I	me	my	mine
you			
he			
she			
it			
we			
they			

Leave this on the board for the SS to refer to. The crossword could be done individually, in pairs or by copying it on to the board it could be done with the whole class.

1

ACROSS	DOWN
1 your	3 Susy's
2 us	4 mine
5 theirs	5 them
7 She	6 he
8 hers	8 him
9 me	

Exercise 2a) This asks SS to think about their learning. Try to get information as to why they did or didn't enjoy previous experiences. However, they may not have the necessary language or the confidence to explain.

Exercise 2b) SS may say it is all important for them especially if they are doing an exam, but you can still ascertain which areas they like studying. You could also try to find out what they are interested in, e.g., music, sport, cinema, computers etc. so you can include these in future lessons.

Extra material and ideas

Your song page 128, 1.4. *Your Song* by Elton John is on the Class Cassette at the end of Unit 1. It is simple and provides good practice for pronouns. There is a gapped and complete version. You might want to pre-teach some vocabulary items: *feeling, to hide, 'sculptor, 'potions, 'travelling, gift, to 'put 'down (= to write), roof, moss, verses, cross, to 'turn 'on, to for'get.*

Spend spend spend!

> ## Students' Book
>
> **General theme:** shopping.
> **Unit topic:** clothes, shops.
>
> **USE YOUR ENGLISH:** public places, requests and answers.
> **SKILLS:** listening and speaking (shopping and souvenirs); vocabulary (guessing meaning from context); writing (spelling rules: -s and -ing endings for verbs).
> **GRAMMAR:** talking about the present; Present Continuous or Present Simple?; adverbs of frequency.
> **VOCABULARY:** buying clothes.
> **USE AND REVIEW:** biographies.
>
> ## Workbook
>
> **GRAMMAR:** Present Continuous or Present Simple?; short answers; question forms; adverbs of frequency.
> **VOCABULARY:** clothes, shops.
> **SKILLS:** reading (a model's clothes); writing (spelling -ing, -s).
> **DICTATION/PRONUNCIATION:** Sound and spelling /ə/; clothes.

USE YOUR ENGLISH
Public places

A► Polite requests and vocabulary for shopping.

L • The politeness of a request is signalled by facial expression as well as structure, intonation and the use of *please*.

• Pronunciation. Weak forms *have* /həv/, *can* /kən/, *could* /kəd/; consonant vowel links: *Can͜ I …?, May͜ I …?* ; assimilation:*Could you* /kədjʊ/; intonation: the pitch starts quite high, and rises on the main stress.

• *May* cannot be used with *you*. We cannot say *May you open the door?* It's most commonly used with *I* or *we*.

Students' Book (page 12)

Exercise 1a) Establish the meaning of *request* by demonstration or translation. Quickly draw these objects on the board and number them.

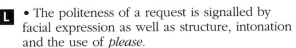

Using the names of the five places in the book, ask *What can I get/buy at a _____ ?* If the students don't know the names of the things you have drawn, they can say the letter labels of the pictures. Read out the requests, remembering to use appropriate facial expression, stress and intonation.

🔑 1 b)   2 c)   3 a)   4 d)

Exercise 1b) You may want to prepare SS for c) before you play the cassette. Ask SS to listen to the intonation. Draw these three pitch starts on the board.

Using one of the requests, model a low, middle and a high pitch start. Ask *Which is more polite?* Explain that the first two aren't impolite, but that the higher the start, the more polite it sounds.

📼 [2.1]

1 A: Have you got a small brown loaf, please?
   B: I'm terribly sorry, but we've only got white bread left.
   A: That's all right. I'll have a white loaf then.
   B: That's thirty-eight p.

2 A: How about a cup of coffee?
   B: Can I have white, no sugar, please?
   A: Of course. I'll just call the waiter. Excuse me... could you get us two white coffees, no sugar?
   C: Yes, of course. Two white coffees, no sugar.

3 A: Could I have ten first class stamps?
   B: Yes, here you are.
   A: And could I send this letter airmail?

4 A: May I change these traveller's cheques?
   B: Certainly. How would you like your money?
   A: In tens, please.
   B: Would you sign here, please?

Exercise 1c) Using the drawings from b) quickly ask SS to say the requests using low, middle and high pitch starts.

🔑 1, 3 and 4 The questions started higher, which makes them sound more polite.

Exercise 1d) Highlight the use of *May* (see L) as well.

Exercise 1e) Demonstrate the meaning of *Here you are. Saeed needs a pen.* (Hand a pen to Saeed.) *Here you are, Saeed.* Again SS practise pronunciation and intonation.

🔑 1 I'm terribly sorry ...
2 Yes, of course.
3 Yes, here you ...
4 Certainly.

21

Exercise 2a) Ask a few SS to read aloud the items on the list. Then do the exercise with the whole class. Highlight the difference between *a library* and *a bookshop*.

🔑 bookshop: Stephen King's new novel;
butcher's: 6 chicken legs; chemist's: cough mixture;
jeweller's: watch strap; greengrocer's: grapes

Exercise 2b) GW. You could write the shop names on the board. Each group is responsible for naming items for one shop only. One person from each group is the runner who writes items for their shop on the board. Encourage runners to write things up as soon as the group thinks of them, not to wait until the end to avoid crowding at the board. Check and allow SS time to write new words in their vocabulary records. See also *Extra material and ideas* 2 below.

🔑 bookshop: dictionaries, reference books, comics, novels, maps etc.
butcher's: chicken, lamb, pork, mince, beef, chops etc.
chemist's: shampoo, have photos developed, make-up, prescriptions, soap, aspirins etc.
jeweller's: watches, rings, necklaces, earrings, bracelets etc.
greengrocer's: apples, oranges, bananas, cabbages, onions, flowers, herbs etc.

Exercise 3 PW. Writing may be a welcome change of pace here. Pairs could exchange their conversations for checking and correcting before roleplaying them. Make a note of any errors, particularly with the structures used for requests. Write errors on the board and ask SS to correct the mistakes. See *Extra material and ideas* below for an alternative approach.

Extra material and ideas

1 WB page 9, Vocabulary, Exercise 6.

 2 Shop bingo page 129, 2.1. Give each S one of the bingo boards. Read out the names of items of shopping: toothpaste, football, suitcase, hairbrush, T-shirt, chair, glove, banana, lipstick, orange, coat, cake, toothbrush, swimming costume, comb, newspaper, bar of chocolate, hat, pencil, necklace, potato, car, apple, skis, socks, watch, chicken, telephone. If SS have that picture, they cover it up. When they have a line in any direction they shout *BINGO!* SS have to say the words when you check their cards. This should generate a lot of vocabulary. Pay attention to pronunciation.

3 GW. For Exercise 2b). Make individual word cards for the items available in each shop. Divide SS into 4 equal groups and put a group of words on a table in different parts of the room. One S from each group goes to a table and collects all the items that belong to his/her shop. They reform the group and discuss whether the words collected by individual SS belong to their shop. Then do feedback with the whole class. Allow SS time to note new vocabulary.

4 What's our shop? You can't buy X at our shop. GW. Each group chooses which shop they want. The group then makes a list of things you can't buy in its shop. In turn each group starts to read out its list. The other groups compete to be the first to guess what the shop is, but each group is

only allowed two guesses. Point out that their lists must help the others to eliminate certain shops, so they can't just list items relating to one shop.

 5 Exploring cultural differences and similarities regarding shops and shopping, page 130, 2.2. In a multilingual class you could use the questionnaire to interview each other. In a monolingual class, you could compare Britain with their country. Here are some facts about Britain:
- Opening/closing times: 9 or 9.30 am till 5 or 5.30 pm. Food shops sometimes open earlier.
- Sunday trading laws: some shops now open on Sundays.
- You can buy stamps in lots of shops now.
- Most people go to supermarkets and shop once a week.
- There are fewer specialist shops, e.g. butcher's, greengrocer's, etc.

6 PW. To complement Exercise 3, give SS a piece of paper and ask them to write their conversations. Set a time limit to encourage them to finish at the same time. SS put their papers on the wall or leave them on their desks. They walk around reading and correcting other conversations until you say *Stop!* They then practise saying the conversation nearest to them. Join in when SS are walking around, helping them with corrections and pronunciation. If it's a small class, SS could roleplay all the conversations. If it's a larger class, while you're monitoring, identify a few of the better conversations. Make sure the SS who practise the conversation are not the ones who wrote it. Conversations could be recorded on audio cassette or video for fun and/or correction work.

 7 Two halves of a crossword page 131, 2.3 GW and PW. Group A get the words for DOWN. Group B get the words for ACROSS. Each group has to make up clues for the words in their crossword. They then give their clues to the other group for them to complete their crossword. Finally they check each other's work.

SKILLS

A▸ • The reading passage introduces the theme and predicts content of the listening passage.
• Listening: for detail; revision and extension of vocabulary from USE YOUR ENGLISH.
• Speaking: vocabulary of shopping and asking questions (revising question forms from Unit 1).
• Pronunciation: recognising and producing weak forms using /ə/.
• Vocabulary: guessing meaning from context.
• Writing: spelling of -s + -ing endings.

Listening and speaking

L▸ • Most of the vocabulary should be familiar but you could check: *souve'nirs, warm, re'lax, de'cide*. DON'T preteach items selected for the vocabulary exercise: *save, 'earrings, 'necklaces, e'normous, co'llect*.
• Although it's important for SS to recognise weak forms for comprehension, production in

their spoken language is arguably less important. However, if your SS are keen to have a more native speaker-like pronunciation, the use of weak forms will help them to achieve better models of sentence stress and rhythm. There are about 40 weak forms in British English, most of them are function rather than content words.

📖 Students' Book (page 13)

Exercise 1 Ask SS what's in the photographs and what they think the article is about. Check the vocabulary.

🔑 1 umbrellas, china, tea 2 cottages, phone boxes, taxis

Exercise 2

📻 [2.2]

INTERVIEWER: What do you spend your money on when you have it, Tanya?

TANYA: Oh, holidays. I don't spend anything for months. I just save and save, then, when I have enough, I go off for a week or two or longer - somewhere I've never been before or just somewhere warm to relax. And when I'm not on holiday I spend money on books.

I: Travel books?

T: Yes, well all kinds of books, really.

I: David, what about you?

DAVID: Well, I'm a student, as you know, so I haven't got much money, unfortunately. What I have goes on music - CDs, mostly.

I: What kind of music?

D: Everything - classical, jazz, pop. I also like going to pop concerts, but they cost a lot, so, you know 'cos the tickets are so expensive. I also love clothes so if there's a sale I buy casual things - jeans, shirts, jackets - that sort of thing.

🔑 1 holidays, books, music, clothes
2 holidays, books
3 clothes, music
4 open question

Exercise 3 Although SS have to recognise detailed information, the exercise asks them to say what kind of thing, not the individual items. However, better SS may want to show that they can remember these items.

📻 [2.3]

INTERVIEWER: What kind of souvenirs do you bring back from your travels, Tanya?

TANYA: I usually buy something for the house or garden - you know, wooden parrots, big plant pots for my garden, small rugs. But it can be very difficult to bring souvenirs back. I once sat on a fifteen hour flight with an enormous plant pot on my knee - so big I couldn't see over the top. Then at the airport I put it down for a second and somebody fell over it and broke it!

I: Oh no!

T: I wasn't very pleased! I also love jewellery so - for example, in South America I bought lots of earrings and big necklaces.

I: And you, David?

DAVID: Well, music of course and also whatever's cheap - clothes in the States are cheap, for example. I collect T-shirts.

I: Really? How many have you got?

D: Oh, I've got about forty of them from all over the world. But you have to be careful - I remember one holiday I spent a long time deciding which T-shirt to buy and when I got back home they had exactly the same one in our local shop!

🔑 1 things for the house, things for the garden, jewellery
2 music, clothes

3 Tanya carried a big plant pot all the way back and then someone broke it at the airport. David spent ages choosing a T shirt and then found a similar one at a shop near his home.

Exercise 4 Begin by telling SS about your best/worst/ most expensive purchase. The same exercise can be done using best/worst/most expensive present they have had.

Exercise 5 Remind SS that they met the schwa /ə/ symbol in Unit 1. Ask them to name a country with that sound in it, e.g., /əˈmerɪkə/ *America*. Introduce the idea of weak and strong words. Write *I want to leave* on the board. Point to the word *to*, ask SS to pronounce it. In isolation you can expect /tuː/. Tell them to listen to the pronunciation when you say the sentence and elicit /tə/. *To* can have a weak or strong pronunciation. Copy the strong and weak men on the board to reinforce the point.

Write the /tuː/ under *strong* and /tə/ under *weak*. Tell them about 40 words can have a strong or weak pronunciation, but usually they have a **weak** pronunciation. If you think that it would help, repeat the sentence *I want to leave*, and ask which is the main stress, and mark it. Then by tapping a pen, or clicking your fingers, show that English rhythm is not equal stress on words, but a pattern of main stressed v. secondary unstressed syllables, the most important stressed syllable often being near the end of a sentence. Be careful not to blind SS with terminology. We feel it is acceptable to talk about big and small stresses at this level to help comprehension. When SS identify the pronunciation of the weak forms, add them to the weak and strong arms on the board using phonemics. This helps the gently, gently approach to recognising the phonemic script if it's unfamiliar.

Vocabulary

📖 Students' Book (page 13)

In monolingual classes SS could guess the meaning of the words in L1. It's the process which is important, and the idea that SS can sometimes guess the meaning of words. Get SS to compare their ideas with others. Then let them check in a dictionary. You may need to use leading questions to encourage them to think about helpful strategies. For example, *Show me your ears*. Ask *What's this on my hand (ring)*. *An earring is jewellery, so what do think an earring is?*

🔑 1 to keep money for later use 2 jewellery for ears
3 very big 4 to bring together

1 Write the names of various countries on the board. As revision of Unit 1, elicit these by giving the first letter only. Tell SS they are going on an imaginary world shopping trip. They must think of all the things that each country is famous for. Write their suggestions on the board.

2 If you have anything you have bought in another country you could take it in. By asking questions SS have to find out as much information as they can using *Where from ...? When ...? How much ...? Why ...?*

Writing: spelling rules

L It often helps SS to remember rules when they know how many they have to remember. This seems to be a linking device for the memory, so tell them they need to remember 2 rules for *-ing* spelling and 3 rules for third person *-s* spelling. For this to work, you need to jog their memories in the following few lessons. Include them in a warmer/revision activity. Ask *How many rules are there for X?* Repeat this question in subsequent exercises to aid memory.

Students' Book (page 14)

As the book uses the terms Present Continuous/Simple here and in GRAMMAR, make sure SS know them. Elicit or supply the question *How do you spell X?* Ask SS to read the rules silently. Tell them to close their books and spell the words which illustrate the rules (*taking, hitting, doing, pushing, marrying*). You can ask why, if you think SS can explain. If not, take the correct spelling as an indication that they either know or understand.

This would be a good opportunity to tell your SS how you are going to deal with spelling mistakes in their homework. If you have decided not to supply the correct spelling, then show them on the board what symbol you will use,

e.g. Sam's wri(tt)ing a letter.
SP

⚷ 1 sitting; writing 2 making; coming 3 goes; flies 4 carries; watches

1 WB page 10, Writing, Exercises 9 and 10.
2 You could begin this whole section with a S to S dictation. Give each S a sentence to dictate to their partner. Include words which test the spelling rules. Tell SS they are not allowed to spell words for their partner. Tell them to put their names on the paper, and then collect them. After SS have done the correction exercise in the book, ask them if they think they made any spelling mistakes in the dictation. Hand the dictated sentences back, ask SS to make any corrections they want to, and then give their paper to their partner who checks and corrects

from the original. The aim is to have no mistakes. Alternatively you could dictate 2 or 3 sentences to the whole class. This will take less time, but won't involve the valuable feedback SS get concerning their pronunciation as they dictate to their partner.
3 Introduce and practise other examples of classroom language. USE YOUR ENGLISH in this unit has practised requests. If possible put the following on card and display them on the wall.
How do you spell X/this word?
What does X/this word mean?
Can/Could you repeat that, please?
I'm sorry, I don't understand.
You will need constantly to encourage and refer SS to them before you can expect them to be used fluently and appropriately in the classroom.

GRAMMAR

A • To revise and compare the form and use of the Present Simple and the Present Continuous.
• Basic adverbs of frequency.
• Further practise of the spelling rules from SKILLS: Writing.
• To preview clothing vocabulary for the following section.

Talking about the present

L • These verb forms will not be new for SS but they will probably be unsure of when to use one as opposed to the other and will overuse the one they have practised most or learnt most recently. Third person *-s* is usually a memory problem. You could draw this on the board and point to it every time the third person *-s* is omitted!

With the continuous form, model and highlight the use of contracted forms, and the weak form of *are* as in *What are you doing?* /wɒtəjʊduːɪŋ/.

Students' Book (pages 14-15)

Exercise 1a) Introduce *fancy dress*. Write *Present Simple/Present Continuous* on the board. Ask SS to look at the photographs and find examples of the verb forms. Write an example of each and highlight the forms and pronunciation features. Use visual effects where possible, colours, boxes, underlining to aid memory.

⚷ Present Simple: I don't usually wear clothes like these. I always casual clothes like these.
Present Continuous: I'm taking the dog for a walk. I'm going to a fancy dress party.

Exercise 1b
1 Present Simple
2 Present Continuous

Exercise 1c
1 I usually wear; I'm wearing
2 He doesn't usually wear; he's wearing

Exercise 2a) You could combine this with Exercise 2b). SS identify what the people are wearing. As you get feedback ask *Does X usually wear ...? So why is he/she wearing Y now?*

1 Peter is wearing a suit and tie.
2 Joy is wearing leggings, trainers and a jumper.
3 Alison is wearing a long black dress and a pointed hat.
4 Mary is wearing jeans, a sweatshirt and boots.

Exercise 2b)
1 No. he's wearing them because it's the first day of a new job.
2 No, she's wearing them because she wants to be comfortable when she's taking the dog out.
3 No. She's going to a fancy dress party.
4 Yes.

Exercise 3 Remind SS of the spelling rules. Jog their memories by asking how many rules there are for Present Simple third person and Present Continuous -*ing* form. Then get examples.

1 walks; is going 2 is putting 3 does Josh live; is staying 4 snows; is raining 5 are you doing; am cleaning

Adverbs of frequency

L Word order can be problematic with frequency adverbs. Show the different possibilities, but suggest SS play safe by following the rules in the grammar box.

Students' Book (page 15)

Introduce '*nervous*. Give SS an example of something you might do when you're nervous, such as twiddling your hair or biting your nails. Ask SS what they know about Princess Diana: *What is she wearing in the picture? What is she doing?* Read the text and SS could follow in the book. Ask a few check questions about the passage. Write **Adverbs of frequency** on the board, then write **always**. Elicit other adverbs of frequency if possible. Then draw a cline on the board (see *Language reference*, page 17). As SS give examples from the text, ask where the adverb should go on the cline. Put the adverbs on the cline where SS suggest. Get them to check in the *Language reference* and make any necessary changes to the cline on the board. Perhaps tell them about your nervous habits or those of your friends. The idea is to keep it light-hearted.

Using your grammar

Students working at the board is a good way of checking exercises like these.

The driver's pushing the bus.
The boys are fishing in the drain.
The policemen are singing and playing the guitar.
The children are playing tennis on the zebra crossing.

You could end this section by asking SS to tell you 2 things about the Present Simple; 2 things about the Present Continuous; 2 things about adverbs of frequency. This kind of mini review often helps the memory.

Extra material and ideas

1 WB pages 7 and 8, Grammar, Exercises 1–4.
2 To practise the Present Continuous and clothing vocabulary. SS form two lines facing each other. They are asked to look carefully at all the people in the opposite line. One line then turns around, with their backs to the other SS. You then ask them questions about the SS behind them. Include questions about hair colour, colour of eyes etc. as well as questions to elicit *He/She's wearing X.* This is then repeated with the other line of SS.

VOCABULARY
Buying clothes

L These adjectives may be new: *plain, striped, checked, 'patterned.* The final sounds in these words may cause problems.

Students' Book (page 16)

Exercise a)
See *Extra material and ideas* for an alternative approach.
'jumper, jeans, dress, 'jacket, shirt, skirt, belt, socks, 'underpants, gloves, 'waistcoat, 'slippers, tights, 'dressing 'gown, 'T-shirt, bra, 'cardigan, vest, scarf, 'overcoat, 'nightdress, vest, 'trousers, py'jamas

Exercise b) *'Try 'on, 'changing rooms, in the sale, size, 'sold 'out* will probably be unfamiliar. You could check the meaning before SS listen but don't present the words in the same order as they appear in the text. However, you could try to elicit them from the cassette and then check the meaning.

[2.5]
CUSTOMER: OK, so I'll take the skirt, the dress, these jeans and that jacket. Oh, wait a minute, is this jumper in the sale?
ASSISTANT: I think so. Yes, it is.
C: Could I *try one on*, in *red*.
A: What *size* are you?
C: Twelve.
A: The *changing* rooms are *over there*.
A: Does it *fit*?
C: No, it's a bit big. *Do you have it in* a ten?
A: No, I'm sorry, we've *sold out*.

Exercise d) Check to see if SS are using techniques which will help them learn the words. Give them reflection time to aid memory.

Using your vocabulary

Exercise 2 Join in this activity. After SS have fedback to the class or group, ask them to guess what's on your list. They could also guess what you would never wear.

Extra material and ideas

1 WB page 9, Vocabulary, Exercise 5; Reading, Exercises 7 and 8. Page 10, Dictation, Exercise 12.

2 To establish what vocabulary SS know, begin by having three teams. When you point to a part of your body, the team thinks of things you could wear on that part of the body. When you say 'Go' one member writes the team's list on the board, while the rest of the team work on the next part of the body you have pointed to. Check what they have written on the board before they add the next list. You could award points.

USE AND REVIEW

• Question words and question forms.
• Countries and nationalities.

Students' Book (page 17)

Exercise 1a) Set a time limit so SS finish at the same time. You may have SS who object to role playing the opposite sex if you don't have an even split, male/female. In which case ask SS to change the passage accordingly. This has the added bonus of SS changing pronouns and possessive adjectives to fit the change of sex.

1 How old are you? Where do you live? How many children have you got? What do you play? Where are you working at the moment? Which composer do you love?
2 What do you do? Who are you engaged to? What does he do? What nationality are you? What (three) pets have you got? What do you like doing in your spare time?

Exercise 2

1 a) Turkey b) China
2 a) Brazilian b) Austrian
3 a) Dutch b) French c) Portuguese
4 Australia
5 France

The family unit

Students' Book

General theme: the family.
Unit topic: family relationships.

USE YOUR ENGLISH: talking about families.
SKILLS: reading and speaking (family relationships); vocabulary (adjective endings; *-al, -ive, -ent, -y, -ous, -ic, -ly*); writing (linking words
- *and, so, because, but*).
GRAMMAR: Past Simple and Past Continuous; questions and answers.
VOCABULARY: personality types.
USE AND REVIEW: shopping roleplay; find the difference between two pictures.

Workbook

GRAMMAR: Present Simple, Past Simple, Past Continuous; prepositions of time.
VOCABULARY: family relationships.
SKILLS: listening (families); writing (linking words).
DICTATION/PRONUNCIATION: weak and contracted forms; giving personal information.

USE YOUR ENGLISH
Talking about families

L
• The names of basic family members should be familiar but remind SS of *'cousin, niece, 'nephew, aunt, uncle*. These may be new: *'brother/'sister-in-law, 'stepmother/father/brother/sister*. Note the stress patterns of these compound nouns.

• The intensifier *quite* can be used with gradable adjectives: *quite good = fairly good* but not *very good*. *Quite* can also be used with non-gradable adjectives: *quite amazing = absolutely amazing*. At this level we recommend highlighting *quite* only with gradable adjectives.

Students' Book (page 18)

Exercise 1a) As a lead-in ask SS *Have you been to a wedding? When was the last one? Was it a good wedding? Was it a relative's or a friend's wedding? How many people were there? Did you buy a present?* etc. See also *Extra material and ideas* for an alternative approach. Then ask them to look at the photograph of Lucy's wedding and speculate. Encourage SS to agree or disagree with each other, giving reasons.

Exercise 1b) Preteach *He/She looks nice* or *He/She seems nice*. Also introduce *quite* + gradable adjective (see L) compared with *very* + gradable adjective and *about* + age.

Exercise 2a) Preteach/check *di'vorced, 'separated, en'gaged*.

[3.1]
LUCY: So this is me standing between my parents, just after my wedding. (All right, yeah.) Mum and Dad are divorced, actually, but they still get on well. My Mum got married again last year and I did invite Philip - my stepfather - but he decided not to come. Then next to Mum there's my sister, Sarah - she's holding her new baby, Claudia, (oh, that's nice) and next to Dad is my brother-in-law, Ken. He's standing behind Ben - Ben's three. Behind them there's my brother Max. He's wearing that hat because he's an actor and likes to look different. (Oh, right.) My older brother Tom couldn't come because he's working in Brazil at the moment - he's an engineer. He's engaged and they're getting married at Christmas. Um... anyway, on Max's right are Granny and Grandad - they're in their eighties now (They look great.) - and they adore Max - he's definitely the favourite. Nana - Mum's Mum - is on the other side. Then at the back are my uncle, my aunts and cousins. Mum's sister Auntie Gill, with Uncle Rob - he's Australian, actually and their twins, Harry and Sam - they're 25. (They look alike, don't they?) Yeah. Aunt Pat is my Dad's sister. She's just separated from her husband, which I'm glad about, because I can't stand him, so he didn't come. Anyway, so that's all my relations.

🔑 Mum and Dad are her parents. Sarah is her sister, Ken is her brother-in-law, Ben is her nephew and Claudia is her niece. Max is her brother, Granny and Grandad are her grandparents (her father's parents) and Nana is also her grandmother (her mother's mother). Auntie Gill and Uncle Rob are her aunt and uncle (her mother's sister and brother-in-law) and Harry and Sam are her cousins. Aunt Pat is her aunt.

Exercise 2b)
1 parents 2 Philip 3 Brazil, engineer 4 Tom 5 Uncle Rob
6 Harry and Sam (the twins)

Exercise 3 Give SS two minutes to ask questions about your family. Note any mistakes in their question forms. You could correct the mistakes as they are made. It can be argued that if correction comes immediately, it is more memorable. However, you could list the mistakes on the board and highlight them all just before SS ask each other questions about their families and draw each other's family trees. Some SS enjoy the opportunity to be artistic when drawing the family trees, so take in coloured pens. You could also draw your own family tree for SS. If possible display the trees on the classroom walls and add a photo of the S to the relevant place on their family trees.

Extra material and ideas

1 WB page 12, Vocabulary, Exercise 6.
2 In advance of the lesson ask SS to bring in photos of their families, particularly any wedding photos. And/Or you take in photos of weddings you have attended. Use these as a lead-in to the unit.

SKILLS

• Speaking: a fluency exercise when SS express their opinions of people in their families.
• Reading: predicting content and reading for detail.
• Pronunciation: the sound /ɪ/.
• Vocabulary: word formation, common endings of adjectives.
• Writing: linking words to encourage SS to move away from using very short sentences, particularly when writing.

Speaking and reading

• Exercise 1 deals with the meaning of *to take after* and *to get on with*. You could also pre-teach these words from the text: *'barmaid, 'posters, to fight*. Write them on the board so SS can recognise their written form in the text.
• Many nationalities have problems with the production of /iː/. It is often replaced by the longer /i/ sound. If your SS have problems, try getting them to push their tongues hard against the palate, then relax the tongue while keeping it in contact with the sides of the palate. You will need to include gestures to help SS understand.
• We believe that at this level SS' reading ability will improve by reading! So the majority of texts presented to them should not be too difficult. If SS have a sense of success when they read a text, it will probably encourage them to read more. If they only meet with texts which are very demanding, there is every possibility that they will become demotivated and consequently avoid reading.

Students' Book (page 19)

Exercise 1 Ask SS *What do these people do?* Start writing names of famous models on the board, but don't begin with the super models. Once SS recognise the link and name the job, ask them to name other super models. Make sure Kate Moss's name is on the board. Then divide the board and write: *Good things about being a model/Bad things about being a model.* SS think of points to list in each column and as they think of things, they write them on the board. Then ask SS to look at the photos of Nick and Kate Moss and answer questions in the SB.

Exercise 2 Address these questions to the whole class but don't give SS the answers until they've done Exercise 3a).

1 Kate is interested in clothes but Nick isn't.
2 Somebody from a model agency saw her at JFK airport in New York and said, 'Do you want to come down to the model agency?'
3 Yes, it is. Women earn a lot of money but men don't.

Exercise 3b) You may want to exploit the text

further after the T/F statements, although, in answering the T/F exercise the SS will probably volunteer extra information. Don't pre-teach *'friendly, 'funny, 'different, 'normal, fan'tastic* and *am'bitious* which are focused on in VOCABULARY, page 20.

 1 T 2 F 3 F 4 T 5 F 6 T 7 T

Exercise 4 Don't include this if your SS don't have problems in recognising and producing the sounds /ɪ/ and /iː/. Note that the adjectives in Vocabulary include the sound /ɪ/ in final and penultimate positions such as *-ic, -ly* or *-y*.

Extra material and ideas

1 WB page 9, Reading is about a model's personal wardrobe.
2 Take in pictures of models on the catwalk. Write the following statements on the board. *It's interesting to read about models and their lives. Women models should earn more money than men models.* Ask SS to agree or disagree with them.
3 The grammar focus of the unit is past forms, so you could ask SS to find the past forms of these verbs in the text: *come, go, stay, say, hit, know, throw, have, can* as a preview activity for GRAMMAR. It should allow you to assess how much the SS know.
4 You could begin a class sound and spelling record system to display on the wall. Have minimal pair characters such as JIM and JEAN on cards. Hand out word cards such as *live, leave, ship, sheep* etc. for SS to decide whether the word belongs to JIM or JEAN. Tell SS that JIM likes swimming but JEAN likes skiing. Then ask them questions and they have to find answers for JIM and JEAN. The answers have to include /ɪ/ or /iː/. *What food do they like? What colours do they like? What jobs do they have? What country do they live in? What cars do they drive?* etc. In both cases the word cards should be displayed under JIM or JEAN. As new words arise in future lessons ask SS to keep adding them to the lists.

Vocabulary: adjectives

• Because *-ly* is also a common ending for adverbs you might want to highlight this for SS.

Students' Book (page 20)

 1 'friendly 2 a'ttractive 3 'funny 4 'different 5 'normal 6 fan'tastic 7 am'bitious

Extra material and ideas

1 SS brainstorm other adjectives with the same endings as those in the exercise.
2 Write the following on the board for further practice. SS have to complete the sentences. If you think they need more help, give the first letter of each word.
A book you can't stop reading is an _____ book. (interesting)

The last page in a book is the _____ page. (*final*)
Hair with lots of curls is _____. (*curly*)
A person who never does any work is _____. (*lazy*)
Food which is really good to eat is _____. (*delicious*) etc.

3 Check to see if SS are keeping good vocabulary records, and try to give them time, to record any new vocabulary from that day's lesson. You could keep the left hand side of the board sectioned off specifically for new vocabulary.

Writing: linking words

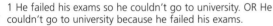

• It's unlikely to be a problem at this level, but SS can get confused between *because* and *because of*. If SS do include the preposition: *I can't come because of I'm working*, underline the verb <u>I'm working</u> and cross out the preposition. Tell SS *of* can only come before a noun or pronoun and not a verb phrase.

• If SS are aware of the structure *So am I* etc., they may be confused to see *so* used as a linking word. Show SS that *so* and *because* are doing similar jobs in a sentence. It's useful to clarify the sequence of reason and result. *I didn't have any money so I went to the bank. I went to the bank because I didn't have any money.* Ask SS to say which was first: going to the bank or no money? If we put the reason first we use *so*. If we put the result first we use *because*.

Students' Book (page 20)

1 He failed his exams so he couldn't go to university. OR He couldn't go to university because he failed his exams.
2 Last year I went to France and Turkey.
3 I saw the car coming towards me but I couldn't stop.
4 I left the beach early because I was very hot. OR I was very hot so I left the beach early.

Extra material and ideas

1 WB page 13, Writing, Exercise 9.
2 Give each group a selection of cards or pieces of paper face down. On each card is written one of the linking words *and, so, but, because*. Make sure each group has a selection, e.g., 3 x *but* cards, 4 x *so* cards, 2 x *and* cards and 3 x *because* cards. Read out a part of a sentence or write it on the board. The group turns over one card and SS have to complete the sentence using the linking word. The winner is the first to complete the sentence with perfect grammar and the correct use of the linking word. To encourage SS to form longer sentences, award 1 point for each word in the winning sentence. Continue supplying incomplete sentences until all the cards have been turned over. Tell SS that they can complete the sentence by putting something before or after the part you give them.
I left work early. I was ill so .... OR .... because I was ill.

Cues
... she went home ...
... she went to bed ...
... Sally phoned Harry ...
... Sam hit Peter ...
... they went to see a film ... etc.

GRAMMAR

 • The Past Simple and the Past Continuous interrupted.
• Question forms.

Past Simple

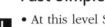 • At this level SS will be aware of Past Simple forms, though they make mistakes with irregular verbs, negatives and question forms **I writed a letter. *I no write to my parents. *Did you went? *Where you went?*
• The pronunciation of *-ed* endings may be a problem. The main issue is usually overuse of the /ɪd/ ending (which they usually pronounce /ed/. Don't spend a lot of time differentiating between /d/ and /t/ which in connected speech is frequently indistinguishable anyway. Concentrate on eliminating the incorrect use of /ɪd/. You could do this by highlighting familiar verbs which do use the /ɪd/ ending, then emphasise that the others do not.

Students' Book (page 20)

Before focusing on the Past Simple, you could begin by asking SS to describe what's happening. This will review the Present Continuous and introduce the vocabulary they need. Note the phrasal verbs *'get 'up, 'wash 'up* and the collocation of *have a 'shower, make 'breakfast, take the dog for a walk*. Point out you can also say *have breakfast*. All the verbs, except one, are irregular. Ask SS to identify the regular verb.

Exercise a)
f) c) b) d) e) g) a

Exercise b)
Liz got up. She had a shower. She made some coffee and toast. She ate her breakfast. She read the paper. She washed up. She took the dog for a walk.

Exercise c)
Draw SS' attention to the Irregular verbs list on page 132.

walked began did decided drank fell sold sat left taught wrote sang felt put went heard played woke

Questions and answers

Exercise a)
If you write examples on the board, draw attention to the changes by using boxes/lines, using colour etc. The changes can be compared with those which occur in the Present Simple.

1 Did Liz have a bath? No, she didn't. She had a shower.
2 Did she wash her clothes? No, she didn't. She washed up.
3 Did she have a cup of tea for her breakfast? No, she didn't. She had coffee.
4 Did Liz watch the television? No, she didn't. She listened to the radio.

Extra material and ideas

1 WB page 11, Grammar, Exercise 1.

2 Verb Bingo page 132, 3.1. Give each S a photocopy of a bingo card. Read the base forms out one by one: teach, come, bring, go, get, fly, ring, take, sell, pay, tell, think, fall, catch, buy, begin, have, stand, become, eat, drive, leave, drink, meet, write, spend, say, hit, wake, be, send, give, swim, find, see, read, lose, break, sit, put, sleep, hear. If a S has the past form he/she ticks it. The winner is the first to get a completed card.

3 Ask SS to think of two or three important dates in their lives. Put them into groups and divide the board into however many groups there are. One person from the group writes all the dates on a piece of paper then puts them on the board (to practise saying dates). You then randomly circle one date per group. The person who put that date forward tells their group what happened. You could get someone else in the group to report back quickly to the whole class.

4 GW. Give each group the base form of between 6 and 10 different verbs on cards. SS have to make up a story using as many of the verbs as they can within a time limit. The verbs must be in the past form. They pass their story to another group which converts the verbs back to the base form. This group then shouts out which verbs they think the first group were given.

5 Picture stories page 133, 3.2. GW. Give each group a set of random pictures which they have to work into a story. When they've written their stories, they cut up the pictures in their set and give them to another group. They then tell that group their story and the listening group has to put the pictures in the correct order. Groups could write the stories for homework.

Past Continuous

• The Past Continuous may be new to SS. The form should not present too many problems if the SS are familiar with the Present Continuous and *was* and *were*. However, the concept and use may be more difficult. The idea that this verb form often acts as a background to a story can be helpful. You will need to use gestures and questions to illustrate the idea. *Yesterday morning Jill went for a walk. The birds were singing and the sun was shining.* Which is the main information – the walk or the birds/sunshine?

• With the Past Continuous used as an interrupted activity, highlight that the action described by the Past Continuous began before the action described by the Past Simple, and the first activity may or may not have continued after the interruption.

• Adverbials *when* and *while* can cause problems. Highlight that *while* is usually used to introduce the continuous form, but *when* can introduce both forms. You may want to mention *as* at the same time which is similar to *when*.

• Pronunciation: weak forms of *was* /wəz/ and *were* /wə/ linking /r/ if followed by vowel should be highlighted and practised. Example: *were‿eating*.

Students' Book (page 21)

Exercise 1 Read the sentence aloud and refer SS to the timeline. Draw the timeline on the board. You can't really emphasise the difference of use too much, so try as many ways as you can to illustrate the concept. Highlight that one action is complete and the other is incomplete at the moment of interruption. Then repeat this idea using the terms *longer* and *shorter* action. Draw dots and wavy lines to signal long and short time spans. Emphasise the idea of the Past Continuous action starting before the Past Simple action. You could add that we need these two forms when we tell stories. The Continuous gives us background information, tells us what's happening behind the completed action. Use gesture and mime.

Exercise 1a) Yes, she did.

Exercise 1b) *The postman arrived* is the short completed action. *Liz reading the paper* is the longer activity.

Exercise 1c) She stopped reading.

Exercise 2a)
[3.3] (sound story extracts)
1 Heavy rain and birds singing, someone snoring gently. Suddenly alarm goes off and someone wakes up.
2 Noise of a shower and a woman singing in it. The phone rings.
3 Someone washing up and the sound of a plate breaking.

1 It was raining. The birds were singing. Liz was sleeping. She was snoring.
2 Liz was having a shower. She was singing.
3 Liz was washing up.

Exercise 2b) longer: the birds were singing, it was raining, Liz was sleeping; shorter: Liz woke up.
longer: Liz was having shower; shorter: the phone rang.
longer: Liz was washing up; shorter: Liz broke a plate.

Exercise 2c)
1 When Liz *woke up* it *was raining* outside and the birds *were singing.*
2 While Liz *was having* a shower the phone *rang.*
3 She *broke* a plate when she *was washing* up.

Exercise 2d) Introduce adverbials *while* and *when* and show how these can combine sentences. Write the following on the board.

I was walking. It began to rain. While *I was walking it began to rain.* When *I was walking it began to rain. It began to rain* while *I was walking. It began to rain* when *I was walking.*

Highlight we can say: *I was walking* when *it began to rain* but not **I was walking* while *it began to rain.*

Exercise 3 A good opportunity to revise prepositions with time expressions. Write the rules on the board with some examples.
at (+ time) 10 o'clock
in (+ month/year) February 1996
on (+ day/date) Thursday 10 February

🔑 1 woke up 2 got up 3 put on 4 went 5 made 6 rang 7 was having 8 didn't answer 9 got dressed 10 took 11 left 12 was driving 13 turned on 14 heard

Using your grammar

Begin by telling SS about yourself. They usually enjoy being nosy! It also offers valuable listening practice.

Extra material and ideas

1 WB page 11, Grammar, Exercises 2–4.
2 Draw the picture cues on the board. SS form sentences using the Past Continuous interrupted by the Past Simple.

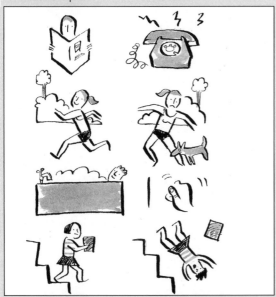

3 Tell a story e.g. the one below which includes both verb forms. One half of the class mimes/gives gestures for the Past Continuous verbs and the other half does the actions for the Past Simple verbs. Younger SS usually like this activity a lot. You can get them walking round the room in a circle as you tell the story. Good way of checking comprehension.

It was a beautiful day, the sun was shining and the birds were singing. John woke up at 7 and decided to have a bath. While he was having a bath he heard a crash in the kitchen. He got out of the bath, put on his dressing gown and went downstairs. While he was running down the stairs he tripped over the belt of his dressing gown and fell to the bottom of the stairs. When he got to the kitchen...

VOCABULARY
Personality types

🇱 • Highlight word stress as some of these adjectives have complicated stress patterns. Consciously review this vocabulary over the next few lessons to help SS remember.
• Intensifiers *a bit* and *quite* are included. You may want to do some work with these and other intensifiers *ex'tremely, very, 'rather* but only if your class are confident and good.

📖 Students' Book (page 22)

Exercise 1a) Before looking at the SB ask SS to write down their favourite colour, and one they don't like. Ask them to look at the colours on page 22 and find the colours they wrote down. This should stop them from reading the definitions first. Or you could write the definitions on the board, ask SS to choose the one they think belongs to the colours they wrote down and then check in the SB.

Exercise 1b)
🔑 inde'pendent 2 'thoughtless 3 imma'ture 4 'lively and ener'getic 5 ex'travagant 6 easy'going

Exercise 2a) To help SS remember, keep backtracking and asking *What do we call a person who ...?*
🔑 1 'honest 2 'generous 3 good-'tempered 4 'patient 5 fun 6 a'ffectionate

Exercise 2b)
📼 [3.6]
TOM: My Grandad always spends his money on other people, not on himself - you know, even if he hasn't got much money he'll buy you what you want for your birthday. And he's never bad-tempered - he always smiles and says nice things. And what I like about my Mum - she waits for ages for my little brother to get ready and tells him the same things lots of times but doesn't lose her temper.
DIANA: The cat's the best person in our family. She always comes and jumps on you and licks you and is really loving. She loves playing - she really seems to enjoy life. The next best is my Dad - he always says what he thinks - he can't tell a lie. If he does, he goes red. I like that.
🔑 Tom: his Grandad and his mother; Diana: her cat and her Dad

Exercise 2c)
🔑 1 generous and good-tempered 2 patient 3 affectionate and fun 4 honest

Using your vocabulary

Exercise 1 An opportunity to look at ways of stating an opinion/agreeing and disagreeing with others: *I think... I don't think... I agree with... I don't/can't agree with...*

Exercise 2 You could write a poem yourself. If possible get SS to display their poems and everyone can walk around and see them. See also *Extra material and ideas* below.

Extra material and ideas

1 WB pages 12 and 13, Listening, Exercises 7 and 8.

2 PW. Get SS to choose adjectives to describe members of their family. They tell their partner, but they have to give a reason. This will also act as revision of *because/so: My X is mean so I don't like her. I don't like my X because she's mean.*

3 Stress patterns GW. Write the stress patterns, not the words, of the following adjectives on the left side of the board:

○ ○ ○ ○ energetic	○ ○ ○ immature
○ ○ patient	○ ○ ○ thoughtless
○ ○ polite	○ ○ ○ ○ affectionate
○ ○ ○ good-tempered	○ ○ ○ ○ easygoing
○ ○ honest	○ ○ ○ intelligent
○ ○ ○ ○ extravagant	○ ○ ○ thoughtful
○ ○ ○ ○ independent	○ ○ ○ impolite

Then write the adjectives, in a different order on the right side of the board. Give the group a different coloured pen. The groups write the adjectives under a stress pattern on the board according to which pattern they think the adjective is. The colour will show which team has written the word. Check and practise saying the words.

4 Write adjective stress patterns on some cards and the adjectives on other cards. Hand one card to each SS and ask them to find their partner or partners. You may give more than one adjective with the same pattern. Use the new adjectives to describe people, but include some SS knew before: *'happy, 'angry, inte'lligent, 'beautiful, good-'looking,* etc.

5 You could extend the poem activity and practise question forms by reading out a S's poem to the class. SS then ask questions: *Where did you meet X? How old is X? Is X your boyfriend?* etc.

USE AND REVIEW

• Revision of polite requests and clothing vocabulary.
• Revision of the Present Continuous.

 Students' Book (page 23)

Exercise 1 Remind SS of the polite requests and other question forms *How much is it? Have you got one in X?* before you begin the roleplay. If you have access to a video or audio cassette recorder you could record SS' conversations for accuracy work later.

Exercise 2 This could be a purely oral activity. Make sure SS don't look at each other's pictures, but make it clear they are cooperating in this activity not competing. You could sit them in tango (see *Introduction*, page 14).

1 The woman is holding some bananas/some apples.
2 The assistant is carrying a box/a bag.
3 The assistant is talking to an old woman/old man.
4 The woman is wearing a blue/red coat.
5 The assistant is wearing an orange/brown uniform.

Extra material and ideas

To remind SS of clothing vocabulary, call out letters of the alphabet and ask SS to write down as many items of clothing as they can which begin with that letter.

Me and my body

USE YOUR ENGLISH

On the phone

A
• Times, days, months, dates.
• Preview of Present Continuous used for future time reference (see Unit 5).
• Revision of requests, accepting, refusing.
• *I'll* and *Shall I ...?* for offers.
• Spelling and pronouncing letters of the alphabet.

L
• Different ways of writing dates: Jan 27(th) or 27(th) January or 27/1/96. American English writes the month first not the day 1/27/96. Recommend that SS write Jan/January 27 if writing to someone in America. You could introduce abbreviated forms of the months: Jan, Feb, Mar, Apr, (May, June, July can't be abbreviated) Aug, Sept, Oct, Nov, Dec.

• The Present Continuous will be familiar (see Unit 2), but SS may not be aware of its use for future time reference (see Unit 5).

• The answers to offers are different: Offer: *I'll ...* Answer: *Thank you.* Offer: *Shall I ...?* (a question) Answer: *Yes, please.* There are intonation differences. *I'll ...* has a falling intonation but starts quite high to sound polite. *Shall I ...?* has a rising intonation.

Students' Book (page 24)

Exercise 1a) Ask SS to tell you the date and write it on the board in different ways (see L). Model the pronunciation and ask SS to repeat. Then ask SS to look at Emma's calendar in SB. Highlight that we can use the Present Continuous for the future, but don't spend a lot of time explaining. It's covered again in Unit 5.

🔑 1 She's seeing her bank manager on Wednesday (the 17th) at half past ten.
2 She's going to the cinema on Saturday (the 20th) in the evening.
3 She's having lunch with her aunt on Sunday (the 21st) at half past twelve.
4 She's babysitting for Tina on Monday (the 22nd) at eight o'clock.

Exercise 1b) Refer back to the date practised above. Ask SS to tell you the difference between the way we write it and the way we say it. Point out the difference between American English and British English when writing dates (see L).

🔑 Dates can be written in different ways (15 August; 15th August; August 15; August 15th) but when they are said we include *the* and *of*. Example: *the 15th of August; August the 15th.*

Exercise 2a) If SS are allowed to write in their books, they can make notes on the calendar.

📼 [4.1]
1 MAN: Good morning. The Bistro, Fulham Road.
EMMA: Hello. Is there a table free on Thursday evening, please, at about eight o'clock? For six people.
M: So that's the eighteenth of August, isn't it? I'll just check... I'm afraid there isn't one free until eight forty-five. Is that too late?
E: No, that's OK.
M: Could I take your name, please?
E: Yes, it's Emma Matthews. That's M-A- double T-H-E-W-S.
M: And may I have your phone number?
E: Of course. It's five four three, one double two.

2 CAROL: Hello, seven one three, four double seven.
EMMA: Hello. Is that Carol? This is Emma.
C: Hi there. Do you want to speak to Simon?
E: Is he in?
C: I think so. Hang on a minute.
SIMON: Hi, Emma.
E: Hi, Simon. How are you? Listen. I think I can get a tennis court for Wednesday afternoon. Would you like to play?
S: Yeah, I'd love to. I've got a meeting that afternoon, but it should be over by five.
E: Shall I book it for five thirty then?
S: That would be fine.

3 RECEPTIONIST: Good morning. Gold Street surgery. How can I help you?
EMMA: Morning. I'd like to make an appointment for my daughter please, with Doctor Brown. For a check-up.
R: Right. When would you like the appointment?
E: Some time next week would be fine.
R: Can you hold, please?... Would two twenty-five next Tuesday be possible?

E: Oh... That's great. That's the twenty-third, isn't it?
R: Yes, and your daughter's name is ..?

🔑 1 The Bistro restaurant on Thursday, 18th August, at 8.45pm.
2 Play tennis with Simon on Wednesday afternoon (17th), at 5.30pm.
3 The doctor's, next Tuesday (23rd) at twenty-five past two (2.25 pm).

Exercise 2b) The receptionist at the doctor's sounds unfriendly and uninterested because of her flat, monotonous intonation. You could ask SS to say what she says using a higher/more polite pitch tone.

Exercise 3 Introduce *Shall I ...?* and *I'll ...* used for offers. Establish that both forms do the same job (offering), then highlight the differences of form. *Shall I...?* is a question. Highlight the different replies (see L). You might like to explore ways of refusing politely: *Thank you but I can do it.* Use a polite tone and stress on *I.* Conversation 1 includes the spelling of a person's name. You may want to extend this to practise the pronunciation of the alphabet. SS could spell the name of a friend or relation for the class. The other SS then say the name.

📼 [4.2]
EMMA: Hello. *Is there* a table free on *Thursday evening,* please, at *about eight o'clock?*
MAN: *I'll just check.*
M: *Could I* take your name, please?
E: Yes, it's *Emma Matthews. That's M-A- double T-H-E-W-S.*
M: And *may I* have your phone number?
E: *Of course.* It's *five four three, one double two.*

Exercise 4 The language and conventions of speaking on the phone come up in this exercise and lead into the roleplay in Exercise 5. How much attention you give to this depends on how likely your SS are to need it. However, it is a motivating context to practise requests, offers etc.

🔑 1 Hello, 713477.
2 Hello. Is that Carol? This is Emma.
3 Hang on a minute. (Could you/would you wait a moment, please?)
4 Would you like to play?
5 Shall I book...?

Extra material and ideas

1 WB page 6, Dictation, Exercise 11 is about dates and times.
2 You could ask each S to write his/her name and birthday on a piece of paper. Then they exchange papers. Two or three of the more confident SS come to the board. Ask *Who can tell me X's birthday?* The S with the appropriate information gives the date. The SS at the board write the date up. Ask others if they agree with the written versions. Correct where necessary.
Ⓟ 3 A history quiz page 134, 4.1. Give each S a copy of the quiz for pair or individual work. SS have to **say** the date when you check their answers in the feedback.

🔑 1 12 October, 1492 2 20 July, 1969 3 11 November, 1918 4 22 November, 1963 5 1876 6 1953 7 1949 8 1928 9 20 September, 1519 10 6 September, 1522

Ⓟ **4 Offers and Requests** page 134, 4.2. GW. Cut up card or pieces of paper. There should be either a tick √ or a cross x on each. Each group is given 12 of these face down on the table. They also get the 12 picture cues from page 134 cut up and face down. One S picks up a request/offer cue card and forms a sentence. He/She can decide whether to make an offer or request. Another S turns over a √ or x card and responds accordingly. The others in the group decide whether they think the sentences were correct. Then two other SS continue by turning over the cards and so on.
5 As part of a routine you could begin each day by asking SS the date. This allows repeated practice of saying different dates.

SKILLS

🔺 • Reading for detailed information.
• Speaking about health and diet.
• Vocabulary: noun/verb collocation.
• Writing: to encourage SS to use a wider range of vocabulary in writing and to review linking words *so, and, but, because* (see Unit 3).

Reading and speaking

🔳 • Noun/verb collocations for health.
• Exercise 2b) practises Present Simple question forms, including negative questions which SS may not have practised much before. *Why doesn't ...?*
• Vocabulary for parts of the body.

📖 **Students' Book** (page 25)

🔑 **Exercise 1a)** 2 c) 3 e) 4 a) 5 b)

Exercise 1b) You could introduce this by showing pictures of hamburgers, chips, coke etc. and asking whether SS like these/eat these/think they are healthy etc. This could then lead into Exercise c).

Exercise 1c) *Give up/cut down on* something. These patterns, *give up/cut down on +-ing* come up again in Unit 8.

Exercise 2a) Before reading ask SS to look at the photographs and predict who has the better/healthier diet.

Exercise 2b)
🔑 Student A
1 F 2 T 3 T 4 T 5 F 6 F 7 T 8 T
Student B
1 T 2 T 3 F 4 F 5 T 6 T 7 F 8 F

Exercise 2c) As well as being an information gap activity, this practises question forms. If SS make mistakes, you can correct individuals as you hear them or make notes of the errors and do remedial work later. If it's just a few individuals making mistakes, we recommend that you do some immediate correction as it's believed to be more effective. However, if the mistakes are numerous, this signals that you need to cover this area of grammar again.

Exercise 3 Draw a simple figure on the board and ask SS to help label the picture with the words from the text. Then ask SS to label as many other parts as they can. This will be useful for VOCABULARY, page 28.

face; stomach; chest; hair; teeth

Exercise 4 SS could interview each other about their diets.

Extra material and ideas

1 WB page 15, Vocabulary, Exercise 5 is about parts of the body. Page 16, Listening, Exercises 7 and 8.
2 Before beginning SKILLS you could ask SS if they think their diet is healthy or not. Then ask them to list everything they ate and drank during the previous day. This can often surprise us. We tend to eat more than we think we do. Collect the lists and read them out for SS to guess whose it was.
3 Simon says game for parts of the body. SS stand up. You say either *Touch your + part of the body* (e.g., *knees*) or *Simon says touch your (knees)*. SS must follow the instruction only if it's preceded by *Simon says*, otherwise they are out. SS are also out if they touch the wrong part of the body. Instructions should be given quite rapidly. Once SS get the idea they can be the instructor.

Vocabulary

Collocation of nouns used with the verbs *take* and *lose*.

Students' Book (page 26)

1 take 2 lose 3 lose 4 take 5 take 6 take 7 take
8 take 9 take 10 lose

Writing: improve your writing

• The focus is on adjectives, to encourage SS not to overuse *good* and *nice*. There is a collocational element, too: *delicious* - food; *comfortable* - room/chair/bed; *friendly* - person/cat/dog/place; *interesting* - person/book/film/job etc. You could explore the collocational possibilities of the adjectives.

• Expect pronunciation problems with: *delicious*, SS often pronounce it /ˈdelɪsɪʊs/ instead of /dɪˈlɪʃəs/; *interesting* - /ɪnteˈrestɪŋ/ instead of /ˈɪntrəstɪŋ/; *comfortable* - /kʌmfɔːˈtɑːbl/ instead of /ˈkʌmftəbəl/; *attractive* - /ætrækˈtiːv/ instead of /əˈtræktɪv/.

Students' Book (page 26)

Exercise a) Write the words *good/nice/bad* on the board and tell SS that these words are banned for the day's lesson. This includes you, so SS can try to catch you out, too! You might

choose to extend this into collocational possibilities of the adjectives (see L).

There isn't a lot of food. It's *delicious*. The people are *friendly*. The bedrooms are *comfortable*. There is a very *attractive* aerobics teacher here. The evening activities are *interesting*.

Exercise b) It would probably be better to do the first sentence combination with the whole class. Then let SS work in pairs.

There isn't a lot of food but it's delicious. The people are friendly and the bedrooms are comfortable. There is a very attractive aerobics teacher here so I'm doing aerobics three times a day! The evening activities are interesting because there are lots of different things to do.

Extra material and ideas

1 WB page 17, Writing, Exercise 9.
2 Ban certain words on different days, or write up words you want SS to use at every possible opportunity in the lesson. Whether this actually works or not doesn't matter. The idea is to raise SS' awareness.
3 You could extend this idea to **Mistakes I don't want to hear today**, e.g., third person -s mistakes. Treated in a light-hearted way this can be a very effective classroom technique.

GRAMMAR

• To extend the concept and use of modal auxiliary verbs *can/can't, should/shouldn't, must/mustn't* and *have to/don't have to*.
• Comparing the language of obligation and possibility and obligation and advice.

Obligation and possibility: *have to* and *can*

• *Have to* + base form of the verb is not strictly a modal because its formal features don't fit those of modals. It uses *do/does/did* in questions and negatives. Modals don't. It can co-occur with other modals: *You might have to* ... Modals can't: **You can might come. Have to*, therefore, isn't necessarily the first verb in the verb phrase. Modals are. However, conceptually there are similarities. *Have/Has to* modifies the meaning of the main verb and it has intrinsic meaning of its own, unlike other auxiliaries *have/be/do*. It uses third person -s, *has to*. Modals don't. Modals don't use *to. Have to* does. The difference of use between *have to* and *must* for obligation can be rather subtle for this level. *Must* is used for obligation from the speaker and *have to* is considered to be obligation external to the speaker.

• Modal auxiliaries can have more than one use, e.g., *may* is used to express possibility in the future and for polite requests. And the same function can be expressed by different modal auxiliaries, e.g. *Can I come in? May I come in?*

35

• Pronunciation of weak and strong forms of many auxiliaries. *Can* /kən/ *you swim? Yes, I can* /kæn/. *You must* /məs/ *go. Yes, I must* /mʌst/. *Have to/Has to* is sometimes contracted by some native speakers but we recommend you don't introduce the contracted form.

• When asking about obligation there is a growing tendency to use *Do you have to ...?* rather than *Must you ...?*

📖 Students' Book (page 26)

Exercise 1a) Ask SS to read the holiday advert. Ask a few comprehension questions. Then write *NECESSARY* and *POSSIBLE* on the board. Elicit the answers and add them to the board. It might be a good idea to put complete example sentences on the board rather than just *have to* and *can*. This should begin to illustrate the difference of form more obviously.

🗝 *Have to* = it's necessary. *Can* = it's possible.

Exercise 1b) Model the pronunciation and get SS to practise. Highlight the use of weak forms *can* /kən/ and *have to* /'hæftə/. Work on the pronunciation of *can't* /kɑːnt/. This will come up again in *Using your grammar*.

🗝 1 have to; don't have to
2 can; can't; have to

Exercise 2a) Add examples to the board and use visual clues and colour to highlight features of form. For example:

I have to go. He has to go.

| Do | you | have to | go? | | Does | he | have to | go? |

| I | | don't have to | go. | | He | | doesn't have to | go. |

I can go. He can go.

Can I go? Can he go?

I | can't | go. He | can't | go.

🗝 1 **Have to**: positive (*We have to pay.*); negative (*We don't have to pay.*); question (*Do we have to pay?*).
2 **Can**: positive (*We can fly.*); negative (*We can't fly.*); question (*Can we fly?*)

Exercise 2c) Focus on the third person *-s* with *have to*. Add this information to the rules you have highlighted on the board.

🗝 **Have to**: positive (*He/She/It has to pay.*); negative (*He/She/It doesn't have to pay.*); question (*Does he/she/it have to pay?*).
Can: no change in form.

Exercise 3

🗝 1 can't; has to 2 Do we have to? 3 can't; have to

Exercise 4 SS could act this out but they will need time to practise.

🗝 1 do we have to pay; you don't have pay
2 We can have
3 Can we walk; you can walk
4 Do we have to have; you can

Using your grammar

Exercise 1a)

📼 [4.4]

SAM: Can we hire a car while we're there?
TRAVEL AGENT: Yes, you can, but remember to take your driving licence with you, won't you?
KAREN: What can we do in the evenings?
TA: Well, you can go to bars and restaurants to eat and dance. Or you can stay in the hotel. There's usually a show there.
SAM: Do we have to get a visa for Romania?
TA: No, but you have to take your passports.

🗝 1 Yes, they can.
2 They can go to bars and restaurants or they can stay in the hotel.
3 No, but they have to take their passports.

Exercise 1b)
🗝 1 /kən/ and /hæftə/ 2 At the end of a short answer.

🗝 **Exercise 1c)** Example questions: Can we hire skis? Do we have to have our own ski boots? Can we hire ski boots? Can we eat at the hotel? etc.

Exercise 2 Encourage SS to give other examples of rules in their country. In a multilingual class this could become a cultural survey.

Obligation and advice: *should(n't)* and *must(n't)*

🔤 • *Must* can be used to signal a strong recommendation: *You really must read that book.* However, we tend to avoid using it in advice situations unless speaking to children, close friends or ourselves.

• *Must* can only refer to a present or future obligation. To refer to the past we use *had to*.

• The negative *mustn't* does not negate the obligation. It is a negative obligation. To remove the idea of obligation we use *don't/doesn't have to = it's not necessary to*.

• Pronunciation *must* and *should* are usually weak: unless we are stressing the modal auxiliary for some reason. The *-t* in *must* is often elided if followed by a consonant, but it's usually retained before a vowel: *must go* /məsgəʊ/ but *must eat* /məstiːt/.

📖 Students' Book (page 27)

Exercise 1 Highlight that modals don't take *to* before the base form of the verb. Highlight the conceptual differences (see L).

🗝 *Must* is stronger.

Exercise 2 Get SS to read their answers aloud, practising the weak forms after they've listened to the cassette.

🗝 1 You shouldn't eat at the hotel because the food's awful.
2 You should buy traveller's cheques because it's difficult to change money.
3 You mustn't take young children skiing because it's too dangerous.
4 You must remember your camera because the mountains are fantastic.
5 You shouldn't pack formal clothes because it's very casual there.

1 WB page 14, Grammar, Exercises 1–3.
2 A visitor's guide to _____. SS could make posters giving advice for visitors to their country. *You should ... You shouldn't ... You must ... You mustn't...*

VOCABULARY
At the doctor's

L • SS often mispronounce *ache* */ætʃ(ə)/* and *temperature* */tempɔːˈrætʒʊə/*. The correct pronunciation is /eɪk/ and /ˈtemprətʃə/.

Students' Book (page 28)

Exercise 1a) Begin by asking SS what their last illness was. This may mean you steal some of the information from *Using your vocabulary,* Exercise 2. However, if you limit it to the last illness, it would still be possible to do Exercise 2. Be prepared to supply vocabulary if SS get stuck. Or if you have a 'good' personal illness anecdote you might like to tell the class. You could add to the list of ailments if SS are not overloaded.

1 d   2 c   3 a   4 b   5 e

Exercise 1b) Check the concept of *symptoms*.
You have a cold or flu.

Exercise 1c)
1 My head/arm/leg aches/hurts.
2 I feel ill/ dreadful/terrible.
3 I've twisted/sprained/broken my leg/arm/foot/wrist.

Exercise 1d) You could introduce *preˈscription.* This would encourage *You should/must get a prescription for ..... from your doctor.*

Using your vocabulary

Exercise 1 Introduce *What's the matter? What's the problem? How can I help?* to start the doctor/patient interview. Remind SS to use *must/should.* With a S, you could demonstrate to the class. Take the role of the doctor. This illustrates clearly that SS with the role of doctor should ask for more information about the illness.

Exercise 2 Begin by brainstorming questions such as *When did this happen? How long were you ill? Did you go to hospital?* Get SS to ask you questions then do a) + b). When SS tell their group the others can then ask for more information. If a S talks about a serious illness, e.g., cancer, it might be better for you to be the sympathetic listener if you sense the others feel at a loss as to what to say.

P 1 WB pages 16 and 17, Vocabulary, Exercise 6.
2 The best and the worst doctor page 135, 4.3. Divide the class into doctors and patients. If you have an odd number of SS, have an extra patient. Get doctors to copy the doctor's form from the board, patients to copy the patient's form.

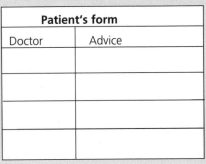

Patient's form	
Doctor	Advice

Doctor's form		
Patient	Problem	Advice

Assign areas around the room as doctors' surgeries. Doctors should go to their surgeries and make sure there is a chair for the patients. Have a waiting room area in case there are no doctors free. Give each patient a problem from page 135. Every patient should try to see every doctor and make notes on their charts. The doctors should fill in their charts before seeing the next patient. When you are sure that all or most patients have seen all or most doctors, group the patients together and group the doctors together. Ask the patients to tell each other their problems first. Then they should discuss which doctor gave the best and worst advice. Tell the doctors they are at a medical conference. They should tell each other what advice they gave the patients. The doctors could also consider who is the easiest and most difficult patient. This is **not** meant to be a serious activity, so if you add ailments choose them carefully. Please note that this activity may take a long time!

P 3 A mingle activity page 135, 4.4. Every SS has a picture cue for an illness and/or word cues (see 2 above). They ask each other *What's the matter?* and give advice.

USE AND REVIEW

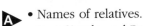
• Names of relatives.
• Past Simple and Past Continuous.
• Linking words: *and, but, so, because.*
• Time expressions: *when, while, at, on, in.*

Students' Book (page 29)

Exercise 1 Give SS a few examples of how they can tell each other about words without saying the targeted word. *Bird live in them = trees. You go to this person when you are ill = doctor.*

1 Not your sister = BROTHER
2 Your brother/sister's son = NEPHEW
3 Your father/mother's brother = UNCLE
4 Your father/mother's sister = AUNT
5 Your female child = DAUGHTER
6 Your brother/sister's daughter = NIECE
7 Married to the husbands = WIVES
8 Married to your father = MOTHER
9 Your uncle/aunt's daughter/son = COUSIN

Exercise 1c) Relatives

Exercise 2 You could get SS to exchange their stories and correct any mistakes. This encourages them to check their own work in future. You could guide them by mentioning what kind of mistakes they could look for, e.g., spelling, prepositions, verb forms. You could, in fact, limit the correction to one thing if this is the first time SS have checked each other's work.

Getting around

Students' Book

General theme: transport.
Unit topic: modes of transport.

USE YOUR ENGLISH: making travel arrangements.
SKILLS: listening and speaking (an unfortunate trip to the seaside); vocabulary (same spelling, different meaning); writing (reference words).
GRAMMAR: the future (plans, decisions and arrangements); *will* and *going to* and the Present Continuous.
VOCABULARY: transport.
USE AND REVIEW: interpreting instructions; body parts; problem page advice.

Workbook

GRAMMAR: *will*, *going to* and the Present Continuous.
VOCABULARY: transport (*trip, travel, journey*).
SKILLS: reading (a place to park); writing (an informal letter).
DICTATION/PRONUNCIATION: /ðeə/ *they're, their, there.*

USE YOUR ENGLISH
Making travel arrangements

A
- Review of *have to* and *could you ...?*
- Preview of the contrast between *would like to* v. *like* + base form + *-ing* (see Unit 8).

L
- *Love, hate, can't stand, don't mind* + base form *+ing* relating to general feelings. *Would like to* + base form refers to a particular future time. As these structures are highlighted in Unit 8 just make sure that SS realise this basic difference.

Students' Book (page 30)

Exercise 1a) If it's appropriate, ask SS how they came to class, and tell them how you come to work. You could revise the infinitive of purpose *You go to work to earn money.*

a) You catch/take a plane from an airport.
b) You catch/take a bus at the bus stop.
c) You catch/take a train at a railway station.
d) You buy/get petrol at a petrol station.
e) You park your car at a car park.

[5.1]
1 A: Thirty litres, please. Four star.
   B: Shall I check your oil as well?
2 A: Do we have to get a ticket? It costs sixty p an hour.
   B: Yes, but there's a traffic warden over there and we don't want a fine!
3 A: The train now approaching platform one is the eleven oh five service to Manchester Oxford Street, calling at...

4 A: Last call for passengers flying to Barbados, flight BA two five five. Please report to Gate Number six immediately.
5 A: What's the fare to King Street, please?
   B: Twenty eight p please, sir.

Exercise 1b)
1d) 2e) 3c) 4a) 5b)

Exercise 1c)
petrol station (30 litres, 4 star, oil)
car park (ticket, traffic warden, fine)
railway station (train, platform 1, service)
airport (last call, passengers, flying, flight, Gate Number 6)
bus stop (fare)

Exercise 1d) You could ask SS to write words to the board as they think of them, but not to repeat words others have written up. However, if they think a word is spelt incorrectly, they can check with you/a dictionary and correct it if necessary.

Exercise 1e) Give SS time to note any words they want to add to their vocabulary records:
petrol station (unleaded petrol, diesel, pump)
car park (parking space)
railway station (carriage, compartment, single/return/season ticket, book/reserve a seat)
airport (pilot, book/reserve a seat/reservations, check-in desk, boarding card, to board a plane, seat belt, return/one-way ticket)
bus stop (passenger, driver, ticket)

Exercise 2 Preteach *don't mind* and *can't stand* + base form +*-ing. Travel sickness* may also be useful. Ask some SS to tell the class what they found out about their partner. Then invite them to ask you the questions. Teachers talking to the class in this way can offer SS valuable exposure to the language as long as you make sure you use language appropriate to their level. See *Extra material and ideas* below for alternative approach.

Exercise 3 These words may be new: *flight, 'aisle seat, 'platform, 'single/re'turn, 'boarding card.* Mark the stress on any words which are new to SS. With flights we say *one way ticket* not *single.* The vocabulary that comes up here will be useful for the roleplay in Exercise 4 below. Before checking with the cassette you could ask some SS to roleplay the conversations or listen to the cassette and then roleplay/read. Ask if other SS agree, then play the cassette.

[5.2]
1 At a railway station
   A: Could I have a ticket to Liverpool, please?
   B: Single or return?
   A: Day return, please. Do I have to change?
   B: Yes, change at Crewe. That's forty-three pounds please.
   A: Here you are. What platform does it leave from?
   B: Number 8.

2 At a check-in desk
  A: Could I have your ticket and passport, please?
  B: Yes, here you are.
  A: Thank you. Would you like an aisle or a window seat?
  B: Window, please. No smoking.
  A: OK. And how much luggage have you got?
  B: Just these two suitcases. Is the flight on time?
  A: Yes, it is. Here's your boarding card. The flight is boarding at ten twenty from Gate eight.

Exercise 4 You could ask SS to write their conversations either as they think of them, or for homework. You could also ask more confident SS to do their roleplay for the class after they have had time to practise.

Extra material and ideas

1 WB pages 19 and 20, Vocabulary, Exercises 5 and 6.
2 Sentence completion PW. Using the cues in Exercise 2, SS could guess and complete sentences for their partner. They then ask questions to see how many of their guesses were correct.
3 Give SS sets of word cards. They have to group them according to the appropriate place/form of transport (see Key to Exercise 1e) above).

SKILLS

• Listening and speaking: predicting the content of a text; listening for gist; listening for detail.
• Fluency practice: telling a story.
• Pronunciation: recognition of weak and contracted forms; recognising main sentence stress.
• Vocabulary: homonyms.
• Writing: anaphoric references to avoid repetition.

Listening and speaking

L • The weak forms practised are *were, a, to, the, he, was, she.*
• Review of past verb forms.
• The reported structure *she knew this would take time* will be new but SS are familiar with all the individual words, and the context should clarify meaning, so don't draw attention to it.

Students' Book (page 31)

Exercise 1a) Begin by asking SS to think of problems old people sometimes have. You could ask them how old the oldest person in their family is. This would give you the opportunity to revise the question *What's he/she like?* and adjectives describing personality. The focus should be on the events of the story. SS shouldn't have any problems understanding the main points but check *sticks, hard shoulder* and *to break down.*

Exercise 1b) It's important that the SS are familiar with the map and can recognise the pronunciation of place names before listening to the story! *Devon* /ˈdevən/, *Tewkesbury* /ˈtjuːksbri/, *Clevedon* /ˈkliːvdən/, *Bristol* /ˈbrɪstl/. Note the M5 is the name of a motorway.

Exercise 1c) [5.3]
NEWS READER: And finally, a woman from Tewkesbury was left waiting for five hours in a car on the motorway yesterday while her forgetful husband went home without her!
  Thomas Brown and his wife Catherine were going to the seaside in their old car when it broke down. They were going on a day trip to Devon. They were travelling along the M5 at Clevedon, near Bristol, when the car broke down. So Mr Brown parked the car on the hard shoulder and went off to find help. His wife knew this would take time as the seventy-three year old man walked with two sticks. But she didn't realise just how long!
  Five hours later the police found Mrs Brown, eighty-four, still in the car on the hard shoulder on the M5! Mr Brown was already at home in Tewkesbury! When he left his wife in the car, he took a bus to Bristol and then a train home to Tewkesbury - a seventy mile journey.
  'I suppose I forgot,' Mr Brown said. 'I was very surprised when the police arrived at home.'

Exercise 1d) Refer SS to the sentence cues. Then play the cassette through. When you play the cassette to check the answers, you may need to pause after each chunk so that SS can check more easily.

1 They were going on a day trip to Devon.
2 They were travelling along the M5 at Clevedon (near Bristol) when the car broke down.
3 Mr Brown took a bus to Bristol and then a train to Tewkesbury.
4 Five hours later the police found Mrs Brown still in the car (on the hard shoulder on the M5).

Exercise 2a) [5.4]
1 *They were going on a* trip *to the* seaside. 9
2 *The old man's got a problem with his* legs. 10
3 *He* forgot *what he was doing.* 6
4 *She was* still waiting *for him in the* car. 9

Exercise 2b) You could ask SS to practise saying these sentences but recognition is arguably more important than pronunciation here.

Exercise 2c) Highlight that in English main stress often, though not always, comes near or at the end of a sentence. You could point out that there is a preference for main sentence stress to come towards the end of a sentence, unless it's a contrastive stress pattern. It may also be helpful to highlight that it's the important information words which carry stress.

Vocabulary

L • Homonyms: *trip, train, fine, change.*

Students' Book (page 31)

Before doing Exercise a) ask SS to think about the word *trip*. Is it a noun or a verb? Write the following sentences on the board:

1 Did you enjoy your trip to London? (noun)

2 Don't leave your bag on the floor. It's dangerous. Someone will trip over it. (verb)

Exercise a) Remind SS that the dictionary will tell them the part of speech: noun, verb etc. The concepts are easily illustrated except *to fine* someone. Present other situations where a fine could occur: for dropping litter in the street (about £200), a parking fine (between £10–£25).

Exercise b)
1 changes (v) 2 change (n) 3 training (v) 4 train (n) 5 Fine (adj) 6 fined (v)

Extra material and ideas

1 WB page 21. Dictation, Exercise 12 and page 60, Vocabulary, Exercise 6.

2 Homonyms If your SS enjoy these, ask them to think of as many as they can and make sentences to illustrate them. Here are some possible words: *file, can, ring, cold, dear, lie, can, fly, saw.*

Writing: reference words

• Subject and object pronouns, the possessive adjective *their*, and *there* referring to place.

Students' Book (page 32)

Exercise 1 If your SS are still unsure of subject and object pronouns you might review this before beginning the exercise (see Unit 1 USE AND REVIEW, page 11. Ask SS why this is similar to the listening text, or ask a few comprehension questions.

1 the Italian man 2 the Italian man's 3 the Italian man and woman's 4 Rome 5 the Italian man's wife 6 the Italian man 7 the reporters 8 the Italian man and his wife

Exercise 2
1 them 2 there 3 their 4 him 5 they

Extra material and ideas

WB page 20 Reading, Exercises 8–10 and page 22. Writing, Exercise 11.

GRAMMAR

• Future plans, decisions and arrangements using *will* + base form, *going to* + base form and the Present Continuous.

The future: plans, decisions and arrangements

• SS may be familiar with these structures, but will probably still be confused about when to use them.

• The difference between *going to* + base form and Present Continuous is not easy to grasp. We offer SS terms such as plans v. arrangements but in fact the differences are subtle and complicated. In the majority of cases the two forms are interchangeable. However, we wouldn't say **I'm killing him on Thursday*, even though this can carry the idea of an arrangement. Here are some guidelines:

- The Present Continuous is very commonly used with verbs of movement: *coming, going, taking, bringing, catching, flying* etc.

- *Going to* + base form often expresses or emphasises determination or a strong resolution while the Present Continuous seems devoid of this. The Present Continuous seems very matter of fact, with no emotional undertones.

- Both structures include an element of the present. They express the idea that there is an existing present situation. *I'm leaving on Tuesday.* (Perhaps the ticket has been booked, I've told everyone etc.)

For SS it is perhaps safest to say very often you can choose either, and then wait for SS to use it where a native speaker wouldn't use it. *I'm killing him tomorrow* sounds strange because the element of determination, strong resolution, is expected. You can often explain these individual incorrect uses, but it's difficult to give a general rule as to when the two forms are not interchangeable.

• Pronunciation difficulties include the contracted *'ll* form *John'll come with us. Won't* is often pronounced as *want* /wɒnt/. The weak form of *to* is used before a consonant *I'm going to see* /aɪm ɡəʊɪŋ tə 'siː/ but the strong form is used in positive short answers. We can't say **Yes, he's. *Yes, she'll.* However, the contracted form is used for negative short answers *No, she isn't. No, he won't.*

Students' Book (page 32)

Exercise 1a) If your SS have met all these forms before, the focus will be on use rather than form. Point out that *will* is a modal and not followed by *to.*

1 Mrs Wilson and Max 2 Tess

Exercise 1b)

[5.5]

MUM: You have remembered it's Dad's birthday on Monday, haven't you?

TESS: Yes, but I really don't know what to get him. He's got everything!

MAX: Well, I've already decided on my present. I saw it in a shop in town. I'm going to get him a video about playing golf.

T: Oh. What about you, Mum?

M: I'm not actually buying him a present. I'm taking him to London for the evening. I've booked a table at a new Italian restaurant I've heard about and then we're going to the theatre. I got the tickets last week but he doesn't know. It's a surprise.

T: Oh, that's an idea! I think I'll buy him something nice to wear then. A new tie or something. What...?

🔑 Max is going to buy him a video about playing golf. Mrs Wilson isn't buying him anything but she's taking him to London to a new Italian restaurant and the theatre. Tess is going to buy him something to wear, perhaps a tie.

🔑 **Exercise 1c)**
1 *will* + base form of verb
2 *be + going to* + base form of verb
3 Present Continuous

Exercise 1d) This is a process exercise. It's important that there is discussion of why SS chose their answers.

🔑 1 I'll   2 We're going   3 I'll   4 I'm going to

Exercise 2a) You may want to emphasise that not always, but very often we can use either the Present Continuous or the *going to* form. If you want to show an example of when it can't be used, give *It's raining tomorrow*. Explore the idea that we can't arrange this, can't write it in a diary. As you check their answers you can point out where the Present Continuous or the *going to* form could have been used – 3, 4, 7.

🔑 1 I'll do   2 I'll put on   3 I'm taking/I'm going to take
4 I'm playing/I'm going to play   5 I'm going to buy
6 I'll go   7 Tom is having/Tom is going to have
8 I'll buy   9 I won't get

Exercise 3a) Encourage SS to use weak forms *are* /ə(r)/ and *to* /tə/. Practise the contracted form *'ll* using the names of your SS. *José'll come. Korina'll come. Mustafa'll come.* They'll probably find this amusing, and the frequent repetition should aid the memory. Listen carefully for the *want/won't* confusion. You could do a minimal pair exercise on these. (See *Extra material and ideas* 2 below.)

Using your grammar

Exercise 1 You could join in by making a list of your New Year's Resolutions.

Exercise 2a)
📼 [5.8]
Tomorrow
I'd really like to *get up early*,
I think I'll *jog to work*,
I'm going to *cycle and swim and run*,
I'm *giving up chips* of course.
Or am I? On second thoughts, maybe I'll wait until the day after tomorrow.

Exercise 2d) An alternative to SS reading their poems out would be to display the poems round the room, and allow SS time to walk around and read each other's.

VOCABULARY

Transport

L • SS may have difficulty with stress and pronunciation of *reliable* /rɪ'laɪəbl/, *comfortable* /'kʌmftəbl/, *interesting* /'ɪntrəstɪŋ/.

• Collocation with verbs *drive, ride, get on/off, get into/out of, to go by.* Some of these may seem illogical to SS. Why do we *get on a bus, plane* etc. but *into a car?* Why do we *go by car, bus, plane* etc. but *on foot?* Highlight carefully.

📖 **Students' Book** (page 34)

Exercise 1 Highlight and mark the word stress on the board. Allow SS to practise saying the words until they feel confident with their pronunciation.

🔑 **Exercise 1b)** dangerous ≠ safe; noisy ≠ quiet; expensive ≠ cheap; slow ≠ fast

Exercise 2a) When you have checked SS' answers, hold up flash cards of the nouns and see how quickly SS can supply the appropriate verb. Speed it up so that they are having to respond more and more quickly. A bit behaviouristic perhaps, but it works as an aid to memory.

🔑 1 *drive a plane   2 *ride a boat   3 *get on/off a car
4 *get into/out of a motorbike   5 *go by foot.

Exercise 2b) 2 a)/d)   3 a)/e)   4 c)   5 b)

Using your vocabulary

Exercise 1 You could join in by completing the sentences and SS can ask you questions to get more information.

Exercise 2 In a multilingual class this could be an interesting information exchange. For a monolingual class, try to find pictures of forms of transport from different countries. Include some of the following: London taxi cabs, double decker buses, British trains and stations. Put the pictures on the board and ask SS to guess the country.

Extra material and ideas

1 WB, page 20, Vocabulary, Exercise 6 and page 20, Reading, Exercise 8.

2 GW. Assign one form of transport per group. Supply SS with poster paper and coloured pens. Each group is the advertising department of a company which sells cars or bikes or motorbikes or scooters or trains or tube trains etc. They should include information on their poster to convince people that their form of transport is better than others. If your SS are bashful artists, they don't have to draw. It could just be a word poster, but it should still be visually attractive. They are the advertising department, after all!! Display the posters, and allow SS time to walk around and look at the others.

3 Write the following on the board and ask SS if they are connected with trains (T) or planes (P).

1 I'll get a drink from the buffet. (T)
2 Where's the check-in desk? (P)
3 Show your ticket to the inspector. (T)
4 We must go through Security. (P)
5 Let's wait in the waiting room. It's cold out here. (T)
6 Put your luggage on the rack. (T)
7 Let's go to the duty-free shop. (P)
8 Fasten your seat belts, please. (P)
9 I can't find an empty compartment. (T)
10 Here's the departure lounge. (P)

USE AND REVIEW

• Modals: *have to/don't have to; can/can't; must/mustn't; should/shouldn't.*

• Vocabulary: parts of the body.

Students' Book (page 35)

Exercise 1 You could elicit/add other examples to the list: Dry Clean only. Not suitable for children under 3 years old. Not for pregnant women. Poisonous, keep out of children's reach. Danger: no entry.

Exercise 2 You could do this as a team game.

2 feet 3 fingers/toes 4 ears 5 waist 6 legs/feet 7 nose
8 teeth 9 thumb 10 eyes

Extra material and ideas

1 You could present the SS with a problem you have in your life, real or imaginary. SS write down advice and suggestions using the modals above. They then try to find another SS who had the same advice. Present another problem. This time they work with the person or people who had similar advice to theirs for the first problem. Together they decide on their advice. (Some SS may still be working on their own if no one else had similar advice. They should continue to try to find like-minded people!) Again SS try to find other pairs/groups with similar advice to form a larger group. Feed in the next problem and so on. In the feedback stage get the SS to retell the problem and offer their advice. You then choose which advice you are going to take.

2 SS write down a real or imaginary problem on a piece of paper with their name. The paper is passed around and SS write their advice on the paper. When there are several pieces of advice the paper is returned to the original S. The SS may or may not want to feedback to the group. Let them choose.

3 Problem page questions page 137, 5.2. Give students extracts from problem page questions. (You could also use real ones if they are not too difficult or in L1 if you teach a monolingual class.) They must give advice using *must/mustn't* or *should/shouldn't* either in a letter or orally.

TEST

There is a progress test, for Units 1-5 on pages 150 and 151 of this book for you to photocopy for your students. See page 158 for the Key.

Unit 6

Daily bread

Students' Book

General theme: food and drink.
Unit topic: eating and drinking.

USE YOUR ENGLISH: eating out.
SKILLS: reading and speaking (how to eat spaghetti); vocabulary (setting the table); writing (instructions and putting information in the correct order).
GRAMMAR: quantity expressions (*a, some, any, a few, a little, a lot, much, many*).
VOCABULARY: food and drink.
USE AND REVIEW: travel advertisements; transport vocabulary.

Workbook

GRAMMAR: countable and uncountable nouns.
VOCABULARY: food.
SKILLS: listening (food); writing (putting information in the correct order).
DICTATION/PRONUNCIATION: sound and spelling /ɔ:/, contractions and weak forms.

USE YOUR ENGLISH
Eating out

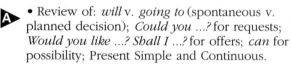

• Review of: *will* v. *going to* (spontaneous v. planned decision); *Could you ...?* for requests; *Would you like ...? Shall I ...?* for offers; *can* for possibility; Present Simple and Continuous.
• Vocabulary of restaurants *bill, 'menu, tip, 'service* including collocation *leave/tip, pay/bill*.

Students' Book (page 36)

Exercise 1a) Don't concentrate too much on food vocabulary here as it's the main focus of VOCABULARY on page 40. Ask SS where they eat when they go out for a meal. If you can, find pictures of different eating establishments, market stalls, pizza huts, motorway cafes, elegant restaurants, McDonald's etc., ask which they would choose for different situations (a meal with friends, a family birthday, a business lunch, lunch while out shopping etc.). Tell them about the last meal you had in a restaurant. If you're teaching in Britain, ask the SS what the differences are between eating out in Britain and in their country. Focus on popular eating times, when restaurants open and close, the cost of a meal, a typical menu, do people leave tips etc. You could add *to book/reserve a table*.

2e) 3b) 4a) 5d) Note in British English we also say *lay the table*.

Exercise 1b) Revises the Present Simple.

Then the waiter/waitress brings you the menu. You look at the menu and the waiter/waitress takes your order. He/She sets the table and then you eat your meal. After the meal you ask for the bill, pay it and leave a tip.

Exercise 1c) Revises the Present Continuous.

1 Two women are having lunch in a pub. A waitress is taking their order.
2 The waitress is setting the table. The women are having a drink.
3 The women are paying the bill. One of them is writing a cheque.

Exercise 2 Revises requests, offers and *will* v. *going to*.

[6.1]
WAITRESS: Are you ready to order yet?
LIZ: I think so. I'm going to have the chicken in cream sauce.
WAITRESS: *Would you like salad or vegetables with that?*
LIZ: Er, salad, please. And some chips. I'm starving.
WAITRESS: And for you?
ANNA: *I'll just have a starter.* The mushrooms, I think.
WAITRESS: Fine. I'll just set the table for you.
(later)
LIZ: *Could we have the bill, please?*
WAITRESS: Certainly. Here you are.
LIZ: OK. That's £16.50.
ANNA: *Is service included?*
LIZ: No, it isn't. So that comes to about £18 including the tip. That's £9 each.
ANNA: *Do they take Visa?*
LIZ: No, but you can pay by cheque.

Exercise 3 Remind SS to use some of the expressions from Exercise 2.

Extra material and ideas

SS could conduct a survey based on eating out and interview family, friends, fellow SS etc. Try to elicit questions they could ask, but here are some suggestions: *How often do you go out to eat? Do you have a favourite restaurant? Why do you like it? Do you go to a lot of different places? Have you had a really bad meal in a restaurant? Did you send the food back to the kitchen? What's the most expensive meal you have had? Do you leave a tip?* It doesn't matter if they conduct the survey in L1, but they should report their findings in English. The class could produce their own guide to eating out in their town/city/area.

SKILLS

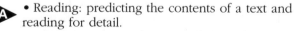

• Reading: predicting the contents of a text and reading for detail.
• Speaking: SS compare acceptable table manners in Britain and their country.
• Vocabulary: revision and extension of words related to food and eating; pronunciation and dictionary work.

• Writing: sequencing words for giving instructions.

Reading and speaking

L

• This is an intensive reading exercise. The article lists instructions for how to eat and how not to eat spaghetti. It is therefore not suitable for gist questions though you could ask an inference question: *Do you think the man enjoys spaghetti?* The answer would appear to be yes. He knows a lot about it. It brings back good memories of his childhood etc.

Students' Book (page 37)

Exercise 1 Write the names of various international food and drinks on the board: *curry, pizza, hamburger, paella, sushi, rice, vodka, borscht, tea, coffee, moussaka, sake* etc. Ask SS to name the country.

You could reverse this, by writing the name of the countries on the board and asking SS what food/drink they associate with each country. Ask SS which of this food they have never tried. Then use the pictures to introduce vocabulary such as *suck*. Note that more work on vocabulary comes up on SB page 40.

1 spoon and fork 2 suck 3 cut with a knife 4 turn spaghetti round a fork

Exercise 1b)
1 He's eating spaghetti with a spoon and fork.
2 He sucked (strings of) spaghetti into his mouth.
3 He's cutting spaghetti with a knife.
4 He's turning spaghetti round a fork.

Exercise 1c)
1, 2 and 3 are not polite ways of eating spaghetti.

Exercise 1e)
He used to suck strips of spaghetti into his mouth. He used a spoon to get the spaghetti round a fork when he was a child.

Exercise 1f)
1 If the pasta is in a soup or if it's very small.
2 Mix the pasta with the sauce.
3 You can break the spaghetti in half before you cook it.
4 The plate should be almost dry.
5 Fish sauce.

Exercise 2 Give good and bad examples of table manners in Britain. You could use gesture to elicit the information. Introduce the word *lap*. Then write on the board:

IN BRITAIN	
DON'T	**DO**
• talk when you have food in your mouth	• put your knife and fork together when you have finished eating
• put your elbows on the table	• say 'Will you excuse me?' when you want to leave the table
• eat with your fingers (unless it's a hamburger or bread, for example)	• put the napkin on your lap

SS then say how things are different in their country. Be ready to supply necessary vocabulary.

Extra material and ideas

In a multilingual class table manners could stimulate a lot of discussion and cross cultural understanding. The discussion could extend into other customs related to eating.

P

International eating habits page 137, 6.1. SS use the questionnaire to interview each other. To collate the information write the names of the different countries on the board with columns to represent some of the questions. When SS have interviewed someone about their own country, or one they know well, they fill in the chart on the board, or they report back to you and you add the information to the board. This then gives an immediate comparison of all the countries represented.

	meal times	knife/ fork	chop-sticks	fingers	in the street	elbows on the table
Thailand						
U A E						
Switzerland		✓				
Spain						
etc.						

With a multinational class this could also be *Guess what they do in X*. SS try to guess another country's habits. Check with someone from that country.

Vocabulary: setting the table

L

Expect pronunciation difficulties with: *fork* /fɔːk/. Make sure that SS use the longer vowel sound /ɔː/ not /ɒ/. *Spoon* /spuːn/. Again it has a long vowel sound /uː/ not /ʊ/. *Suck* /sʌk/, /ʌ/ not /æ/ and *knife* /naɪf/. Point out *k* is silent/elided.

• The phonemic alphabet (SB page 132) is needed for Exercise 2.

Students' Book (page 37)

Exercise 1 You could begin Exercise 3 by asking SS to draw a typical place setting from their country. Even monolingual classes will probably produce different drawings. Some SS could work at the board so you have an immediate reference point. Ask *Do you agree? Is it the same in your country/home?* Alternatively, you could draw the cutlery, photocopy it, cut it up and ask SS to name the pieces and place them as they think a British place setting would be. They then check with the picture in the SB.

1 sideplate 2 napkin 3 fork 4 dessert spoon 5 plate
6 wine glass 7 knife 8 soup spoon

Exercise 2 When SS practise these words, be particularly careful that they use the long /ɔː/ and not the short /ɒ/ in *fork*. You could follow on from the elided *k* in *knife* and do more work on silent letters: *write, wrong, knee, wrist, hour, comb, thumb, which, when* etc. Also see WB, page 44, Writing, Exercise 11.

🔑 1 knife 2 spoon 3 glass 4 napkin

Exercise 3 See notes in Exercise 1 above.

Writing: instructions

🇱 • Imperatives and negative imperatives.
• Sequencing words: *first, next, then, after that* and *finally* to order instructions.

📖 **Students' Book** (page 38)

Exercise 1a) You could tell SS that *should* and *must* can also be used for giving instructions.

🔑 Mix it with the sauce; push the pasta to the side of your plate; turn the fork; put it into your mouth; don't let the spaghetti hang out of your mouth; don't put cheese over a fish pasta sauce.

Exercise 1b) Point out the shell on the prawn.

🔑 4 = Then 2 = Next 1 = Then 6 = After that
3 = Finally. *Then/next/after* that are more or less interchangeable.

Exercise 2 Be prepared to supply necessary vocabulary: *to peel, re'move, crab, snails, 'artichokes, as'paragus, 'pineapple, 'orange* etc.

Extra material and ideas

1 WB page 25, Writing, Exercise 11.
2 Each S writes a few instructions on a piece of paper. They should not be **complete** instructions and they mustn't say what the instructions are for. They write their name on the papers which are then passed around the class. Each SS tries to guess what the instructions are for. If they can they write their name and idea on the paper. Then the papers are passed back to the original S who sees if anyone guessed correctly. If they can't think of anything you could suggest: *making a cup of tea, mending a puncture, blowing up a balloon, cleaning a car.*
Alternatively, you could write short incomplete instructions and place them round the room.
Put it in water, then turn it round until you see bubbles in the water. (mending a bicycle puncture)
Pour the boiling water on the bag and leave it for 1 minute. (making tea with a tea bag in a cup)
The water must be boiling when you put it in. Then leave it for about 8 to 10 minutes. (cooking pasta)
Make sure the + is at the + end and the − is at the − end. (changing a battery)
SS walk around and write their guesses on the papers. Collect them, see if anyone guessed correctly and ask SS to give the missing information.
3 Take in things to make a sandwich. Ask SS to give

you instructions. Do exactly what they tell you to do. This usually causes much laughter. For example, they tell you to put the butter or cheese on the bread, so you literally lift the butter or cheese on to the bread! You will need to add vocabulary such as *to spread, to slice* etc. so that they can give you more precise instructions. Don't forget that they should use sequencing words. Tell SS you will not do anything if the instruction isn't introduced by a sequencing word.

GRAMMAR

◤ • To review and extend SS' recognition and production of quantifiers: *a, some, any, a few, a little, a lot (of), much, many.*

Quantity expressions

🇱 • We often expect that *a, some, any, much* and *many* are fairly familiar forms at this level. However, SS are unlikely to be accurate, and what we perceive as countable and uncountable will continue to be a mystery for some.
• It is tempting but not advisable to give absolute rules. For the use of *some* and *any* it is neat to offer a hard and fast rule: *some* in the positive, *any* in the negative and question forms. However, this ignores a large body of language which includes: *I'll take any you can spare. Would you like some? Is there someone there who can help me?* In the SB, care is taken not to flag any of the analysis as an absolute rule. However, we do point out that *some* is used in questions where we expect the answer *yes* (ie. offers or requests, rather than information questions.)
• The *of* in *a lot of* is only used if a noun follows: *I need some shampoo. Don't worry I've got a lot.*
• We often use *a bit of* to replace a *little* or we can add it to *little*: *I need a little butter. I need a bit of butter. I need a little bit of butter.*

📖 **Students' Book** (pages 38-39)

A, some and any

Exercise 1 You could begin this section by raising SS' awareness of countable v. uncountable nouns by giving pairs a number of picture or word cues. Each pair should have different cues. SS are asked to divide these into two piles. They exchange with another pair who says which pile is countable and which uncountable. If the second pair thinks some are in the wrong pile, they should hand these to you to deal with later with the whole class. Point out that dictionaries will also tell them whether a noun is un/countable. The same cues can be used in Exercise 4.

a cheque book, some cassettes, a radio, some stamps, some writing paper, some shampoo, some money, some toothpaste, a toothbrush

Exercise 2 Refer the SS to the *Language reference* on page 41. You could read the explanations aloud.

Exercise 3

1 any sugar; some honey   2 any good restaurants
3 some coffee   4 a cup of tea   5 any information

A few, a little

Exercise 4 After checking the concept, if you used the picture and word cues in Exercise 1 above, you could ask SS to mix the piles up and put them face down. (GW x 3.) S1 picks up a card and asks *Is/Are there any X?* S2 has to reply. *There is a little/are a few left.* S3 listens and corrects any mistakes they hear. Encourage SS to do this as quickly as they can. The roles of SS1, 2 and 3 should rotate each turn. This idea would also work for Exercise 5 below, using different cues.

a few; a little

A lot (of), much, many

Exercise 5 If you don't think your SS are experiencing overload, you could introduce the use of *a bit of* (see L) or use it in a review and extend part of a later lesson.

a lot (of); (not) many; (not) much

Exercise 6

1 much   2 a little; a lot of   3 much   4 a few   5 much; a lot

Exercise 7a) Make sure SS look carefully when they refer to the picture. If they don't, there will be too many possibilities for this gap exercise. SS could roleplay or read the conversation for extra practice.

[6.2]
ALICE: Have you packed *any/some* shampoo? I've run out.
AMY: Yes, but not *much*. Why? Do you want *some*?
ALICE: Yes, please. What about writing paper?
AMY: Well, I've got *a little*. How *much* do we need?
ALICE: *A lot.* We have to write to all our clients. Oh, and we need stamps. I've only got *a few* left.
AMY: It's OK. I've got *a lot of/some* stamps.
ALICE: Don't forget to bring *some* cassettes for the car journey, will you?
AMY: Well, I haven't got *many*. I usually listen to the radio.
ALICE: And I forgot to go to the bank. I hope you remembered to get *some* money?
AMY: No, I didn't, but you've got *a cheque book*, haven't you?

Using your grammar

Exercise 1 You will need to circulate and help SS with vocabulary. Make sure they understand that you don't expect exact quantities. In a multilingual class, if possible, let them work in nationality pairs.

Exercise 2 Go round and monitor how well SS are using expressions of quantity. Perhaps make a note of mistakes and begin the next lesson with a *Spot the mistake* exercise.

Extra material and ideas

1 WB pages 22 and 23, Grammar, Exercise 1-4. Exercise 4 is loosely based on the Red Riding Hood story and could be used as a gap dictation in class. It would help SS to see the humour in the passage if you talked about what is considered to be healthy and unhealthy food.

2 True/false Get your SS to do an exercise with these sentences on the board:
1 We use <u>much</u> and <u>many</u> for questions and negatives sentences. (T)
2 We use <u>a lot of</u> only for positive sentences. (F)
3 We usually use <u>any</u> for questions and negative sentences. (T)
4 We use <u>some</u> for questions when we expect the answer to be yes. (T)

3 I went to market and bought ... SS have to repeat the items said by previous SS and then add one to the list. They can't use the same quantifier as the previous 2 people, but they can include a negative if they want. Example:
SI *I went to market and bought a pen*
S2 Repeats 1 adds *some cheese*
S3 Repeats 1+2 adds *a lot of pears*
S4 Repeats 1+2+3 adds *but they didn't have any bread*
S5 Repeats 1+2+3+4 adds *but they didn't have much milk*, etc.
Because this is complicated by the quantifiers you could help by drawing the items on the board.

4 Sentence completion Write the following on the board:
Yesterday
  1 I ate a.....................................
  2 I ate some...............................
  3 I had a lot of...........................
  4 I didn't eat any.......................
  5 I didn't eat many....................
  6 I didn't eat much....................
  7 I also had a few......................
  8 I didn't drink any....................
  9 I didn't drink much.................
 10 I didn't drink many.................
 11 I drank a lot............................
 12 I drank a few..........................
SS should copy the sentences and complete them. Collect the SS' papers and begin reading out the sentences. When SS think they know who wrote them, they shout out the name. Include one for yourself but don't let SS know that beforehand. Note

that *Using your vocabulary* Exercise 2a) asks SS to interview each other about their previous day's food intake, so you couldn't use both activities.

VOCABULARY

Food and drink

L • Fish is the most common plural of *fish,* though the plural *fishes* does occur occasionally.

• There may be pronunciation difficulties (particularly if SS have similar words pronounced in L1 differently). If the problem involves both stress and sound mistakes, focusing on word stress will often correct the sound mistakes because stress can affect the pronunciation of surrounding vowel sounds.

📖 Students' Book (page 40)

Exercise 1a) You may want to take in pictures of food which is relevant to your SS to add to these lists. Encourage SS to use word trees and other ways of recording vocabulary (see *Introduction,* page 12 and Unit 1 *Extra material and ideas* 4 page 17 and allow them time to make a record of new words).

🔑 1 Fruit: pears, a 'melon, grapes, 'strawberries.
2 Vegetables: a red 'pepper, green 'beans, 'onions, 'mushrooms
3 Fish: a 'lobster
4 Meat: lamb 'chops, beef

🔑 **Exercise 2a)** 1 an oven   2 a grill   3 a frying pan
4 a saucepan

🔑 **Exercise 2b)** 1 an oven   2 a frying pan   3 a saucepan
4 an oven   5 a grill

Exercise 2c) Begin by telling SS about the food you like and extend this into food SS don't like, have never tried, are not allowed to eat, etc.

Using your vocabulary

Exercise 1 Check the meaning of *to snack/a snack* before SS begin.

🔑 1 Three meals. 2 Breakfast, lunch, dinner. 3 Bananas, apples, cup of tea.

Exercise 2c) The SS could display their paragraphs round the room and walk around and read each other's.

Extra material and ideas

1 WB page 23, Vocabulary, Exercises 5 and 6 and page 26, Listening Exercise 7.
2 Team game. Call out a letter of the alphabet. SS have to write down as many words as they can, related to food beginning with that letter, in 1½ minutes. SS only score points if they can spell and pronounce the words correctly.
3 Taking each letter of the alphabet, SS have to name an item of food. S1 apple, S2 banana, S3 cauliflower etc. Perhaps miss out the more difficult letters.

USE AND REVIEW

L • Revision of vocabulary related to clothes, souvenirs and food.
• Revision of ways of expressing future plans and decisions.

📖 Students' Book (page 41)

Exercise 1 If possible take in some real holiday brochures for South Africa, Italy, Singapore and Malaysia and Britain. In fact, any brochures would be relevant in terms of scene-setting. Display these round the room and let SS wander around and have a look at them. You could read the advertisements aloud to SS. SS could work alone, or if there are other SS who want to go to the same place, they could work in pairs or groups.

Exercise 2

🔑

Extra material and ideas

SS imagine they have been on holiday at their chosen destination for a week. Get them to write a postcard to a friend.
You could draw the prompts on the following page to help them.

Or ask questions to guide them: *Where are you staying? What is it like? Which places have you visited? What food have you eaten? Who have you met? What have you done? What are you going to do next?*

Note: WB page 17, Writing, Exercise 9 has an example format for a postcard.

How do you feel about ... ?

Students' Book

General theme: opinions.
Unit topic: expressing opinions.

USE YOUR ENGLISH: saying what you think.
SKILLS: speaking and listening (young people talk about their lives); vocabulary (guessing words in context); writing (when to use *the*).
GRAMMAR: Present Perfect Simple or Past Simple?; time expressions (*just, ever, never, yet*).
VOCABULARY: feelings and opinions: *-ing* and *-ed* adjectives.
USE AND REVIEW: bingo.

Workbook

GRAMMAR: Past Simple and past participles; Present Perfect or Past Simple?; *been* or *gone*?
VOCABULARY: adjectives and prepositions.
SKILLS: reading (finishing relationships); writing (*a* or *the*?).
DICTATION/PRONUNCIATION: questions and pronunciation.

USE YOUR ENGLISH
Saying what you think

A
- Adjectives for opinions and feelings.
- Verbs for opinions and feelings.

L
- Many of the extreme adjectives don't collocate with the adverb *very*. We can use *very* with *nice*, *'boring* and *'clever*. With the extreme adjectives we can use *'absolutely*, *'absolutely fan'tastic*. However, all of the adjectives collocate with *'really*.

Students' Book (page 42)

Exercise 1 Begin by asking SS to describe any pictures they have on their walls at home. Or take in a variety of art postcards and ask SS to say which they wouldn't have on their walls. Then ask some confident SS to work at the board. When they have finished the exercise ask other SS if they agree and correct where necessary. Elicit and mark the word stress then practise those adjectives which are new. You could add more adjectives to the lists: *'terrible*, *'fabulous*, *'brilliant, ter'rific* and remind SS of the adjective endings covered in Unit 3.
VOCABULARY, page 46 focuses on *-ed/-ing* adjectives.

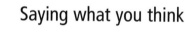

1 Good: great, fan'tastic, 'lovely, nice, 'wonderful
2 Bad: 'awful, 'dreadful, 'boring
3 Not good or bad: not bad, all right

Exercise 1b) Once SS have had time to form opinions about the posters this could be a mingle activity where they have to find other SS with the same, similar or completely different opinions. Feedback could be conducted according to how you have set the activity up. Either, *why did you both like this poster*, or *why did you like it but your partner didn't?*

Exercise 2 [7.1]
JUDY: I don't think the first poster is very exciting, I'm afraid. It's all right, but it's not the kind of thing I would sit and look at.
ANDREW: Really? I think it's great! It's clever, and quite funny.
A: I don't mind the picture of the man and the baby. I suppose it's quite sweet.
J: Oh, yuk! I can't stand it. It's dreadful!
J: This one is lovely. It makes me feel calm and relaxed, and the colours are fantastic.
A: Yes, it's quite nice. But it's not really my taste.

Judy: c   Andrew: a

Exercise 3 The gap fill exercise focuses on adjectives. Ones which may be new are *'clever*, *re'laxed* and *sweet*. You could preteach these or focus on them after the gap fill has been completed. The idea that an adjective can describe one's feelings (*relaxed*) as well as the thing itself, is introduced in the context of the dialogue (VOCABULARY, page 46 also deals with this).

[7.2]
1 JUDY: *I don't think* the first poster *is very exciting*, I'm afraid. It's *all right* but...
   ANDREW: Really? I think *it's great!*
2 A: *I don't mind* the picture of the man and the baby.
   J: *I can't stand* it. It's *dreadful!*
3 J: This one is *lovely*. It *makes me feel* calm and relaxed.
   A: Yes, it's *quite nice*. But it's not really *my taste*.

Exercise 4 The pieces of music are jazz, rock, rap, classical music, opera.

Exercise 5 This could be introduced by taking in a CD, film video, photos of actors and singers. An alternative would be to write the cues on the board (music/films etc.), and the question, WHICH X DO YOU LOVE/HATE? Invite SS to ask you questions. You then model the verbs *can't stand* and *don't mind* etc. when you tell them about your likes and dislikes before they work together.

Extra material and ideas

1 In advance of the lesson, or for some future lesson, ask SS to bring in things they like and dislike, a favourite possession, CD, picture etc. and tell the class why it means so much to them. Even if it isn't possible to bring the items in, SS could still interview each other about their favourite things.
2 Invite SS to bring a piece of music they like, and each day begin or end the lesson with a S's choice.

SKILLS

A
• Speaking and listening: predicting from headlines, listening for gist and detail; stating opinions on problems facing young people.
• Vocabulary: guessing meaning from context.
• Writing: accuracy, the definite article *the*.

Speaking and listening

L
• Some of the vocabulary in the listening will be unfamiliar but **don't** preteach: *fed up, to change one's mind, smart, second'hand, dye* and *to pick someone up* as these form the basis of the VOCABULARY exercise. You could check *veg* (for vegetables), *ripped, to en'courage* and *to stop someone doing something*.

Students' Book (page 43)

Exercise 1 Do this as a whole class exercise.

Exercise 2 Ask SS to explain the headlines in their own words. Ask if these problems exist in their country.

Exercise 3 Do this with the whole class and write their suggestions on the board.

Exercise 4 Check SS understand the vocabulary in the lists before they begin. If it's appropriate, you could divide the class into male and female groups to see if the sexes have the same opinion about what is important for girls and for boys.

Exercise 5a) Check SS' answers before going on to b).

[7.4]
INTERVIEWER: What's it like being a teenager these days? Do you worry about what's happening in the world?
CHRIS: Well, I watch the news and so on but I don't really care about politics - I don't think about it that much. I do worry about the environment, though - it seems to be getting worse and worse all the time.
PENNY: So do I. *These days it's even dangerous to go out in the sun.* I worry about animals, too, and how they're treated - that's why I'm a vegetarian. My Dad is fed up with me not eating meat - he likes the typical meat and two veg - and *he hopes I'll change my mind and start eating meat again,* but I won't.
C: But really it's everyday things that worry kids of our age, you know, how you get on with your parents and so on.
I: Do you argue with them?
C: Well, we argue about clothes because they like me to wear smart clothes and I like old ripped jeans. But I usually wear what I want in the end. *It's important to me to look good and be in fashion.*
P: I wear jeans or go to second-hand shops for my clothes. You can get really cheap clothes there which are nearly new. But I do care about what my parents think of me. My Mum doesn't mind if I dye my hair - *I dyed it red last week* and she said it looked nice - but she wouldn't let me wear a ring in my nose.
C: We argue about housework, too. I hate it and they're always telling me to do the washing up.
I: Do they stop you doing anything?
P: Well, I can only go out at the weekend. *My Dad usually picks me up in the car at eleven* and I feel stupid in front of my friends. Young people have to learn to be independent and try different things. A lot of the young people at my

school smoke, for example, but their parents don't know. I have smoked but I gave up. A lot of the boys drink, too. I think it's better if parents just let them do it - not encourage them but not stop them either.
I: What about the future?
P: Well, *I'm going to art college in the autumn.*
C: *Maybe I'll get married, probably at twenty-eight and I'll have two kids.* I'd like to be rich, I don't want to live in Britain, because there's not much work and *it's cold and boring.*

🔑 politics, the environment, relationships with parents, clothes and appearance, housework, going out, smoking, relationships and marriage.

Exercise 5b) Elicit the answers and write them on the board exactly as SS said them. As they check their answers, ask them to correct any mistakes of content on the board. You then listen again and focus on grammar mistakes.
🔑 See tapescript above.

Exercise 6 Ask SS if they would hear similar things from teenagers from their country.

Vocabulary

L
• Point out that *fed up* can be used transitively but needs the preposition *with*: *I'm fed up **with** the weather. Smart* is a homonym and can also mean *intelligent. Second-hand* can collocate with individual items as well as shops, *a second-hand car.* Highlight the spelling of *dye,* a regular verb. Compare it with *die.*

Students' Book (page 43)

It's important that SS see this as a process rather than a test. It aims to show SS that, as with L1, they can sometimes guess the meaning of vocabulary by looking for language and context clues within the text. Ask SS to justify their answers but if they are restricted by a lack of language, they could use L1. With multilingual classes, SS could quote the parts of the tapescript which helped them to guess.
🔑 1b) 2b) 3a) 4b) 5b) 6a)

Writing: *the*

L
• The exercise limits the focus to general v. specific: *boys* v. *the boys.*

Students' Book (page 44)

Exercise 1 Begin by writing on the board *When to use THE, When NOT to use THE.* Read the explanation to the class, and check their understanding by writing an example on the board *Cats can live for many years. The cats next door are very old.* and ask SS to explain the use of the definite article. It's important to point out that numbers 1, 3 and 5 refer to general things.
🔑 1 I spend all my money on t~~he~~ books.
2 The books on this shelf are quite useful.
3 T~~he~~ water is very good for your health.
4 The water in this country tastes awful.

5 Sue doesn't usually like t~~he~~ Indian food.
6 The Indian food in the restaurant is great.

 Exercise 2 All over the world t~~he~~ women still do not have the same opportunities as t~~he~~ men. The men in my office always get better jobs. T~~he~~ young people in my country worry about t~~he~~ jobs and t~~he~~ money.

Exercise 3 If appropriate, SS could work in nationality groups. Previous discussion should have generated enough ideas for them to concentrate on the language rather than having to decide on the content. You could ask them to limit their letter to one subject such as unemployment. Circulate the letters to other groups to check for grammar and spelling mistakes.

Extra material and ideas

1 WB page 29, Writing, Exercise 8.
2 Point out that often we can't see our own mistakes easily, and that if we show others our writing, they can often help up to improve it. You could then set up a S checking system where any writing, other than simple exercises, is given to at least one other S to check before it's handed to you for marking. You need to offer some guidelines, *don't write on the paper,* and *use pencil which can be erased.* Ask SS who checked the piece of writing, to initial it at the top to show that it has been seen by someone else first. They can ask you if they aren't sure who is correct. The idea you're hoping to implant is that when they hand their work in to you, it's the very best they can do. Allow them a few minutes at the beginning or end of the lesson in which you intend to collect it in. This may have the added bonus of getting SS who don't usually do homework to do it, as they know there will be this checking time in class.

GRAMMAR

A
• Present Perfect Simple for past experience and recent changes compared with the Past Simple.
• Adverbs *just, ever, never* and *yet.*

Present Perfect Simple

L
• SS may have difficulties with the concept and use of the Present Perfect. Problems also arise in manipulating the form. Highlight the general concept of **before now.** The Present Perfect views past time from time **now,** whereas the Past Simple has the feeling of being distanced, removed, over there, away from the present. With the two uses focused on in this unit it is quite easy to see how they fit into this general concept. With the Present Perfect used for experience, we're often relating the fact that **now** we know something because of an experience which happened **before now.** With the concept of recent changes we relate it nearer to time **now,** we don't yet view the action as

removed or distanced. A visual representation may help support your illustration of concepts.

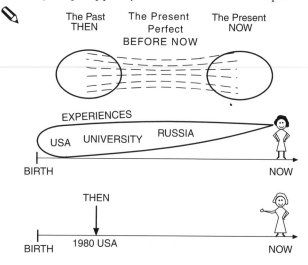

Students' Book (page 44)

Exercise a) Highlight the language aims by writing on the board *Present Perfect Simple* and *Past Simple* and add an example of each. Use the picture to elicit that the couple have just moved in. Check vocabulary from the letter '*furniture,* '*curtains,* '*carpet and paint.* You could read the letter while SS follow in their books. This way all are guaranteed to finish at the same time.

Exercise b) As SS find the meaning and use of the Present Perfect quite problematic, begin by immediately focusing on this. You could draw visual illustrations to aid understanding (see L). The letter should give the sense of recent time but it's advisable to keep asking SS questions to reinforce the idea of **near time now.** The reference to carpets gives us an example of the Present Perfect and Past Simple. You could refer back to these examples later to check understanding.

1 On Monday.
2 We don't know exactly - sometime before now.
3 We don't know exactly - sometime recently before now.
4 Yesterday.

Exercise c) Highlight the concept that the Past Simple is concerned with **then** and **time**.

The Past Simple: We moved in on Monday. We bought it yesterday.

Exercise d) Highlight that the Present Perfect is more concerned with the event than the time but it's still clear that it happened **before time now.**

The Present Perfect: The furniture hasn't arrived yet. We've borrowed a CD player. A friend has just given us some curtains. I've never put up curtains before. We haven't laid it yet. Have you ever laid a carpet?

Exercise e) You will need to check that SS understand the meaning of *still.*

No, they haven't.

Present Perfect and Past Simple

Exercise 1 You could use the timelines in L above to reinforce the different uses of the verb forms. Repeat these questions throughout the lesson: *Which one tells us this happened before now but not exactly when? Which one do we use for experiences in our lives but not for time? Which one do we use to tell when the experience happened?* Perhaps when SS come to produce the verb forms these questions will come to mind and help them to decide on which form to use. Highlight the use of *yet* in the questions but point out that it isn't necessary, we could also say *Has the furniture arrived?* See *Extra material and ideas* 2 below for more work on the Present Perfect Simple.

[7.5]
MOTHER: *Has your furniture arrived yet?*
LOUISE: Yes, it has.
M: *When did it come?*
L: It came yesterday afternoon.
M: And *have you finished painting the sitting room yet?*
L: Yes, we finished this morning.
M: Oh, good. And *have you put up the curtains yet?*
L: Yes, we have. David's just done it. And they haven't fallen down yet!
M: *Have you laid the carpet yet?*
L: No, we haven't had time.
M: Don't worry. We'll do it for you.

Exercise 2 Draw attention to the Irregular verbs list on page 132.

saw/seen, drank/drunk, did/done, put/put, spoke/spoken, began/begun, wrote/written, went/been or gone, met/meet, ate/eaten

Exercise 3 Ask SS to explain why they chose the answer they did. This could be in L1 if it's a monolingual class.

1 I saw 2 Have you finished 3 has arrived 4 I went
5 I've done 6 I've lost

Time expressions with the Present Perfect

• Adverbs *just, ever, never* and *yet.*

just = close to time now/recent. It can be used in questions but it's more commonly used in statements. *I've just finished. Have you only just finished?*

ever = in your life up to now. It can be used in questions and statements. *Have you ever seen a live whale? It's the biggest fish I've ever seen.* Note that without using *ever* in these examples the meaning remains the same. *Ever* seems to emphasise the idea of *at any time.*

never = emphasises **not at any time.** Compare *I haven't been to Siberia* and *I've never been to Siberia.* Note it can be used with *before* to mean this is the first time. *I've never been to Siberia before.*

yet = up to time now. *She hasn't finished yet. Has she finished yet?*

Exercise a) Write the adverbs on the board and ask SS to find examples of them in the letter on page 44. As you go through the exercise add the these visuals under the words:

1 ever 2 never 3 yet 4 just

Exercise b) Draw attention to the position of adverbs in a sentence. Write jumbled sentences on the board and ask SS to put them in the correct order *never been to has Scotland Jack Jack's never been to Scotland.*

Already has not been included here as there is quite a lot for SS to take in. However, if it arises or you feel your SS won't be overloaded, you could introduce it. It is used in statements to emphasise a completed action: *I've already read it.* It is often used in a question to signal surprise and/or check that the action has been completed: *Have you finished already?*

Using your grammar

Exercise 1a) [7.6]
1 She hasn't finished her drink yet.
2 They've never heard that word before.
3 He's not at home.
4 We've just said that!
5 He's just told me the news.
6 It's an old house.

Exercise 1b) 3 and 6

Exercise 1c) *he's = he is* in 3 but *he has* in 5; *it's = it is*

Exercise 2 You could begin by drawing some quick sketches on the board which depict experiences in your life (you've flown a plane, you've worked as a waitress, you've visited the tower of Pisa). SS try and guess what things you've done. The worse the drawings, the more humorous this becomes!

You may like to give written cues with the pictures in the book: *go/opera, dye/hair, fly/India, eat/Chinese restaurant.*

b) She's been to the opera.
c) She's been /flown to India.
d) She's dyed her hair black.
e) She's been to/eaten at a Chinese restaurant.

Exercise 3 Invite SS to ask you the questions. This allows you to check question forms, and by listening to your answers, SS are reminded about the verb form, which will not be familiar or accurate yet.

1 Have you ever ridden a donkey? 2 Have you ever had a fight? 3 Have you ever spent a lot of money? 4 Have you ever won a prize?

Extra material and ideas

1 WB pages 26 and 27, Grammar, Exercises 1–5.

2 Page 138, 7.1. Give SS copies of the picture and tell them that a week later Louise and Daniel are going to have a house-warming party. Ask them: *What have Louise and David done?*, *What has changed?*

1 They've laid the carpet. 2 They've put up the curtains. 3 The furniture has arrived. 4 They've finished painting. 5 They've put up the pictures.

3 For further practice of the Present Perfect for recent changes, line SS up so they are facing each other in two lines. Tell them to look carefully at the person opposite them. Look at what they're wearing, jewellery, etc. One line turns so their backs are facing their partners. The other line of SS changes something about their appearance. The less obvious the better – tucking the hair behind an ear, putting a ring on the finger next to the finger it was on originally, turning a collar up or down, opening a button etc. Then the others turn back again and try to find the difference. *You've moved your hair* or *Have you moved your hair?* This is then repeated with the other line turning round while their partners change something. Be ready to help SS with vocabulary: *cuff*, *'collar* etc.

4 SS take 2 pieces of paper each. They write 2 good things they've done on one piece (Example: *I've given up smoking.*) On the other they write 2 things they haven't done yet but would like to do. (Example: *I haven't been to China yet.*) Then GW. They mix up the papers and guess who wrote the sentences.

5 Team game page 138, 7.2. Photocopy the cue cards and cut them up. In turn a member of each team rushes to collect a cue card. They mime the situation stated on the card for their team. The team members try to guess what was written on the card. They begin their guesses with: *You've just ...* The team with the most correct guesses wins.

VOCABULARY

Feelings and opinions

L • -ed/-ing adjective endings. This is often an area of confusion for SS and one which can cause unintentional humour *I'm boring/exciting* when the S intended to say *I'm bored/excited*. The difference is often described as being inside and outside the person which is easy to see in

examples such as *It's exciting/I'm excited.* However, when SS come across examples such as *He's boring* the above explanation is confusing. It's perhaps clearer to distinguish between feelings and opinions *He's bored = that's how he feels*, but *He's boring = my opinion of him.* You could highlight *I'm bored = how I feel* v. *I'm boring = my opinion about myself.*

Students' Book (page 46)

Exercise 1 Write on the board **What's the difference between he's bored and he's boring?** to highlight the focus.

2 She's surprised 3 He's excited 4 He's frightened 5 She's depressed 6 She's embarrassed

Exercise 2 Keep checking the difference throughout the exercise *Is this a feeling or an opinion?* Refer back to the question on the board and elicit answers. Warn SS of the possible danger of using the wrong one.

2 surprising 3 exciting 4 frightening 5 depressing 6 embarrassing

Exercise 3 Ask SS to justify their answers according to feeling or opinion.

1 worried 2 tiring 3 interesting 4 annoyed

Using your vocabulary

Exercise 1 You could complete the sentences and SS could interview you at the end of the lesson.

Exercise 2 This would be a good opportunity to transform sentences to reinforce the feeling/opinion differentiation. *I feel bored when ..., I think ... is boring.*

USE AND REVIEW

A • Quantifiers.
• Food and cooking vocabulary.

Students' Book (page 47)

Exercise 1 Do a trial run for the Bingo on the board. Highlight that SS have to change the prompt into a question *doesn't eat much meat* → *Do you eat much meat?*

enjoys cooking.	hates cooking.	eats a lot for breakfast.
never eats breakfast.	never eats fruit.	doesn't drink tea.
had a meal in a restaurant last week.	can name three ways to cook eggs.	can make bread.

Exercise 2 Elicit some names and put them on the board, *Sonia doesn't eat much meat,* so SS know which questions to ask which SS. Monitor the activity and note mistakes in question forms and pronunciation. Do correction work.

All work and no play ...

USE YOUR ENGLISH
Making arrangements

• Review and extend the language of offers, acceptance and refusal.

• Asking for details about place, time and content.

• *Would you like to ... ?* (neutral tone) and *Do you fancy ...ing?* (informal tone) would commonly have a rising intonation for friendliness.

• Accepting an invitation *I'd love to ...,* and refusing politely, *I'm afraid I ... .* It's common to begin a refusal with *I'd love to but I'm afraid ...* and a lower starting pitch than that used to signal acceptance, when we often use a high fall on *love* to signal enthusiasm, with appropriate facial expressions. Demonstrate to SS the effect a stern expression and a low pitch range would have on the listener. Highlight that we can say *I'd love/like to. I'd love/like to come.* But we can't say only *I'd love/like.*

• Suggestions, *Let's ..., Shall we ...* and *Why don't we ... ?* Point out that the full form is *let us* and is not followed by *to.* Word order is a common problem with *Why don't we ... ?* SS often say **Why we don't ... ?* This is followed by the base form of the verb. It is often helpful visually to guide SS away from these potential

errors. You could illustrate them like this, using colour, if possible.

Let's ✗ go to.

• Questions asking for details *Who's in it? What's it about? When does it start? Where's it on?* offer a good opportunity to practise consonant vowel links, simple rhythm and sentence stress patterns and to highlight that a falling intonation is frequently used with questions involving question words.

Who's_in_it?
/zɪnɪt/
What's_it_about?
/sɪtəbaʊt/

📖 Students' Book (page 48)

Exercise 1a) This subject gives ample opportunity for SS to personalise language. They could tell each other what they do at the weekends, the last film they saw etc. An alternative would be for you to tell them about yourself for listening practice. If you remember to use gesture, repetition, redundancy, recycled language and mainly familiar vocabulary, SS can tolerate a little new language. If you can add an element of surprise and/or humour into your anecdote, all the better. See *Extra material and ideas* 1 below for further suggestions. You could preteach the questions for the conversation by writing them on the board and jumbling up appropriate responses. Ask SS to match the questions and answers. Include the question *What's it like?* to recycle the adjectives learned in Unit 7.

Focus on rhythm, sentence stress and intonation. Alternatively you could immediately ask SS to complete the dialogue and deal with problems as they arise. However, we would recommend some practice of pronunciation.

Exercise 1b)

🔊 [8.1]

DIANE: Do you fancy seeing *Four Weddings and a Funeral* tonight?
MARK: I don't know anything about it. Who's in it?
D: Er - *Hugh Grant and Andie McDowell.*
M: What's it about?
D: Well, *it's a love story but a comedy as well.*
M: It sounds good. Where's it on?
D: *At the Odeon.*
M: OK. I've got a meeting that finishes at half past five. What time does the film start?

D: *At quarter past six or twenty past eight.*
M: Let's go to the early show, shall we?
D: All right. Shall we try that new Italian pizza place afterwards? My sister says it's great.
M: Fine. Why don't we meet at the cinema at ten past six?

Exercise 1c) Remember to highlight features mentioned in L.

1 Do you fancy seeing...?
2 Shall we try that new Italian pizza place? Why don't we meet at the cinema?

Exercise 2a)
1 The Museum of the Moving Image.
2 The Imperial War Museum.
3 The Sealife Centre.
4 Alton Towers.

Exercise 2b) Highlight the language used for accepting and refusing an invitation (see L). Ask 4 SS each to pick one of the advertisements and invite you to go with them tonight. Ask the other SS to write exactly what you say. To each invitation choose one of the following responses: *Oh yes, I'd love to. Oh, I'm afraid I can't. I'm working tonight. Oh, I'd love to. Oh, I'd love to but my parents are visiting us tonight. No, I don't want to.*
Don't forget to allow time for SS to write down what you say. Then you invite four other SS to go out with you this evening, and they each use a different response which you dictated. Write *ACCEPT REFUSE* and *IMPOLITE* on the board. Ask SS where you should write the responses – under accept, refuse or impolite? Write the responses on the board, highlight features of grammar and pronunciation mentioned in L. You could also take in advertisements applicable to the local environment but make sure they include appropriate cues.

Extra material and ideas

1 If you use the personal anecdote suggestion in Exercise 1, you could design it around four truths and a lie. Tell SS they have to guess which fact about your weekend was a lie. They could then tell their partner about their weekend based on four truths and a lie.

2 If you are teaching a multilingual class encourage SS to bring in information, photos, etc. about their town/city or country and tell the class where they would take foreign visitors.

3 SS plan what they would do on their perfect day off. They are only allowed a few minutes and they can't choose outrageously expensive events. They then try to find someone else who had a similar list of events/activities. Alternatively, they could try to find someone who had a very different idea of what a good day's activities would include.

SKILLS

A • Reading and listening: predicting the gist of a passage from a headline; reading and listening for detailed information.

• Vocabulary: antonyms of basic adjectives and contrastive stress.
• Writing: formal and informal letters.

Reading and listening

L • In Reading, the colloquial expression *to keep an eye on someone/thing* might cause problems.
• Other items which may need clarification are: *a'wards, 'doorsteps, home 'grown* and *leave us notes.* You could highlight these words before reading the text or ask SS to guess the meaning from context after they have read it.
• In Listening, these items might cause comprehension difficulties: *'nervous, a 'lone, a 'day 'off, 'hedgehogs* and *'squirrels.*
• Collocational features *co'llect the 'money, 'post 'letters, 'peel po'tatoes.* Remind SS collocational information is available in dictionaries.

Students' Book (page 49)

Exercise 1 Before looking at the book draw these on the board.

Ask SS which they can have delivered to their homes in their country and whether the person who delivers them is usually a man or a woman.

Exercise 1a) As SS give suggestions ask them to say why they think that.

Exercise 1c) If you want to get some idea of how quickly SS can locate and process information in a text, you could do the first few questions together with the whole class. They then continue in pairs or on their own.

1 She wakes up at 3.50 am.
2 She doesn't mind getting up early.
3 She finishes by 8.30 am.
4 She sleeps for five hours a night.
5 Customers give her cakes and vegetables.
6 She collects the money on Friday afternoons.
7 She looks after some elderly people.
8 To check if they're all right.
9 She posts letters, peels potatoes, all sorts of things.

Exercise 2 You could let the SS read the text first which will make the listening easier, but don't do this unless you have a group who really are lacking in confidence. Get SS to underline the mistakes in pencil in their books and ask them to correct the information. However, this is testing memory. It's unlikely that at this level they will have been able to note the correction down at the same time as listening. To get the correct information you may need to play the cassette again, stopping after each identified mistake. This text has such a personal flavour it might be nice to get the SS' reactions to Irene. Do they know people like her? etc.

[8.2]

IRENE: I'm not nervous when I'm out by myself in the dark. When our two boys were little I took them with me. They loved it. It seems to have given them a healthy life and both of them are milkmen now. I sing as I go along the quiet empty streets. I like hymns and Elvis Presley. I love the night. You see some wonderful things, like ducks going in a line down the main road. There are hedgehogs and squirrels, too.

  Everything is so peaceful and still. You see a few people, policemen, nightworkers and so on but sometimes you're all alone. I think a lot while I'm out - usually about the past.

  I haven't had a day off in eleven years. I'm never ill - it's all the milk I drink! Even when we went to London to get the award we got up at two in the morning to deliver the milk before we went.

She has two sons, not three. She took them with her when they were little. She didn't leave them at home while she was working. She isn't nervous when she's out at night. She sometimes sees a few people, policemen and nightworkers. She's never had a day off work.

Extra material and ideas

You could take the opportunity to talk about jobs which are traditionally done by men and those usually done by women. Ask SS to say if they think any jobs have to be done by one sex or the other. However, as the vocabulary focus for the unit is jobs, you could keep this discussion for later, but some kind of preliminary discussion will give you an idea of how much vocabulary SS know on the topic.

Vocabulary: opposites

• We are beginning the task of sensitising SS to the idea of partial antonyms and synonyms so the opposite of *light* can be *dark, heavy, serious* etc. depending on the context. The contexts in the unit are those which we would probably associate with the required antonym even without a context.

• Revision of intensifiers: *quite, really* and *very*.

Students' Book (page 49)

Exercise a) Page 139, 8.1. Before doing the exercise in the book, photocopy the adjectives and cut them up. Give each SS an adjective and ask them to go around and find the person who has a word which means the opposite. When the SS have found their partner, one of the pair says their adjective and the other SS predict the word on the partner's card. Finally the partner says what's on his/her card.

  To introduce the concept of partial antonyms take the adjective *light* and ask SS to complete these sentences with a word which means the opposite. Write the sentences on the board:

Hurry up. I want to get home before it gets _____. (dark)
Can you help me carry these books. They're very _____. (heavy)

Don't delve any further than this initial awareness-raising. However, when you come across partial antonyms/synonyms at their linguistic level, point them out.

1 difficult 2 wrong 3 generous 4 dirty 5 safe
6 light 7 expensive 8 poor

Exercise b) SS may stress more words in B's reply than necessary, e.g. they may stress *I* or *thought*. Try to keep the pitch level and the stress fairly even before the contrasted word. At this stage there's no harm in exaggerating the stressed syllable to make your point. Add a visual element to this exercise by writing the sentences on the board and using colour/boxes etc. to mark the stressed word in each sentence including A's sentences. Get SS to work in pairs to practise the sentences. First take the part of A and choose a confident S to take the part of B. Remind SS to swap roles.

Extra material and ideas

1 PW. Each pair needs a clean piece of paper. Using the adjectives in Exercise a) above assign two adjectives to each pair. SS then write four sentences, two for the adjectives they have and two for their antonyms, with gaps where the adjectives would be. Then pairs exchange papers. The SS try to guess what the missing adjectives are. When they feel sure they know, they write them at the bottom of the paper, not in the gaps. When each pair has written as many adjectives as they think will go in the gaps, they return them to the original pair who mark the answers.

Some sentences will suggest many alternatives to the SS: *This is a _____ book. This is a _____ book.*

Possible adjectives could be: long/short; interesting/boring; cheap/expensive; big /small. Obviously, if SS give more clues the alternatives should be reduced: *This is a _____ book. I really enjoyed it. This is a _____ book. I really hated it.* This activity highlights the idea that antonyms are context sensitive and practises common adjective/noun collocations.

2 Contrastive stress page 139, 8.2. Photocopy the sentences, cut them out and hand one to each S. Ask SS to look at their sentences and point out that the word in the box is the stressed word in the sentence. Then tell them to memorise the sentence. Count to three and ask SS to shout their sentences out. They then check they have said them correctly. Again count to three and ask them to whisper the sentence and check to see if they got it right. When you feel confident they can remember the sentences, collect them in. SS then go round the class saying their sentences and try to find their partner according to the stressed word they hear. If your SS need to keep their sentences with them, allow them to, but try to make sure they listen for their partner rather than just showing each other the stressed word. When everyone who can has found a partner, the pairs say their two line dialogues to see if they have the right partner. You could then hand out part or all of the exercise and get SS to practise the various examples of contrastive stress and discuss the meaning differences.

Writing

L

• The focus is on the language rather than the layout of formal/informal letters. (For layout of formal letters see WB page 33.)

This is an awareness-raising activity. We are not expecting the SS to produce the language of formal letters, only to demonstrate the language difference. However, by coupling the sentences with less formal, and in this case, easier language, SS should be able to understand the meaning of the formal sentences.

• Conventions of formal letters include: no abbreviated or contracted forms, not using first names in the greeting, closing with *Yours faithfully* if the greeting is *Dear Sir/Madam*, *Yours sincerely* if the greeting uses the person's surname, *Dear Miss Smith*. There is a tendency to use longer phrases/sentences in formal writing.

• Vocabulary in the advertisement may be unfamiliar: *volun'teers, preser'vation, 'habitats, grant.*

Students' Book (page 50)

My friend Jack — the bank manager

Exercise 1 Introduce the exercise by drawing these on the board to illustrate the idea of informal/formal letters. Tell SS they are going to read an advertisement for an unusual job and then a letter answering the ad. Preteach unfamiliar vocabulary from the advertisement (see L). If there is an advertisement or situation more relevant to your SS, you could base the exercise around that. Quickly check comprehension of the advertisement before moving to the letter. You could get SS immediately to try and identify the more formal sentences and then highlight the conventions listed in L. Or highlight the conventions before they attempt the exercise. The choice depends on how analytical your SS are.

1 b)   2 a)   3 a)   4 b)   5 b)   6 a)

Exercise 2 A good part of this will be SS copying the basic sentences in the given letter and simply changing the details to fit themselves as they are or would like to be. Encourage them to be inventive about themselves, e.g., *I've had ten years' experience with gorillas.* Allow time for SS to exchange and check each other's work.

Extra material and ideas

1 WB page 33, Writing, Exercise 12.
2 Job interviews roleplay using their letters as the basis. This would be very effective if they have been imaginative with the information they have given about themselves.
3 Try to make the practice of SS checking each other's written work a standard procedure. Even if it's done as homework, allow an extra day before collecting the written work so they can check with another S. Make it clear that any suggestions for improvement should be written in pencil only, and changes can only be made by the original S. Point out that this isn't just a technique we employ in language classrooms but an advisable thing to do with any written work.

GRAMMAR

• Sentence patterns with verbs followed by *-ing* and *to*.

Verbs followed by *-ing* or *to*

L

• When these sentence patterns are pointed out to SS there is usually a sigh of relief because they are at a point where they realise there are different patterns but they have no understanding of what governs the choice of the form which follows the verb or adjective plus preposition.

• This unit focuses on verbs which are consistently followed by either *-ing* or *to* or verbs which can take either with a minimal change in meaning. Those verbs where the choice is dependent on meaning have been avoided e.g. *remember.*

• Although it is inadvisable to explore the difference at this level, *try* and *forget*, do have a change in meaning when followed by *-ing* but the *to* form is more common. This is the form we focus on here. *Try to swim/swimming.* The *to* form suggests the objective is to swim, that is the goal. The *-ing* form suggests swimming is a means to an end but not the goal. Compare: *The sea was very rough. John tried to swim back to shore but ...* (objective/goal/implies it's difficult) and *I've got terrible backache. Have you tried swimming? I've heard it's good for the back.* (experiment/doesn't imply difficulty).

Forget to do/doing. The most common use is the *to* form, which usually has a forward reference. That is, the memory is the first reference then the action. *I forgot to put the cat out. Don't forget to take your key.* This means first the memory then the action. With the *-ing* form the action precedes the reference to the memory. *I'll never forget going to the doctor's for the first time.* This means first the action then reference to the memory.

• Those verbs which can take either *to* or *-ing*

with a minimal change in meaning include *like, love, hate*. The meaning difference centres on the idea of general or specific. Compare *I hate interrupting people* and *I hate to interrupt you but,...* In many instances the difference would be less obvious. Compare *I hate to see you cry* and *I hate seeing you cry*. Again, it's inadvisable to explore these differences with this level. They serve to confuse rather than enlighten. However, be careful not to state absolute rules as SS will undoubtedly meet examples which contradict them. A real danger with these verbs is when they are preceded by *would*. In these cases the *to* form will follow *I'd hate to live there* and *I'd love to work here*. Point this out to SS as they will already be familiar with the *like + -ing* form.

• The general v. specific guideline also works for adjectives. Compare *I'm happy sleeping on the floor* (generally) and *I'm happy to sleep on the floor* (on this occasion). However, it is probably better to limit the information you give and suggest the *to* form after the bare adjective *I'll be sad to leave*, and the *-ing* form after an adjective and preposition *I'm interested in buying a new computer*.

Students' Book (pages 50-51)

Exercise 1a) Introduce the grammar focus by writing on the board:

1	2	3
verb + -ing	+ to + verb	-ing and to

You may want to limit it to two columns depending on how much information the SS can take. The power of positive thought wouldn't go amiss here! Acknowledge the problem SS have with this area of grammar and suggest that by the end of the lesson they will understand it better. Remind them that the context is continued from the writing exercise in SKILLS. Ask questions to elicit any information they can remember. Then tell them they are going to hear an interview with Andrew. Ask them to predict the answers before listening. You could let your SS work in pairs immediately after the listening. However, if they are unlikely to achieve success, conduct a verbal comprehension check before they do the exercise to guide them by using the form in the question, *What did he decide to do?* Highlight the rule *would + like/love/hate* (see L).

[8.4]

ANDREW: I've decided to sell my house and give up my job because I want to do something different. I'd like to study how the gorillas live and then I hope to write a book about it.
Maybe some people think I'm mad but I really feel I just need to do something useful with my life.
INTERVIEWER: What about living in difficult conditions? How do you feel about that?
A: I don't mind living in difficult conditions - that's no problem. The only thing is I'll miss seeing my friends. I've promised to write to them every week and tell them about it.

1 to sell   2 to do   3 to study   4 to write   5 to do
6 living   7 seeing   8 to write

Exercise 1b) Tell SS to start a new page for the columns so they can continue to add to them in the future.

Exercise 2 Preteach *en'dangered*. To check comprehension quickly after SS have read, you could ask: *What new information do we learn about Andrew ?*
To form a different working group, you could assign a letter to each S - A, B, C, D. Each group (As, Bs etc.) is responsible for finding the answers for that particular section. They would then regroup so that each group now had an A, B, C and D representative. The SS would then teach each other. Do a plenary check at the end, so that you can highlight the grammatical features. Don't forget to allow time for SS to add this new information to their lists from Exercise 1b).

a) enjoy doing, help to do, expect to do, finish doing
b) interested in, fed up with c) -ing d) to

Exercise 3a) Highlight the preposition rule again before this exercise.

1 with   2 of   3 about   4 on   5 about   6 at

Exercise 3b)
2 sleeping in   3 doing   4 working with   5 giving up
6 speaking

Exercise 4 You could ask a more confident pair of SS to work at the board. Allow SS time to add new information to their lists.

1 to be   2 to find   3 to help   4 working
5 to see (seeing)   6 to remember   7 to stay
8 to come   9 to write   10 to phone

Using your grammar

Exercise 1 Get a secretary to write each group's story down. This will allow you to collect and check their work, and/or let the groups exchange papers and check for mistakes.

Exercise 2 Do an example with the whole class first.

Extra material and ideas

1 WB pages 30 and 31, Grammar, Exercises 1-4.
2 Grammar. Write all the verbs and the adjectives + prepositions from the unit on separate cards. For the next few lessons use these to revise this area of grammar. Open or close the following lessons by dividing the class into two teams. You flash the cards and the first team to shout -ING or TO correctly, gets the card. The winning team is the one with the most cards. Or you could give a mixture of cards to teams and they divide them into -ING or TO lists. The winning team is the one which finishes first with no mistakes.

VOCABULARY
What do you do?

L

• Pronunciation focuses on recognition of syllable and word stress. It's interesting that there isn't a definitive description of what a syllable is. However, you can guide SS by telling them a syllable has to have a vowel sound in it (*y* can be pronounced as /ɪ/), and it can be a vowel on it's own, *again*.

• Point out that compound nouns stress the appropriate syllable in the first word, *'travel agent*.

Students' Book (page 52)

Exercise 1 You could begin with a game to elicit what they know. Write the letters of the alphabet on the board. In groups SS try to find as many jobs as they can beginning with each letter of the alphabet. As they think of them, one member of the group writes them on the board. They can't repeat any that another group has already written. Leave these on the board so that after checking the exercise you can add any they didn't get.

1 pilot   2 accountant   3 travel agent   4 photographer
5 politician   6 journalist   7 mechanic   8 actor
9 librarian   10 architect   11 engineer

Exercise 2a) You will need to isolate the syllables visually and vocally to prepare SS for this activity. Write and say : 'pi lot , 'ar chi tect , 'tra vel a gent. Be careful NOT to change the stress or vowel sounds as you do this.

2-syllable words: actor
3-syllable words: accountant, journalist, mechanic, engineer
4-syllable words: photographer, politician, librarian

Exercise 2b) If you have used the alphabet game in Exercise 1, then use the words from that to give further practice of syllable identification.

Exercise 2c) Try to elicit the word stress pattern for the words in Exercise 2a) which have first syllable stress. Then play the recording.

1 'pilot   2 a'ccountant   3 'travel agent   4 pho'tographer
5 poli'tician   6 'journalist   7 me'chanic   8 'actor
9 lib'rarian   10 'architect   11 engi'neer

Exercise 3 When feeding back, ask SS to say why they think a job is exciting, boring, romantic, etc.

Exercises 4 and 5 You could join in. Let SS ask you what you think. You could also tell them why you became a teacher, and discuss the good and the less good things about the job or get SS to predict the good and bad aspects!

Using your vocabulary

Exercise 1 If you have any SS who work, ask them to tell the class about their situation. Or ask SS to talk about a member of their family who works.

Exercise 2 Get the SS to work with a partner to do the quiz. Again you could join in and let the SS interview you.

Extra material and ideas

1 WB page 31, Vocabulary, Exercises 5 and 6.
2 If you haven't already discussed it, you could get SS to look at traditionally male jobs and female jobs. Then discuss whether this is tradition or necessity.
3 If you work with a multilingual class, you could do a cultural exchange activity. Write questions on the board:

What age do people stop working in your country? Does the government help people who don't have jobs? How many people don't have jobs? Which jobs are well paid? etc.

List the SS' countries on the board and columns for the questions. You or the SS add the information to the board, and the facts are compared.
4 SS choose the best jobs for a person who:
a) is creative
b) likes working alone
c) likes working with his/her hands
d) is hardworking
e) is clever
f) is patient
g) is energetic
h) is good at communicating
i) enjoys working with people
j) likes working outside
k) likes every day to be different
5 Write these two lists on the board:

A	B
well paid	interesting
badly paid	boring
hard work	glamorous
easy	dangerous
needs a lot of training	exciting
doesn't need much training	fun
energetic	varied
unusual	important

In pairs SS think of a job and choose one adjective from list A and one from B that best describes that job. They write the jobs on a piece of paper and the adjectives on another piece of paper. They pass the jobs list to another pair who try to guess what adjectives the first pair wrote down for each job. After that they then check against the paper with the adjectives on. It's important that SS number the job paper and the adjectives the same, so that it's clear which adjectives belong to which job e.g.

| 1 vet | | 1 well paid   dangerous |

USE AND REVIEW

 Present Perfect v. Past Simple.

Students' Book (page 53)

Exercise 1 You could use other real world events of the moment or events relevant to the local situation you are teaching in.

Exercise 2 If you have the facilities, record the news programme on video or audio cassette.

A place of your own

Students' Book

General theme: housing.
Unit topic: choosing a place to live.

USE YOUR ENGLISH: talking about preferences (where you'd like to live).
SKILLS: reading and speaking (describing possessions in a room); vocabulary (guessing meaning from context); writing (adjectives or adverbs?).
GRAMMAR: opinions (*will, won't, might, may*); First Conditional.
VOCABULARY: rooms and furniture.
USE AND REVIEW: *to* v. *-ing*; First Conditional.

Workbook

GRAMMAR: *might, will* and *won't*; First Conditional and *might*.
VOCABULARY: furniture.
SKILLS: listening (Home, sweet home!); writing (telling a story).
DICTATION/PRONUNCIATION: word stress; contracted forms.

USE YOUR ENGLISH
Talking about preferences

• Vocabulary for different types of houses.
• Prepositions of position.

• Recycling of *I'd like to ...* from Unit 8 and introduction of *I'd prefer to...* in the listening. The difference between the two is that *prefer* is used when more than one option is available, illustrated by the frequent use of than: *I'd prefer to live in the city than the country*. However, *I'd like to ...* isn't limited in the same way. Highlight that *I'd prefer* is also followed by *to* + base form.
• Pronunciation difficulties are usually with the contracted form *'d* and the resulting consonant cluster. However, don't exaggerate or voice the *'d* as this will sound awkward and worse than if it is omitted. Try to encourage SS to use an aspirated *'d* sound. It often helps to repeat *I like/I'd like* and *I prefer/I'd prefer* so that SS hear the difference and produce a more accurate realisation of the whole phrase. Expect difficulties with the consonant cluster in *detached* /dɪ'tætʃt/.
With the question forms note that if the question includes an alternative *Would you like/prefer to live in the city or the country?*, there is a tendency to rise on *city* indicating incompleteness, and fall on *country* indicating

completion. If we don't mention an alternative, there is a tendency to rise slightly on the main stress.
• Unfamiliar vocabulary includes: *'spacious, de'tached, 'semi-detached, 'bungalow, two-bedroomed, ex'tensive, e'state agent, spare, 'fairly, 'countryside. Bedroomed* is an adjectival form describing the house. If you offer the synonym *big* to guide SS to the meaning of *spacious*, point out that it is used for rooms, cars, houses etc. and it means *big inside*. Then give an example that isn't a possible collocation, **a spacious book*. SS may not recognise that *the countryside* means not in a city or a town. We also say *I live in the country*. Highlight that the definite article is always used when the meaning is NOT *city/town*.

Students' Book (page 54)

Exercise 1a) Page 140, 9.1. Before turning to the book, hand out copies of different types of houses around the world. In groups SS try to guess the country. If they have difficulty, you could list all the countries on the board in the wrong order.

A Greenland B the USA C Malaysia/Indonesia D the USA (or any modern capital city) E Britain F Switzerland/Austria G France H Japan I Nigeria

When you have checked the answers, focus on other new vocabulary, (see L). You could leave it to the SS to choose which words they want you to focus on.

A 3 B 2 C 1 D 4

Exercise 1b) You could extend this into *I wouldn't like to live... because...* You could also introduce the concept and form of *I'd prefer to live... than...* which comes up in the listening, Exercise 2b).

Exercise 2a)
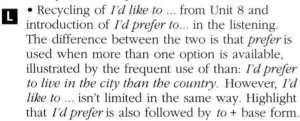
[9.1]
1 ESTATE AGENT: Are you looking for a fairly big place?
WOMAN: Well, no, now we've retired we don't need so much space - but John's leg's bad so we'd prefer to have a bungalow. We'd like to live in the country or by the sea, and we need a spare bedroom for when our son comes to stay.

2 ESTATE AGENT: So you are looking for a house with what - about three bedrooms?
MAN: Yes, it must have three bedrooms and also a garden for the dog. Otherwise the only important thing is to be quite near schools, for the kids, and shops and so on.
ESTATE AGENT: And are you looking for an old house, or a modern one?
MAN: We'd rather have an old detached house but we haven't got enough money so we'll have to go for a semi, I suppose.

3 ESTATE AGENT: How can I help you?
YOUNG WOMAN: I'm looking for somewhere cheap to live

while I'm at college. I don't care too much, because I'll sell it when I leave. Something in the centre of town, with a modern kitchen.

a) 1 c   2 a   3 b

Exercise 2b)
a3   b2   c1

Exercise 2c) SS have to justify the choices they made in b).

The retired couple want a bungalow, in the country or by the sea with a spare bedroom for their son. The couple with children want 3 bedrooms, a garden and to be near schools and shops. The student wants somewhere cheap in the centre of town with a modern kitchen.

Exercise 2d) Give some authentic listening practice by telling them about where you live, the type of house, where you would prefer to live etc. Allow SS to ask questions as this gives feedback on how much they have understood.

Exercise 3 If possible take in adverts for houses from a local paper. If you're in a non-English speaking environment, take in pictures and location information. The SS can create the details. Elicit some examples of possible question forms and practise them for stress and intonation *Would you prefer to live in a city or the country?* (see L).

Extra material and ideas

1 Page 140, 9.2 PW. This is an alternative to Exercise 3. SS take the role of estate agent or potential tenants. Give each the appropriate photocopy. Example:
TENANT: Has it got a bath?
ESTATE AGENT: No, it's got a shower.
Has it got a double bed/single bed/central heating/a fridge/a washing machine/a cooker/a TV? Is it near a station?/How much is the rent?/How much is it per month?

2 A pyramid discussion PW. Cut out pictures of homes from magazines. Give two very different types of dwelling in different locations to each pair. Tell them they are looking for a place to share. Each S must try to persuade the other that they should rent the home in their picture. Allow two minutes and insist on a conclusion. They then take the winning home and join another pair of SS. Now a group of four SS have to choose between these two pictures. You can continue so that you then have eight SS arguing about two pictures etc. Give a time limit for each discussion.

3 Ask SS to draw a sketch of the building where they live. They exchange their drawings with another S. In pairs they try to get as much information as possible about their partner's home in a set time. They then choose another partner and they have to tell them all about their first partner's house. Again set a time limit. Choose a few SS to feedback information they got from the second pairing. This is by now third-hand information. When they have finished ask the original SS if the description was accurate.

4 In a multilingual class you could get SS to interview each other using these questions.

- At what age do most people stop living with their

parents in your country?
- What kinds of homes are popular?
- Do people usually buy or rent their homes?
- Where do elderly people live ?

SKILLS

- Reading: scanning a text to identify the topic of a paragraph; reading for detailed information; simple interpretation of a text.
- Speaking: about possessions.
- Vocabulary: guessing meaning from context.
- Writing: accurate use of adjectives and adverbs.

Reading and speaking

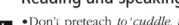

- Don't preteach *to 'cuddle, to stir, 'jealous, to 'nick something, 'furious* as they are the basis of the Vocabulary exercise.
- The following may be unfamiliar: *to hide, to 'straighten, a fringe* (on a carpet), *frame,* (of a window), *'miserable, 'boarding school, stone* (the material), *to run a country, a base* (as in *camp*), *a pot, to re'mind, car'toon.*
- The context is familiar but for the level it is fairly long.
- The fluency activity focuses on the listener's role. Point out features of discourse such as encouraging the speaker by using sounds, *aha;* an interested facial expression; nodding the head to show you're following; using tag questions to encourage the speaker to continue; asking questions for clarification etc.

Students' Book (page 55)

Exercise 1a) Set the scene by talking about one of your favourite possessions: what/where it is, where or who you got it from, why you like it so much etc. Try to elicit adjectives to describe how SS feel about the room rather than just *I like/don't like it.* E.g.: *I think it's awful/great/wonderful/terrible* (Unit 7). Tell them your opinion.

Exercise 1b) You may need to cue this, *Do you think a rich/tidy/intelligent/old/young person lives here?*

Exercise 1c) Make sure SS know the names of the items in the room: *fringe on the carpet, pot, cartoon* and before SS do the exercise write the following on the board: *carpet, matches, cat, painting, cartoon, pot.*

Exercise 2 You could give or elicit information about Mrs Thatcher (British Prime Minister 1979-90. She was the first woman to hold that office. The article is about her daughter.) before the reading or let them discover the references to her in the text. Tell SS they shouldn't read all the text at this time. They will read it in more detail later. They are only trying to find which paragraphs talk about the objects listed on the board, so they should only try to find those words. Point out that often the first sentence of a paragraph tells us the topic.

2 C   3 F   4 G   5 D   6 B   7 E

Exercise 3 Preteach some of the unfamiliar vocabulary (see L), as too many unfamiliar words can make some SS give up. Remember to write the words on the board so SS can recognise the written form in the text.

1 T   2 F   3 F   4 F   5 T   6 T   7 T

Exercise 4 SS have to interpret the text and identify that Carol's relationship with her parents has changed for the better now she's an adult. This is different from the previous exercise which didn't ask them to piece information together.

1 She didn't see much of her parents when she was a child. They didn't have much time for her and her brother, but she's closer to them now.
2 Carol's mother worried about details like straight fringes on the carpet. She works harder than her husband.
·3 Her childhood wasn't particularly happy. She wasn't allowed any pets.
4 She isn't very close to her brother or her parents.

Exercise 5 Before SS do the exercise highlight some basic features of discourse related to the listener (see L). This is a skill SS will have in L1 but may not transfer to L2 because they are often concentrating on the message and not on their role as listener. Draw this on the board.

Ask SS what a good listener does to help the speaker (see L). SS should refer to L1. If they seem unclear, mime a good listener and a bad listener. Ask SS to use encouraging features as they listen to each other, and the speaker can give feedback as to whether he/she was helped by the listener or not. Obviously, if your SS are animated/encouraging listeners already, there's no need to do this. If you're not sure, begin the activity and monitor the SS carefully. Interrupt the activity if necessary. Then ask SS to close their eyes and visualise their favourite possession. Ask questions to help them. *How big is it? What colour is it? Where do you keep it? Can you use it or is it just to look at?* etc. They then tell their partner about their favourite thing. You could do some feedback, *Were there any surprising/interesting possessions?* Be careful of the timing.

Vocabulary

L • Highlight that *to nick* is an informal verb, and that *furious* doesn't collocate with *very*.

 Students' Book (page 55)

Get the SS to justify their guesses by referring back to the text. They could check their guesses in the dictionary.

1 cuddle   2 stir   3 jealous   4 nick   5 furious

Extra material and ideas

WB page 36, Listening. Exercises 7 and 8.

Writing: adjectives or adverbs?

L • Problems include adjectives and adverbs which share the same form, *hard, fast,* and words ending in *-ly* which look like adverbs but are in fact adjectives, *friendly.*

• Position of adjectives and adverbs. At this level it is essential to deliver this highly complex area of grammar in small, manageable chunks without convincing SS that they have the total picture. When giving guidelines use words like *often, usually, sometimes.* It's tempting to say adjectives come before the noun but even at this level that's unacceptable in examples such as *she's happy.* So by saying adjectives **often** come before the noun we suggest to the learner there is more to know. Highlight the most common positions for adjectives and adverbs as SS can immediately use this information.

• Adverbs can qualify adjectives and other adverbs, *She's very intelligent. She works extremely fast.*

Students' Book (page 56)

Exercise 1 Read aloud the information in the box emphasising that not all words ending in *-ly* are adverbs. Draw attention to the position. Point out that we can't say **He quietly speaks.** A *child quiet.*

Exercise 1a) The adverbs are 2, 3 and 6.
Exercise 1b)
Well and *hard* don't follow the *-ly* rule.
Exercise 2
1 quick, carefully   2 polite   3 well   4 kindly   5 fast

Extra material and ideas

1 WB page 37, Writing, Exercise 10.
P **2** Page 141. 9.3. Give SS copies of the paragraph with 9 mistakes in the use of adjectives and adverbs for them to identify and correct.

In the middle of the night Sandy woke up sudden**ly**. She heard a **loud noise** outside her window. She got out of bed quick**ly** and walked quiet**ly** to the window. Careful**ly** she opened the curtains a little, but she couldn't see anything because it was **dark outside**. She fell asleep again quick**ly**. She didn't sleep very **well** because she had some **terrible dreams**.

GRAMMAR

A Expressing opinions, levels of certainty and conditions about future events and the First Conditional.

Opinions and conditions

• Question forms: highlight that we can use *will* when asking for another's opinion about future certainty, but we cannot use *may* or *might*. We can say *Will John be there?* but we don't say **May/Might it rain tomorrow?* This would be expressed by *Do you think it will rain?*

• Different modal verbs suggest different levels of certainty when referring to future time. *Will* is more certain than *may* or *might*.

• Modal verbs are centred around the speaker's opinion about the future at the time of speaking. Compare *She's coming* (statement of fact) with *She'll come* (in my opinion, at this moment).

• Remind SS of the formal characteristics of modals: no inflection followed by the base form of the verb; no auxiliary in negatives and questions; they can't co-occur in the verb phrase. We can't say **He may can come.*

• SS have met these modal auxiliaries before in Unit 4 and various sections focusing on functional exponents so the focus here should be on meaning and use.

• Pronunciation: the contracted form of *will*, if it's followed by a consonant, causes a cluster that is difficult for some SS. They often pronounce *won't* /wəʊnt/ as *want* /wɒnt/. Remedy this by getting SS to repeat *no* /nəʊ/ move to *wo* /wəʊ/ and finally *won't* /wəʊnt/.

Students' Book (page 56)

Will and *won't* for opinions

Focus on the time reference and the meaning. Draw the following:

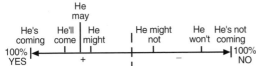

Oh, the FUTURE without him?

Tell SS that the lesson is about the future and how sure we feel about what will happen. Using the cartoons in the book ask: *Does the person know for sure? Does the person feel sure?* Highlight the degree of certainty by adding *will/won't* to the certainty cline.

```
                    He
                    may
He's      He'll  He         He might      He    He's not
coming    come   might       not          won't coming
100% |————————————|——————————|———————|————————→|100%
YES        +                              —       NO
                             |
```

Let SS read the explanation in the box and ask *How can we make this less certain?* and add this

to the cline.

1 'll/will rain   2 won't be   3 'll/will forget   4 'll/will be
5 'll fail/will, you won't   6 won't go, will   7 'll/will help, won't
8 won't start, will

May or *might* for opinions

Use the cline above to emphasize the meaning of *may* and *might*.

MR SURE: I'll earn a lot of money. I'll go out with a lot of women. I won't get married. I'll have a big car. No problem!
MR UNSURE: I may buy a small house. I might get a dog. I may meet a nice woman. I might have two children. I'm not sure.

First conditional: *if* + present + *will*

Exercise 1 Name a politician SS will recognise and ask: *What's his job?* Then introduce po'litical 'candidate, 'general e'lection, po'litical 'party. This will establish the context. Write *Toothfield* on the board. Explain that this is a town with a lot of problems. One of the problems is unemployment, no jobs for people. A candidate for the Drongo Party is asking people to vote for him in the election, and he's making promises. SS then read the speech bubble. Ask a S to read it out for you and write it on the board. Using the concept questions from the book highlight the form and meaning.

Yes/No?	Definite/Sure
If we win,	we'll reduce unemployment.

1 Present Simple   2 The future   3 No   4 Yes, provided he wins   5 The future with *will*

Exercise 2a) Ask SS to read the newspaper extracts and elicit other problems in Toothfield. Then ask them to predict what the candidate will say before doing the exercise.

[19.2]
POLITICIAN: If we get in, we'll employ more teachers. It's very important that young people should have the best start in life. If you elect us, we promise we'll spend more on transport. We badly need a more efficient system.
   If you choose us, you have our word that we'll build more houses. We, too, are very worried about the number of homeless people on the streets.
   We'll ban dogs in public places if we win. This won't be popular with many people but the health of our children must come first.
   Vote for us, the Drongo party.

1 get in, 'll employ   2 elect, 'll spend   3 choose, 'll build
4 'll ban, win

Exercise 2c)

Example: If we win, we'll provide more hospital beds. We'll clean up the streets if we win.

Exercise 3 This exercise moves away from the political context and requires negative forms in the *if* clause.

1 If you aren't/you're not careful, you'll fall off that wall.
2 If you vote for us, we'll reduce unemployment.
3 If you tease the dog, he'll bite you.
4 I'll scream if you don't stop singing that stupid song.
5 If you don't slow down, you'll have a crash.

Using your grammar

Ask SS to make a list of problems in their local environment, and put them on the board. In groups SS then discuss what their party would do to improve the situation. If possible, give the groups large sheets of paper on which to write their manifestos. Then display them around the room. One member of each group stays next to their manifesto to answer questions. The others walk around, read the manifestos and ask questions. At the end there could be a class vote. Each S has two votes. One to vote for their own party and one to vote for the manifesto they think is the best (not their own!).

Extra material and ideas

1 WB pages 34 and 35, Grammar, Exercises 1-4.
2 The election in *Using your grammar* could be based on the school the SS are studying in. They could vote for a class/school president.
3 There are more examples of future time clauses followed by the present in Unit 9. *Unless* is also included in Unit 9.
4 Jazz Chant page 141, 9.4. Note that this is at the end of Unit 9 on the cassette. The chant focuses on rhythm and is intended to be a fun activity. The first reading is greatly exaggerated and nearly all content words are stressed. The second reading has a more natural rhythm and each line has one main stress. With this level, concentrate on main stress and don't draw attention to secondary stress. (You may want to remind SS that unstressed words become weak or contracted.)

VOCABULARY
Rooms and furniture

• The picture of the bedroom could generate an extensive list of vocabulary. Establish how much SS know and then concentrate on the unfamiliar items: 'bedside 'table, 'chest of 'drawers, 'waste 'paper 'basket, 'dressing table, 'slippers, 'windowsill. Highlight the stress patterns carefully.

• Prepositions of place: there may be problems with *over, above.* Both can be used when the meaning is *higher than.* When there is movement we use *over. The photo's **above/over** the fireplace. The plane flew **over** the Atlantic.* Only point this out if a problem arises.

• The kitchen and bathroom vocabulary is equally extensive. Unfamiliar items may include: 'toaster, taps, 'cupboard, 'towel rail, 'dishwasher, 'teapot, 'kettle, sink (in the kitchen) v. 'washbasin (in the bathroom).

Students' Book (page 58)

Exercise 1 Walk around and check SS' spelling. If you do a plenary feedback you might ask SS

to spell some of the more difficult words. Check double consonants *sli**pp**ers, dre**ss**ing gown/table.*

1 The bed is against the wall/in the corner. 2 The wastepaper basket is next to the dressing table/wardrobe. 3 The bedside table is next to the bed. 4 The slippers are under the bed. 5 The cat is on top of the wardrobe. 6 The poster is on the wall above the bed.

Exercise 2 Take this opportunity to check if SS are keeping their vocabulary records up to date. When they have finished and checked their answers, ask them to make a word tree for the bedroom vocabulary from Exercise 1.

1 Bathroom: 'shower, soap, taps, bath, 'cupboards, 'towel rail, 'toilet, 'table, 'washbasin
2 Kitchen: 'washing machine, 'dishwasher, soap, 'freezer, fridge, sink, 'toaster, 'cupboards, 'cooker, 'towel rail, 'microwave, 'teapot, 'kettle, 'table

Using your vocabulary

1 Before you begin, ask each S to draw a plan of their bedroom. They then exchange plans with a partner. If your SS say they can't draw, tell them just to write the words in the appropriate place on the plan.

Extra material and ideas

1 WB page 36, Vocabulary, Exercise 5.
2 Draw a plan of your room on the board and ask the SS to copy it. Get two SS to work at the board. Describe your room and its contents to SS. When you have finished all SS check to see if they agree with the SS who worked at the board.

USE AND REVIEW

• To review sentence patterns *-ing* v. *to.*
• First Conditional.

Students' Book (page 59)

Exercise 2 You could make this a matching exercise. Write the different clauses on cards and ask SS to match the result clause with the *if* clause. They can then find which picture it belongs to.

a) If the sky is red in the evening, the weather will be fine the next day.
b) If you have a money/very small spider on you, you'll have good luck.
c) If a black cat walks in front of you, you'll have good luck.
d) If you you catch the bride's bouquet at a wedding, you'll get married next.
e) If you put up an umbrella in the house, you'll have bad luck.

Britain and the British

1 b) 2c) 3c) 4a) 5c) 6b) 7c) 8b) 9c) 10c) 11c) 12d) 13b) 14b) 15a)

Exercise 2 If you have a monolingual class, you could assign a country to each group. If there aren't any reference books available, you could set this for homework and begin the following class with their quizzes.

USE YOUR ENGLISH

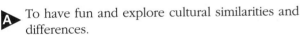

To have fun and explore cultural similarities and differences.

The language in this section should be familiar. However, you might want to check *tra'ditional* and *'super'sonic*.

📖 Students' Book (page 60)

Exercise 1 Try choosing a different way of grouping SS which will signal that this is meant to be fun. It could be male against female/under or over a certain age/hair or eye colour/SS who always do their homework against those who don't etc. As a warmer, ask each group/team to draw an outline of Britain and Ireland, mark the borders of Scotland, Wales and Northern Ireland, mark London, Liverpool, Edinburgh, Cardiff and Belfast. Tell them these maps will be collected and awarded a mark out of 20 to be added to the score they get in the quiz. This adds an element of suspense at the end. If there is a danger of SS taking this too seriously, create other scoring systems, e.g. the best behaved/the quietest/the most modest/the nicest shirt etc. This way they should accept the humorous nature of the quiz. Here is a quick reference for you to check against.

Extra material and ideas

Guess the country. PW. Begin reading the facts below out but DON'T give the name of the counrty. The clues become easier as you go down the list. If a pair think they know the answer they shout STOP. They don't say the country out loud, they write it down and you check. If they are correct, they get points for each clue they DIDN'T need to hear. So, if they guess correctly after clue 3, they get 7 points. If they don't guess until the last clue, they only get half a point. Continue giving facts until either you reach the end or all the SS have guessed the country.

1 China
1 The third biggest country in the world.
2 The currency (money) is called Yuan.
3 Next to the Yellow Sea.
4 The people invented fireworks.
5 A Communist country.
6 It grows lots of rice.
7 The home of the panda bear.
8 The capital is Beijing.
9 A famous leader was Mao Tse-tung.
10 The biggest population in the world. More than 1 billion.

2 Canada
1 The second largest country in the world.
2 The currency (money) is dollars.

3 It makes a lot of paper.
4 The population is 27,296,859.
5 89% of the country hasn't got any people.
6 It has many very large lakes, e.g. Lake Superior, Lake Winnipeg.
7 People speak French and English there.
8 Eskimos live there.
9 The capital is Ottawa.
10 It shares a border with the USA.

3 Pakistan
1 The religion is Islam. 97% of the people are Muslim.
2 It has the second highest mountain in the world called K2.
3 It has lots of rain in the summer.
4 The population is 121,664,539.
5 The currency is the Rupee.
6 The language is Urdu.
7 It grows a lot of rice and cotton.
8 Before 1947 it was part of India.
9 It's capital is Islamabad.
10 The largest city is Karachi.

4 New Zealand
1 The country is two islands.
2 The population is 3,347,369.
3 74% of the people live in the North Island.
4 It's famous for wool.
5 The currency is dollars.
6 It has a lot of earthquakes and volcanoes.
7 It's between the Tasman Sea and the South Pacific Ocean.
8 Maoris live there.
9 The capital city is Wellington.
10 It's near Australia.

5 Australia
1 It's the sixth largest country in the world.
2 The population is 17,576,354.
3 The currency is dollars.
4 There are 5 states in the country.
5 It's surrounded by the Indian Pacific Ocean.
6 It sells a lot of wool.
7 Aborigines live there.
8 The capital is Canberra.
9 It has a very famous opera house in Sydney.
10 Its most famous animals are kangaroos and koala bears.

SKILLS

•Reading, listening and speaking: reading a text for specific information (scanning); stating personal opinions; listening for gist; exchanging information.
• Vocabulary: dictionary skills; understanding idiomatic expressions.
• Writing: organising a letter to achieve its communicative function.

Reading, listening and speaking

L • The texts are quite short and simple with mainly familiar vocabulary except possibly: cre'ative, crea'tivity, con'ventional, 'humour

• SS will need adjectives which describe character.

 Students' Book (page 61)

Exercise 1 As a lead-in ask SS to name as many famous British people as they can, alive or dead. List them on the board, making sure that everyone knows why they're famous. See if SS can find anything they have in common. You could then ask if they think certain nationalities have certain talents. Most SS will probably have an opinion about the British, albeit a stereotypical one, based on films, books or magazines. You could also ask them why the picture shows a lion which is obviously ill/injured.

Exercise 2a) Before SS read the texts check they understand the reference to Amnesty International, an organisation which works to free political prisoners. Remind them they should be able to locate the information they need very quickly.

 1 kind, friendly and creative 2 relaxed and unconventional 3 polite and funny

Exercise 2b) Obviously if your SS haven't had any contact with British people they may have very little to say here so don't do it.

Exercise 3a) This is a jigsaw listening. If you don't have access to more than one cassette recorder, it could be done as a whole class exercise. SS could still be responsible for taking notes on one of the recordings. Make sure they know what Oxfam is. You may need to preteach RSPCA (Royal Society for the prevention of cruelty to animals) to Group B.

🔲 [10.1]
Group A
MAN: Yes, it's true British people seem more relaxed - in public, anyway. For instance, if a train is late with no explanation, people don't complain or get angry, they just carry on reading their newspapers. But it's not because they're relaxed - they're probably furious inside. It's because they hate showing their feelings - they hate people looking at them. If a small child is screaming in a supermarket, for example, the mother looks embarrassed - you shouldn't show your feelings in public! I do agree about the sense of humour. British people love playing with words - they can be very funny, and they can tell a joke without laughing - they can keep a completely straight face. I don't agree that people are polite though - maybe in small towns, but not in big cities like London. Drivers and shop assistants can be very rude.

🔲 [10.2]
Group B
WOMAN: Yes, when I'm away from Britain I miss the people because they're so unconventional - they're all different. You can see it in the way they dress - young people don't follow fashion. They're all individuals. I'm sure that's why there are so many different accents and cultures all over Britain, too - people don't like being the same. Yes, I think in general people are kind. In a village post office they will probably take the time to ask a little old lady, 'How's your knee?' And they are always ready to help and give money if there is a disaster and also to Oxfam and other charities - especially animal charities like the RSPCA! They can seem unfriendly,

or a bit cold at first, to people they don't know, but they're not really. A lot of British people are very friendly indeed.

Exercise 3b)
The man says people seem relaxed but they're not really. They don't like showing their feelings. They are funny and love playing with words. The woman says they're unconventional, kind and friendly.

Exercise 3 If SS have problems remembering, let them read the tapescript in the SB.

Exercise 4 Introduce the idea of stereotypes. However, if you have a multilingual class be careful that it doesn't become offensive. Avoid this by getting SS to write adjectives to describe a nationality not represented in the class and then one to describe their own nationality. Put these into a box, pull one out and read it to the class. SS try to guess the nationality.

Vocabulary: idioms

• Point out that although the temptation to use idioms might be great, if SS make a mistake or use them in the wrong context they can sound ridiculous. However, because they are so common in everyday speech it's important to understand them. The purpose of this exercise is to show SS how to access meaning in a dictionary.

Students' Book (page 62)

SS will need dictionaries. They may have difficulty in identifying the key word. You could tell them it's often the noun, though in the example it's the adjective! If your SS are not very adept at using dictionaries, lessen the load by assigning different ones to different SS and then letting them teach each other.

1c) 2e) 3b) 4d) 5a)

Writing: organising a letter

• SS may not know *pleased, to look forward to -ing, term.*

Students' Book (page 62)

Exercise 1 The focus is not on layout but on organising ideas. Tell SS they are looking at ordering information so that the reason for the letter is clear. Begin by asking them why we write to friends: to get or give news, to ask for favours, to invite, to congratulate etc. They won't use those terms but they should be able to come up with the ideas.

1d)
2a) B b) C c) D d) A

Exercise 2 C B D A

Exercise 3 Less imaginative SS may need some guidance about what to include in the paragraph giving news. Allow them to work with a partner, and encourage them to exchange papers with other SS to check for mistakes.

Extra material and ideas
WB page 40, Writing, Exercise 7.

REVISION OF UNITS 1 - 9

To check and revise grammar, pronunciation, vocabulary, functional exponents from USE YOUR ENGLISH sections and features of written discourse from the writing sections. It's important that you don't ask SS to do any sections which they have not covered for one reason or another. Check this before you begin. This isn't intended to be a test as such. It hopes to inform teacher and SS of areas which need more attention. There are more formal tests on pages 150-157 of this book.

GRAMMAR

• Question forms for Present, Present Perfect, Past and Future.
• *Must/have to* and *can*.
• Mixed verb forms: Present, Present Perfect, Past, Future, First Conditional, *-ing* or *to*.
• Quantity: *much, many, a little, a few, some, any*.

Students' Book (page 63)

Explain to SS that the aim is to find areas that need to be checked again. They should make a note of where they have difficulty so they can work on their own revision programme.

1 Question forms

Revision of question forms (Units 1,2,5,7). This is a conversation so SS could work in pairs and act it out. Comment on their intonation.

1 A: What did you do last night?
2 A: Was it interesting?
3 A: What are you doing tomorrow night?
  B: Do you want to come?
4 A: Do you know James?
5 A: Are you going to invite him to your party?
6 A: Have you seen him this week?
7 A: When did he get back from holiday?
8 A: Have you got his telephone number?

2 Obligation

There shouldn't be any problems here. However, tell SS that they should use all the verbs. If, for example, they use *have to* in 2, discuss why *must* would be more appropriate and why the reverse is the case in 3.

1 mustn't 2 must 3 Do we have to 4 don't have to
5 can 6 mustn't

3 Mixed verb forms

This will be more challenging as SS have a greater field of choice and they really have to think why one form is appropriate and others not. Many SS actually prefer this way of checking as it gives them better feedback on how well they're doing. Again, there are examples where more than one form is just about acceptable (*Going to* + verb or Present Continuous in 2), so remind SS of the differences in use and meaning.

2 is staying/is going to stay 3 to improve 4 is going to study 5 is living 6 going 7 have told 8 aren't 9 has never been 10 goes 11 'll/will cost 12 to come 13 to be 14 'll/will miss

4 Quantity

It is likely that this area of language from Unit 6 will continue to cause problems for some time because there are so many aspects to remember. Encourage SS by pointing out that they have made progress and because it's a complicated area they shouldn't expect themselves to be completely accurate yet.

1 some, a little 2 much, a little 3 some, much

> **Extra material and ideas**
>
> **1** WB pages 38 and 39, Grammar, Exercises 1–4.
> **2** Let SS work in pairs. Dictate a short passage with 6-10 mistakes in it. Choose mistakes you hear and read frequently from your SS. Tell SS how many mistakes they are looking for. SS mustn't write the mistakes down. Their paragraph should be accurate. Choose a S to dictate their corrected paragraph and write it on the board. Ask other SS if they agree and correct accordingly.

Pronunciation

Students' Book (page 63)

Weak forms and contractions

Exercise a) and b) Get SS to say the sentences and emulate the stress and rhythm.

1 *What time's he meeting us at the* shop? (9 words)
2 *Do you want a cup of* coffee? (7 words)
3 *Are you going for a* walk *with him?* (8 words)
4 *She was having her* lunch *when he arrived.* (8 words)

VOCABULARY

L
•For the sake of brevity and because it's perhaps less threatening for SS, the term *phrasal verb* here is inclusive of phrasal, prepositional and phrasal prepositional verbs.

• The phrasal verbs in this section have all come from previous units but have not been focused on as a group before or described as idiomatic and non-idiomatic. The non-idiomatic phrasal verbs are often related to movement. Only one verb appears in both sections *pick up*. This is a gentle introduction to the idea that some can be idiomatic and some more literal. At this level it's probably better to leave it at that. We also believe that it's more appropriate to focus on meaning than on grammar at this level. Only

highlight the issue of separable and inseparable if a problem arises.
• The vocabulary game draws on a variety of items from the previous units.

Students' Book (page 64)

1 Non-idiomatic phrasal verbs

Ask SS what they think a phrasal verb is. If they don't recognise the term give them an example. Highlight that it's a verb with two or three parts. Then divide the board into *EASY to understand/ less EASY to understand*. Give an example of each: *take off* (a watch) v. *fall out* (have an argument with a friend).

1 down 2 over 3 off 4 on 5 up 6 round 7 in 8 away

2 Idiomatic phrasal verbs

Walk around and monitor the SS as they do this. Note any particularly good example sentences and ask the S responsible to write his/her sentence on the board.

1 try on 2 hang on 3 rub out 4 break down 5 pick up 6 give up 7 get on with 8 take after

3 Noughts and crosses

Have a trial round with the whole class to establish the rules and procedure for noughts and crosses. SS may be familiar with the game but not be able to see how it works as a language game.

> **Extra material and ideas**
>
> **1** WB page 39, Vocabulary, Exercise 5.
> **2 Outburst** GW. Assign each group a different lexical area covered in Units 1-9 – clothes, body parts etc. Each group has to choose 10 words in their lexical area and make a list. Two groups sit opposite each other. Name them Group A and Group B. When you say GO, group Group A tells Group B their lexical area and Group B has 30 seconds to shout out as many words as possible from that area. Their aim is to try to guess all the words on Group A's list. When you say *stop!* Group A tells Group B their score. The process is then repeated with Group A trying to guess Group B's list. The group that guesses the most words are the winners. This is an excellent way to review vocabulary. However, beware, it isn't called OUTBURST for nothing. It can be very noisy!

Use your English

Functional exponents reviewed in this section are introductions, requests, invitations, suggestions, offers, making excuses.

Students' Book (page 65)

During the feedback ask one S from a pair to say A's line and another S from another pair to say B's, to see if they had similar or completely different sentences. This could be done as a whole class activity or SS could form groups of four or six. Take the opportunity to check rhythm and sentence stress. Choose a couple of the dialogues, ask SS to identify the stress, point out any consonant/vowel or vowel/vowel links, and get them to practise.

1 A: Can I have/Could you get me a black coffee, please? (Unit 2)
  B: Yes, certainly/of course.
2 B: It doesn't matter. (Unit 1)
3 B: How do you do? (Unit 1)
4 A: Could we have the bill, please? (Unit 6)
  B: Certainly. Here you are.
5 A: Could I have 10 first class stamps, please? (Unit 2)
  B: Yes, here you are.
6 A: Would you like to go to the cinema? (Unit 8)
  B: Yes, I'd love to.
  A: Shall we/Let's/Why don't we meet at the cinema at six?
  B: Shall I pick you up?
7 A: Do you fancy going to a restaurant on Saturday? (Unit 8)
  B: I'm afraid I can't. I'm going to see my grandmother this weekend.
8 A: Hello, 780 2395. (Unit 4)
  B: May I speak to Colin?
  A: Hang on a minute. I'll get him.

Writing

The mistakes focus on punctuation, spelling, anaphoric references, lexical substitution, word order, the use of the article, adjectives v. adverbs.

Students' Book (page 65)

Do the first sentence with the whole class. You could make a list on the board of the types of mistakes included.

I came home last Thursday. My flight was twelve hours late so I felt very tired when I arrived. When I came out of the airport I saw my family. They were waiting for me and it was wonderful to see them. I liked eating Brazilian food again. (Yesterday) we went to the beach (yesterday). I often think of our school and all the fun I had there. Is the class working well? I will continue studying English because I really want to speak it well.

LEARNING REVIEW

To encourage SS to assess themselves at the mid-way stage in the course and reflect on areas they feel they are weaker in/need to revise.

Extra material and ideas

If you can have individual tutorials with SS this exercise could form the basis for discussion. You could assess them on the same basis and compare your conclusions.

TEST

There is a progress test for Units 6-10 on pages 152 and 153 of this book for you to photocopy for your SS. See page 158 for the Key.

Enjoying life

Students' Book

General theme: pastimes.
Unit topic: sports and hobbies.

USE YOUR ENGLISH: filling in a form.
SKILLS: listening (a lucky escape); vocabulary (noun/verb collocation); writing (spelling).
GRAMMAR: comparative and superlative adjectives; *as...as*.
VOCABULARY: hobbies.
USE AND REVIEW: functional/social language; public places.

Workbook

GRAMMAR: comparative and superlative adjectives.
VOCABULARY: noun/verb collocations; compound nouns.
SKILLS: reading (collecting autographs); writing (spelling and silent letters).
DICTATION/PRONUNCIATION: spelling and the alphabet.

USE YOUR ENGLISH
Filling in a form

• Recognition of and responding to information prompts on forms: *Surname, Present occupation, Previous experience* etc.
• Responding appropriately to information prompts.
• Pronunciation of the letters of the alphabet.
• Revision of question forms.
• Revision of saying dates and numbers.

Students' Book (page 66)

Exercise 1 Begin the lesson with some work on the alphabet. Hand out cards each with a letter of the alphabet to SS. Begin by saying A /eɪ/, then they have to say their letters in the correct order. For more able SS start from Z and work backwards.

Ask SS *What was the last form you filled in?* Elicit as many different kinds of form as you can and then ask pairs of SS very quickly to make a list of the type of information you have to give. Then check against the forms in the SB. SS probably won't supply the vocabulary used on the form, so you could ask them to identify the prompts *Where do they want you to write your family name?* (SURNAME) etc. This whole exercise should be done quickly. Alternatively, list some headings (Nationality, Education etc.)

and get SS to match particular forms (Immigration, Job application etc.).

Exercise 2 Focuses on an immigration form. Be prepared to explain vocabulary such as *length*, *'purpose, 'signature*.

Exercise 3a)
1 Length of stay 2 Date of birth 3 Nationality
4 Purpose of visit 5 Present occupation

Exercise 3b) Ensure the register is correct for the situation, so 4 is *What's the purpose...* not *Why are you here?*

1 How long are you staying in this country?
2 When were you born? OR What's your date of birth?
3 What's your nationality? OR Where are you from?
4 What's the purpose of your visit?
5 What's your job?

Exercise 3c) Get SS to practise the conversation. It involves dates and numbers.

[11.1]
IMMIGRATION OFFICER: Hello.
SALLY: Hi.
IO: Where are you from?
S: Canada.
IO: So... nationality... Canadian. Right. What's your surname?
S: Jones.
IO: And your first names?
S: Sally.
IO: Fine. How long are you staying in this country?
S: Two weeks. Until the nineteenth.
IO: And when were you born?
S: 4th of July 1972.
IO: OK. 4th of July 1972. And what's your job in Canada?
S: I'm a Sales Manager.
IO: Fine. What's the purpose of your visit to England?
S: I'm here on business.
IO: OK. Let me see your passport. Where's the number? Ah yes. Seven nine six four two one dash nine three. Thank you very much. Can you just sign at the bottom, please? Good. Thank you. Enjoy your stay.

Exercise 4 Get SS to change roles so that they fill in forms for each other. Remind them that there is often more than one way to ask for the same information.

Extra material and ideas

1 WB Unit 8, page 33, Dictation, Exercise 11 about filling in a job application form.
2 GW For pronunciation of the letters of the alphabet. Write the following phonemics on the board:

1 /eɪ/	2 /iː/	3 /e/	4 /aɪ/	5 /əʊ/	6 /uː/	7 /ɑː/
a	b	f	i	o	q	r
h	c	l	y		u	
j	d	m			w	
k	e	n				
	g	s				
	p	x				
	t	z				
	v					

Ask SS to go through the alphabet and put the letters in the column with the appropriate vowel sound. You will need to demonstrate two or three, then ask SS to work in small groups, one group at the board. When the SS working at the board have finished, ask other groups if they agree. Correct accordingly and then practise saying the letters as they appear in the columns. When SS seem confident with the vowel sounds, ask them to say the alphabet as quickly as they can with a partner in the correct order. The partner should have access to the alphabet order to check.

3 PW. SS form a new club – a debating society, sailing club, dance club, holiday club, golf club etc. They design a membership form to help them to get the kind of people they want for their club. Divide the class so that there is one interviewer from each pair ready to interview any S who wants to join their club. They interview as many of the other SS as they can in the designated time. They then report back to their original partner as to how many suitable applicants they interviewed. If there is a club no one wants to join, you could fill the gap and play the role of a prospective club member.

Feedback could be cause for humour. Who was allowed in, how many people wanted to join etc. but it's important to keep this light-hearted.

SKILLS

- Listening: listening for gist and for discrete language items.
- Vocabulary: verb/noun collocations.
- Pronunciation: sound and spelling *sh* /ʃ/.
- Writing: spelling, silent letters.

Listening and speaking

L • You could preteach the following if you think they will cause comprehension difficulties and/or help to build confidence: *'pastime, fan'tastic, a'mazing, deep, to breathe, ex'cept.*

• Although the information in the listening is quite dense, the exercises don't ask SS to remember the details so they should manage to answer the questions quite easily.

Students' Book (page 67)

Exercise 1 Don't get too involved with the vocabulary of hobbies as this comes up in VOCABULARY on page 70. *Deep-sea 'diving* is illustrated in the picture and without giving too much away of the story, elicit the word *shark*. You could ask more confident SS to say what they think happened, and ask others if they agree.

[11.2]
PHILIP: Sarah and I don't spend our free time doing crosswords. We lead a very active life. When we're not working we enjoy rock-climbing or parachuting or going on safari in Africa. I've even learnt how to fly a plane. I suppose our favourite pastime though is deep-sea diving. Especially in the

Caribbean. I remember once we took the boat into the Gulf of Mexico. The water wasn't very clear. We all went in except Jules. He stayed on the boat. There were some fantastic sights. Amazing creatures I'd never seen before. It was magic with the light on. A kind of wonderland. It wasn't very deep and we were near the bottom. Then all of a sudden I saw Sarah waving her arms at me. She looked frantic. I didn't realise what it was at first. I thought she couldn't breathe or something. Then I saw it. This incredible great shark coming towards me. I've never moved so fast in my life. Luckily, it wasn't interested in me. It just went straight past. Perhaps it wasn't a man-eater or it was short-sighted or something.

Exercise 2a)
He met a shark when he was deep-sea diving but the shark didn't attack him.

Exercise 2b)
Camping

Exercise 2c)
Philip and Sarah's lives are very *active*. Once, in the Gulf of Mexico, they were *near* the bottom of the sea when Sarah *saw* a shark. When she *waved* her arms at Phil he thought she *couldn't* breathe. When he realised what the problem was he moved *quickly* but the shark *wasn't* interested and swam *past* him.

Exercise 3 If you think this pronunciation exercise will interrupt the flow of the lesson here, or you haven't got enough time, you could use it as an opening or closing activity in the following lesson. As well as sound and spelling, it would be useful to focus on word stress. The word *machine* (oO) is an unusual stress pattern for two syllable nouns which commonly have initial stress. The words also include examples of the *schwa* (/ə/) which you could review: *information* /ɪnfəˈmeɪʃən/, *especially* /ɪˈspeʃəli/, *profession* /prəˈfeʃən/, *machine* /məˈʃiːn/.

parachuting

Exercise 3a) ch

Exercise 3b)
infor'mation, es'pecially, pro'fession, 'finish, ma'chine

Exercise 4 Begin by eliciting the verb for the noun *form* (*fill in a form*), a collocation used in USE YOUR ENGLISH. Then ask what other noun we can use with *fill in (a questionnaire)*. The main area of difficulty with this exercise is likely to be the article: *tell **the** time, tell **a** joke, tell **a** lie, tell **a** story, tell **the** truth.*

   You can remind the SS of ONE v. ONE of MANY as a guideline: the time – one time now; the truth – one for a situation; the others refer to one of many – lies, stories etc.

2c) 3e) 4b) 5a)

Writing: spelling

• Expect problems with: the double vowel in *choose*; double consonants in *'luggage, es'pecially, 'travelling* (note: American spelling = *traveling*); sound/spelling differences of *ea*rn, *wea*ther; silent letters in *weigh*; i before e in *nie*ce, compared with *recei*ve (following c with sound ee /i:/).

• Suggest some spelling tips. If SS can visualise words, they are more likely to be accurate spellers.

📖 **Students' Book** (page 67)

[11.4]
1 How much do you *earn*?
2 What lovely *weather*!
3 How much does it *weigh*?
4 I like travelling by *bus*.
5 I've got a lot of *luggage*.
6 Which bag did you *choose*?
7 I don't go out, especially at *night*.
8 Will you hire a *bike*?
9 How old is your *niece*?
10 You look *awful*.

GRAMMAR

• Comparative and superlative adjectives.
• (*not*) *as* + adjective + *as*.

Comparatives and superlatives

• The basic comparison of adjectives may be familiar to the SS but they are unlikely to be accurate. Main difficulties are:

a) Remembering the syllable rules for comparatives. This problem is compounded by the confusion, even for native speakers, involved with two-syllable words. Certain two-syllable words can take -*er* or *more than*: *handsome, stupid, quiet, pleasant, cruel, clever, gentle* etc. However, adjectives ending in -*y* consistently take the -*er* form. This is perhaps a reasonably safe guideline: apart from adjectives ending in -*y*, SS should use the *'more X than'* form with two-syllable words.

b) *The* is not used when a superlative follows a genitive form: *Jane's best poem is* ... We don't say **Jane's the best poem...* Don't mention this unless the mistake arises at this level.

c) Spelling one- and two-syllable words which add -*er* + *than*: *big* → *bigger* → *biggest, hot* → *hotter* → *hottest, ugly* → *uglier* → *ugliest* etc.

📖 **Students' Book** (page 68)

Exercise 1 You could start with a team game where SS list as many animals as they can in 45 seconds. Points can only be scored if the spelling is correct. Then ask SS to name the animals in the SB. Preteach the meaning of *short-sighted*.

1 A cheetah. Cheetahs can run at 60 mph.
2 A rhino. Rhinos are very short-sighted.
3 A giraffe. Snakes are deaf.
4 An elephant.
5 A giraffe.

You could add a further question which leads to the structure *more* + noun + *than*. *Which animal needs more sleep, a lion or an elephant?* Answer: a lion needs more sleep. They sleep 21 hours a day.

Exercise 2 Try to elicit the rules for comparatives from the examples before referring SS to the grammar box.

1 short-sighted   2 faster   3 heavier

Exercise 3 Then get the SS to match the example and rules in the box.

a) 2   b) 3   c) 1

Exercise 4 You could include more examples of one- and two-syllable adjectives: *big, 'ugly, clean, 'dirty, 'heavy, 'noisy, fast, thin, fat*. You could also choose two animals from the box and in pairs SS use as many of these adjectives to compare the animals as they can. If your SS are already familiar with the rules you might choose to include the use of *less* + adjective + *than* though this has not been included in the SB: *English is less difficult than Chinese*.

Exercise 5 You could introduce the superlative with further questions based on animals. *Which animal is the tallest/heaviest/the most intelligent? The giraffe is the tallest* etc.

Exercise 6 Note that SS will have to work out *hot* from the *big* example in the *Language reference* on page 71.

1 better, the best   2 worse, the worst
3 hotter, the hottest

Making comparisons

L • The structure *(not) as* + adjective + *as* will probably be new to most SS at this level. Conceptually this shouldn't cause any difficulties if a clear illustration is given, and indeed the form is easier to manipulate than comparatives as there are no changes to the actual adjective, irrespective of the number of syllables: *as hot as, as expensive as*. However, you will need to highlight features of pronunciation such as weak forms *as* /əz/, and the frequent linkage which occurs *as thick as* /əz θɪkəz/.

How much work you do with your SS on producing these features will depend to some extent on how good SS themselves want their pronunciation to be. However, by spending time practising, you will help them to recognise this structure when they hear it. Note the alternative form: *isn't/aren't as* + adjective *as* v. *'s/'re not as* + adjective *as...*

Students' Book (page 69)

Exercise 7 Begin by asking SS to give you one of the comparative sentences again. Write it on the board to illustrate the concept of *not as* + adjective *as*: *A giraffe is taller than an elephant*. Then add = *An elephant isn't as tall as a giraffe*. Point out that we can also say: *An elephant's not as tall as a giraffe*.

Then draw these figures:

Liz   Jenny   Mike

Point to the *not as* + adjective + *as* example above and ask SS to make a sentence about Jenny and Mike using this structure. Then point to Jenny and Liz. Ask students to compare them. They will probably use the word *same*. Highlight that we can express the idea of *the same* using Jenny's *as tall as* Liz = Jenny and Liz are the same. Highlight the important features of pronunciation at this point (see L above). Point out that SS are being asked for their opinion, especially for 3 and 4.

Exercise 8 Before doing this exercise review the features of pronunciation. Write the example from the SB on the board and use visual clues to illustrate the linkage and contracted forms.

Spring's wetter than autumn.
               /ðən/

No, spring isn't as wet as autumn.
                /təz/   /təz/

It's often helpful to backchain to push this point home. Begin by getting SS to repeat:
as /əz/ then *wet as* /wetəz/ then *isn't as wet as* 'ɪzntəz'wetəz/ then the whole sentence *Spring isn't as wet as autumn* /'sprɪŋ 'ɪznt əz 'wet əz 'ɔːtəm/.
You could repeat the use of visual clues and backchaining for other examples until SS are at least able to recognise these features when they hear them.

[11.5]
1 A: Tom's taller than Bill.
   B: No, Tom isn't as tall as Bill.
2 A: Russia's bigger than China.
   B: No, Russia isn't as big as China.
3 A: Mary's lazier than Jane.
   B: No, Mary isn't as lazy as Jane.
4 A: Jeans are more comfortable than trousers.
   B: No, Jeans aren't as comfortable as trousers.
5 A: French is more difficult than German.
   B: No, French isn't as difficult as German.

Exercise 9
2 lighter   3 better   4 as expensive as   5 worse than
6 the wettest   7 most enjoyable   8 healthier than
9 the best

Using your grammar

Exercise 1 Here are more examples: Precious stones – rubies, emeralds, diamonds. Pets – mice, dogs, cats.

Exercise 2 Once the SS have made their decisions about the people, they could work in groups and see if they have the same opinions by asking *Who do you think is tidier, Anne or Bill?*

Exercise 3 You could add some more adjectives from Exercise 2 but beware of sensitive issues (*fat, short* etc.).

Extra material and ideas

1 WB page 4, Grammar, Exercises 1-4.
2 If you want to check SS' knowledge of comparatives and superlatives before beginning this section, you could do this general knowledge quiz orally. Write the answers on the board in the feedback. Then ask SS to form the question that produced the answers.
  1 Which is colder the North or the South Poles? (The South Pole)
  2 Which planet is nearer the Sun, Pluto or Mars? (Mars)
  3 Which is the largest country in the world? (Russia)
  4 Which is more expensive to buy, platinum or gold? (Platinum)
  5 Which is the widest river in the world? (The Amazon)
  6 Which country has the largest population? (China)
  7 Which is the highest city in the world? (Lhasa in Tibet)
  8 Which is the biggest city in Africa? (Cairo)
  9 Which American state has the smallest population? (Alaska)
  10 Which city is bigger, New York or London? (New York)
  11 Which is older, the Parthenon or the Colliseum? (The Parthenon)

P **3 Making quizzes** page 142, 11.1. GW. The photocopiable material is for 2 groups, but you could divide the information further for 4 or even 6 groups. Give SS photocopies of pieces of information to write a quiz for the other groups. This activity is useful for extending vocabulary. You will need to encourage SS to use dictionaries to find the meaning. Demonstrate that SS should offer alternatives in their quizzes; e.g. 1) Which country has the most radio stations? a) Australia b) China c) the USA. You could give this as homework, giving each member of a team one or two questions to work out. They then come together as a team and ask their opponents the questions.

P **4** Page 143, 11.2. GW Give SS photocopies of the 3 photographs. Ask them to write as many comparative and superlative sentences as they can. The winning group is the one with the most correct sentences.

VOCABULARY
Hobbies

L • Compound nouns generally have the stress on the first syllable: *'ice-skating*.

76

• The suffixes for the person who does something are *waiter, artist, musician*.
• USE YOUR VOCABULARY reviews *like/enjoy/be quite keen on* to base form + *-ing* from Unit 8.

📖 **Students' Book** (page 70)

Exercise 1 Remind SS that *rock-climbing* came up in SKILLS. Point out the stress pattern.
1d) 2c) 3b) 4e)

Exercise 2a) Other hobbies you could elicit/ present are *entering competitions, ballooning, sailing, flying kites, travelling, yoga, amateur dramatics*, etc.

a) hang gliding b) computer games c) painting d) stamp collecting e) music f) ice-skating g) bicycling/cycling/biking h) bird watching i) skiing j) (horse) riding k) canoeing l) fishing m) walking/hiking

Exercise 3 SS need dictionaries to check the word stress.
  You could use gesture/mime to elicit other examples: *weight-lifting/lifter, skydiving/diver, art/artist, dress-making/maker, bungee jumping/jumper, body-building/builder, scuba diving/diver.*

dancing/'dancer; cycling/'cyclist; photography/pho'tographer; cooking/cook; music/mu'sician; acting/'actor

Using your vocabulary

Exercise 1 You could begin by letting SS interview you about your hobbies, past and present. They then interview each other in pairs.

Exercise 2 This could also be a free writing activity.

Extra material and ideas

1 WB, page 42, Vocabulary, Exercises 5-7.
2 SS do a survey on hobbies linked to the grammar. Help SS to prepare a questionnaire. Give them prompts on the board to form questions.
Have/hobby?
How much time/spend on hobby per week?
What hobby/would like to do but don't?
Which hobby/would never do?
Which hobby/most dangerous?
For homework SS interview as many people as possible to feed information into the class survey. Even if you are teaching in a monolingual situation, SS could collect data using L1. As the questionnaire has been compiled in English this would mean SS would have to translate the questionnaire for the interviewees who didn't speak any English which is useful practice. Before the next lesson prepare the board in advance. Write up prompts, *Most people thought X was the most dangerous/exciting hobby. Most people spent more/less than (time) per week on their hobby. Only a few people thought X was the most ...* etc.
SS feedback their results which are added to the board.

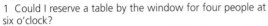

USE AND REVIEW

 • This section includes revision of USE YOUR ENGLISH, Units 1–10.

 Students' Book (page 71)

You could treat Exercises 1–3 as a test or a group competition.

Exercise 1

1 Could I reserve a table by the window for four people at six o'clock?
2 Could I have/I'd like chicken and salad and some red wine, please.
3 Could I have the bill, please? Do you take Visa? Is service included?
4 Do you come here often?
5 Do you fancy going to the cinema?
6 Would you like to come to the cinema?

Exercise 2

2c)   3d)   4a)

Witness

Students' Book

USE YOUR ENGLISH: making conversation.
SKILLS: reading and speaking (an undercover policewoman); vocabulary (noun endings *-ation*, *-ing*, *-ment*); writing when to use *the*.
GRAMMAR: Second Conditional.
VOCABULARY: crime.
USE AND REVIEW: comparatives and superlatives.

Workbook

GRAMMAR: Second Conditional; giving advice (*If I were you...*).
VOCABULARY: nouns from verbs (meet, meeting).
SKILLS: listening (a burglary); writing (punctuation).
DICTATION/PRONUNCIATION: grammar and pronunciation; sound and spelling /v/ and /w/.

USE YOUR ENGLISH
Making conversation

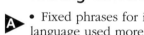

• Fixed phrases for informal conversation; language used more for social bonding than for conveying any vital meaning.

• Point out that with everyday greetings such as, *How are you?*, it's customary to reply *Fine, thanks.* We don't usually give any real account of how we feel. If you really don't feel well you might name the illness *I've got a cold.* Then it's up to the other person to enquire further, or cut the conversation short. A general response which suggests that all is not well is *Not bad.* Again, it's up to the listener to enquire further if there is genuine interest. Point out this greeting is for someone we already know.

• *I hope so/not.* The meaning here is *This is what I want/don't want.* Again, these phrases help the conversation along and allow it to be extended more than giving vital information.

• There is more message value in the fixed phrases *I think/don't think so.* Compare *Is Jane coming tonight? I hope so. /I think so.*

• *I hope so* doesn't really answer the question at all, it states a preference. However, *I think so,* suggests that the speaker has some reason to believe Jane is coming, but he/she is not absolutely sure. We can use this with other pronouns and proper nouns *John doesn't think so. I expect/imagine/believe so* convey a similar meaning to *I think so* but these are more commonly used in the positive and usually limited to pronoun *I.*

• Pronunciation. These phrases have a reasonably predictable stress and intonation pattern. Encourage SS to learn them as set phrases with set phonological features.

Nice to see you again.
/juːwəgen/

How are you?
/waːjuː/

I'm fine, thanks.

How about you?
/wəbaut/

I hope so. I hope not.

I think so. I don't think so.

📖 Students' Book (page 72)

Exercise 1a) Ask SS to talk about the last party they went to. While they think, write guide questions on the board: **Where was it? What was the reason for the party? How many people were there? Did you know all the people? Was there music, dancing, food, drink? When did it start/finish? Was it a good party?**

After some feedback, ask SS to think about how conversations start at parties. Is it easy to start a conversation? They may not come up with anything but you have now set the scene and identified the linguistic area. Using the pictures in the book elicit information about the time of day, (probably lunch time) weather, (cold, snowing a little) who looks friendly etc.

[12.1]
1 A: Nice to see you again.
  B: Hi! How are you? I hear you've not been very well.
  A: I'm fine now, thanks. How about you?
2 A: Hello, Sally.
  B: Hello. Thanks very much for Tom's present. It was just what he wanted.
  A: You're welcome.
3 A: Is Colin here?
  B: Colin who?
  A: You know. Colin Wilson. I want to see him.
  A: I don't think so. I haven't seen him.
4 A: It's a bit chilly today, isn't it?
  B: Yes, I think it's going to snow.
  A: I hope not. We're playing football later.

🔑 1b) 2d) 3c) 4a)

Exercise 1b) When you have checked and practised what SS have written, practise some of the other phrases from the conversations (see L).

Exercise 1c) Remind SS that facial expressions also carry information about friendliness as well as words and intonation. Obviously, we aren't telling them anything they don't know, but when SS are so focused on the actual words, they tend to ignore body language and intonation. If you allow them time to feel confident about the words, you can then ask them to think about facial expression and intonation. This is usually welcome, especially if you do an exaggerated expressionless version to demonstrate.

🔑 In conversations 1, 2 and 4 the people are pleased to see each other. We know by the range of pitch they use.

Exercise 2 Ask concept/context questions, too. *Does the man want it to snow? Why not? What does he say?* Highlight the difference in meaning between *I hope so* and *I hope not*, *I think so* and *I don't think so.* Point out that the expressions with *hope* mean *I want or don't want something to happen.* Expressions with *think* mean *it's my opinion.*

Highlight the difference in form:
Negative of *hope* so = *hope* not
Negative of *think* so = *don't/doesn't think* so
You could point out other aspects (see L), but this may be all SS can absorb at the moment. You could give further information as you review this area at a later date. The principle is review and extend. Give SS a global idea of the new area of study, then later add more detail.

🔑 1 The woman thinks it's going to snow.
2 The man doesn't want snow because he's playing football later.

🔑 **Exercise 3**
1 I hope so.   2 I think so.

Exercise 4a) Expect SS to choose the wrong phrase here because they haven't differentiated between wanting something and opinion about something. Write these questions on the board to guide them.

Does the person want something to happen ? Is it the person's opinion?

🔑 1 I think so. 2 I hope not. 3 I don't think so. 4 I hope so.

Exercise 4b) Give visual guidance for pronunciation by marking linkage and stress on examples on the board (see L).

Extra material and ideas

1 WB page 46, Vocabulary, Exercise 6.
Ⓟ 2 Match the conversations and find your partner page 143, 12.1. PW. Photocopy the sentences and cut them up. Give each S a line of dialogue. They memorise the line. They then walk around repeating it until they think they have found their partner. Each pair says their dialogue while the other SS decide if they fit, what the situation is, if they are friends or strangers, what the problem is, etc. Or cut up the dialogues and give them to groups of four who match the lines. With either approach, when the dialogues are correctly matched, ask SS to extend the dialogue with two more lines. Then get them to mime what happens just before the dialogue begins, say the dialogue then add their extensions.

SKILLS

• Reading and speaking: predicting; finding the main points; reading for detail; personal opinions of a text.
• Vocabulary: word formation verb ↔ nouns.
• Writing: accuracy, use of the definite article.

Reading and speaking

🄛 • Crime involves complex concepts and vocabulary but these have been kept to a minimum in the text. The following vocabulary may be new: *ar'rest, con'fused, con'fession, 'evidence.*

📖 **Students' Book** (page 73)
Exercise 1 Deals with key vocabulary items in the text and is the basis for the prediction exercise so meaning is very important. Ask questions to check SS have understood *What do you want if you write a lonely-hearts advertisement? When can the police arrest you?* etc.

🔑 1 a)   2 c)   3 e)   4 b)   5 d)

Exercise 2 Avoid the temptation to introduce a lot of courtroom vocabulary. It isn't necessary for the prediction exercise or the text. If SS offer conflicting ideas about what they think happened, write these on the board as an added incentive to read the text.

Exercise 3 The article is based on a true story and raises a serious legal issue about what is admissible evidence in court. Get SS to read the text quickly for the main points and check their predictions.

Exercise 4 This exercise requires reading for detailed information. Get SS to read the statements first so they'll know what they're looking for. When they give their answers, get them to say where the information is in the text. Cue this with *Which line is it in ?*
🔑 1 F 2 F 3 F 4 T 5 T 6 F 7 F

Exercise 5 It is unlikely that SS will have sufficient language to explore these issues in great detail but it's worth attempting. Begin by voting on each statement and asking SS to say why they voted that way. For correction during this kind of fluency work, you could reformulate their sentences as we do when we are clarifying information we're listening to. Ask SS if they would do what Pat did and why/why not.

Vocabulary

🄛 • Explain that these suffixes aren't the only ways to form nouns from verbs, but they are common ones.

• Pronunciation. The stress stays the same, apart from those words ending in /ʃən/, when we stress the syllable before: *'STAtion, exami'NAtion, poli'TIcian.* Also point out that the sound /ʃən/ can be spelt *-tion, -tian, -sion, -sian, -cian.*

 Students' Book (page 74)

Highlight word stress (see L above). Ask SS to practise saying the words.

 improvement, feeling, argument, examination, saving, explanation, pronunciation, warning

Extra material and ideas

WB page 46, Vocabulary, Exercise 5.

Writing

 • Geographical features often don't take the definite article, but some do: *Mount Everest* v. *The Alps.* When there is a group of mountains or when a country is made up of a group of what are seen to be individual parts we often use the article: *the USA* v. *America, the Philippines, the UK* v. *Britain,* but *Indonesia.*

• Some nationalities will have greater difficulties with this area than others. If SS' L1 doesn't use articles, expect to deal with this area again and again. Little and often is a good rule of thumb. It's also important to help SS to acknowledge where they have improved so they will not see the task as impossible.

 Students' Book (page 74)

Exercise 1 Refer back to Unit 7, Writing, page 44 and the indefinite article. Let SS read the language summary while you write the following on the board.

> THE ???
> I went to the France last week.
> I went to France last week.
> The moon is really bright tonight.
> Moon is really bright tonight.
> She lives in London.
> She lives in the London.
> She speaks the English well.
> She speaks English well.
> The River Nile is in Egypt.
> River Nile is in Egypt.
> She climbed the Mount Everest.
> She climbed Mount Everest.
> She went climbing in the Alps
> She went climbing in Alps.

In pairs ask them to choose which sentence they think is correct. When you have established the right answers, ask questions to help elicit the general rules.

> *What is London?* (a city)
> *Do we use THE with cities?* (no)
> *What is the Nile?* (a river)
> *Do we use THE with rivers?* (yes)

Is there only one River Nile? (yes)

Continue with this guided discovery approach until you have covered all the examples on the board. SS then look at the grammar box on page 74 and find other rules. Finally get SS to do the exercise to check.

1 A: Have you been to Italy?
   B: Yes. It's the only country in Europe I would like to live in. I also speak Italian.
2 A: What's the name of the place you're moving to?
   B: Oldham.
   A: Oh, I was born there.
   B: We've bought a house in Park Road near the river.

Extra material and ideas

1 WB page 47, Grammar and Pronunciation; Exercise 9.
2 In pairs get SS to write 6 sentences to illustrate the rules for the definite article. Some of the sentences should be correct and some incorrect. They exchange with another pair who try to find and correct the mistakes. While they prepare the sentences, they can refer to the book, but when they exchange papers and try to find the mistakes, they should not.

GRAMMAR

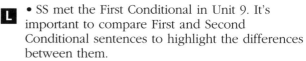

 • SS met the First Conditional in Unit 9. It's important to compare First and Second Conditional sentences to highlight the differences between them.

a) **Time** The First Conditional refers to a future event/time, the Second Conditional doesn't really refer to time as such because it's focusing on a hypothetical situation. However, we could see the hypothetical event in terms of present or future.

b) **Possibility** The speaker and listener understand the First Conditional to mean the outcome of the *if* clause could go either way, a 50:50 chance. However, when the Second is used, we understand that the chance of the *if* clause being fulfilled is either very slim or non-existent.

c) **Form** The formula for the basic First Conditional is *if* + present + *will* + base form.

The basic Second Conditional is *if* + past (subjunctive) + *would* + base form. (Note there are other forms: *If you were walking … If you were to walk…Were you to walk …* and modals, *If you could …*)

It's often hard for SS to accept that the First Conditional, which uses a present tense, refers to future time, and equally hard to accept that the past subjunctive in the Second Conditional isn't referring to past time. This really has to be highlighted frequently. It sometimes helps to give an example of a Third Conditional to show there is a way to refer to past time. However, it's inadvisable to go any further than giving an example.

Although traditional grammars tell us the correct form with the verb *to be* is: *If I/he/she/it were …*, in fact both *was* and *were* are common in everyday speech and should be accepted.

• Pronunciation. The contracted form *'d,* when followed by a consonant, is a difficult consonant cluster for many nationalities. By repeating a comparison such as *I buy/I'd buy* you can help SS to hear the difference and this helps them to produce the different sounds. The sheer length of a sentence can cause pronunciation problems. Give SS time to rehearse the examples and commit them to memory before focusing on phonological features such as contracted forms, stress, rhythm.

📖 Students' Book (page 74)

Exercise 1 Elicit information from the pictures. Ask questions: *Is it common/usual to find money this way? Do we find lost diaries every day?* We're hoping for the answer *No* to introduce the idea of limited possibility. Then focus on the idea of imagination which is asked for in the questionnaire. Let SS read the concept questions silently, then check their answers.

🔑
1 She's imagining it.
2 The future or the present.
3 The Past Simple.
4 If I find £20, I'll keep it = it's possible.

Exercise 2 The focus is on form. Note that this is not a rigid rule. There are alternative forms (see L above). However, don't mention them unless SS raise them, as they could be confused. Ask SS to write the rule in their own words, encouraging them to use a 'personal grammar'.

🔑 The Past Simple; a modal like *would*.

Exercise 3 You could add other situations: *You meet someone you really like who is much older than you, would you lie about your age?*

🔑
3 asked, wouldn't say, would lie
4 booked, was, wouldn't steal, would leave

Exercise 4 Get feedback from one pair for each question, and then ask the others if they have something different. Encourage SS to ask you what you'd do in these situations. This allows more practice of questions forms and offers extra listening practice.

Using your grammar

Exercise 1 Other possible questions: *What be/ the first thing/do ? What/ do /weather was bad?* You could also go into the negative *What/not do? What/not drink or eat?* In feedback, focus on the contracted *I'd.*

🔑
1 Who would you go with?
2 How would you get there?
3 Where would you stay?
4 What would you have to eat and drink?
5 What would you like to do?
6 Who would you send a postcard to?

Exercise 2 Further suggestions: *You can meet anyone you like. You can be a champion of any sport you like. You can give a lot of money to any charity you like. You can change one thing in your life that you're not happy with.*

Exercise 3 Begin, if possible, by dividing the class into men and women. Ask the women to think of three reasons why it's easier to be a man than a woman and three reasons why it's harder. Ask the men to do the same about women. This can often result in some humorous but heated discussion. You will have to help with vocabulary. As the sexes give their opinion, ask the opposite sex if they think they're correct. If you don't have both sexes in the class, you can still use the same cues. Then go to the question in the book and get SS to interview each other.

🔑 Exercise 4
GROUP A
1 What kind of music would you sing if you were Pavarotti?
2 Which city would you go to if you wanted to visit the Vatican?
3 What languages would you speak if you lived in Singapore?
4 Where would you be if you were at Harvard?
GROUP B
1 Which sport would you play if you were at Wimbledon?
2 What would you see if you visited the Louvre?
3 Where would you be if you were at Copacabana?
4 What would you do if you had a balalaika?

Extra material and ideas

1 WB page 44 and 45, Grammar Exercises 1-4
2 The following gives a strong visual representation of the conceptual difference between the First and Second Conditional. Many SS need this kind of visual support. You need a hat or box, and a lot of small scraps of paper. Write on the board:
The lottery prize is £2,000,000.
If I win, I'll buy …
     (will)
IF I won, I'd buy …
     (would)

Ask SS what they know about national lotteries. *How many people win?* So the chance is X million to 1. Not good. Then tell them this is a class lottery. Get them to write their names on one of the slips of paper and put it in the hat/box. As they do this, keep repeating they have a good chance, only a few people, this money could be theirs. Point to the two sentences on the board get a few SS to complete the First Conditional sentence. Then keep adding more and more and more scraps of paper to the hat/box. As you add more and more keep asking, *What about your chance now ?*

The SS see the shift from reasonable chance to very little chance. Refer back to the board and ask which sentence we would say now. Get a few to complete the Second Conditional sentence. End by picking a piece of paper out (try to make sure it's a blank one). (Note that this might be offensive to those whose religion forbids gambling.)

VOCABULARY

Crime

L • This is an area of human interest for most SS but in terms of collocation and complicated concepts, there is a danger of killing this interest. It is important to structure the lesson tightly and keep the amount of vocabulary to a manageable chunk.

• Highlight the collocational features of *rob* v. *steal*. *Rob* a person or a place and a car or house, but *steal* is what you actually take (*a pen, money, a bag, a watch*). The difference can be highlighted by: *to rob a car* (the car is still there but the radio is gone, the bag's gone etc.) v. *to steal a car* (the car's gone). Compare *to rob a bank* and *steal a bank*. The latter would be impossible. Other potential problems include collocation of *to burgle*. This is limited to buildings, you can't burgle a person. It involves breaking in. *Theft* describes the general crime. It also collocates with car. *Car theft is very common now.*

📖 Students' Book (page 76)

Exercise 1 As a lead-in write the word *crime* on the board. Ask SS to give examples. You may need to cue this with an example, *murder*. This will tell you how much vocabulary they already know and will help them predict the vocabulary they are going to learn. Then go to the book.

Exercise 1a)
🔑 1 b) 2 c) 3 a)

📼 [12.2]
1 ANNOUNCER: Last night in Windsor a burglar broke into a house and stole a mobile phone. Later he rang the owner offering to sell it half price for two hundred pounds...
2 Yesterday morning at Burnham a robber tied up a bank manager and took thousands of pounds. The bank manager dialled nine, nine, nine with his tongue and called the police. The police later arrested the robber.
3 A thief walked into an electrical shop in Hitchin and loaded a washing machine into his car. He calmly drove away. The man has been sent to prison for six months.

Exercise 1b)
🔑 a) thief   b) burglar   c) robber

🔑 Exercise 2
burglar burgle burglary
thief theft
robber rob robbery

Exercise 3 Highlight basic collocations. You could also do more work on collocations. Show SS that this information can be found in a good dictionary. How much you do will depend on

what you think your SS can take in (see L). However, it's advisable to highlight the difference between *rob* and *steal* to avoid potential mistakes such as *I've been stolen.*

🔑 1 burgled 2 rob 3 theft

Exercise 4 Preteach *footsteps* and *send someone to prison* as these come up in the text. Highlight that *to steal* is an irregular verb *steal, stole, stolen*.

🔑 arrest, committing, thief, prison, stole

Exercise 5 You could introduce *to break in* though it can be avoided. An opportunity to revise linkers and past tenses used in narratives.

🔑 (This is a suggested answer but accept appropriate alternatives)
One day a young man broke into a language school. He climbed in through a window and stole a cassette recorder and a video recorder. He went back to his car, but he couldn't drive away because two other cars were too near his car. In the end a policeman arrested him.

Extra material and ideas

1 WB page 47, Listening, Exercise 8.
2 SS read local papers for homework and try to find articles about crime. The next lesson could begin with a news report about current crimes. SS could then continue to follow the story and keep the class up to date on what was happening.

USE AND REVIEW

A • Comparative and superlative adjectives.
• Vocabulary of hobbies.

📖 Students' Book (page 77)

Exercise 1 Get feedback by asking SS to tell you everything they know about Sandra and Helen.

🔑 Exercise 1b)
Example answer:
Helen is the tallest. Rebecca is the smallest/youngest. Mark is the fattest/oldest. Steven is taller than Rebecca etc.

Exercise 2 After SS have done this in pairs, you choose one of the people in the pictures and see how quickly they guess. You can also name each character and ask what hobbies people had for them. Are any the same? Are they completely different or similar?

Love is all around

Students' Book

USE YOUR ENGLISH: giving and understanding directions.
SKILLS: listening (song 'Love is all around'); reading and speaking (monogamy and romance); vocabulary (rhymes); writing (reference words).
GRAMMAR: defining relative clauses (*who, which, that, where*); adjective word order (size, shape, colour); *We use a ... for ...-ing.*
VOCABULARY: describing people; relationships.
USE AND REVIEW: crime situations, *What would you do if...?*

Workbook

GRAMMAR: defining relative clauses; directions; adjective word order; *We use a ...for ...-ing.*
VOCABULARY: opposites.
SKILLS: reading (how two couples met), writing (pronouns).
DICTATION/PRONUNCIATION: rhyming words; vocabulary.

USE YOUR ENGLISH
Finding the way

• To understand and give directions.
• Vocabulary related to roads.
• Prepositions of place.
• Use of the imperative.
• Sequencing words.

L • Pronunciation. Word stress may cause difficulty: *'traffic lights, 'T-junction, pe'destrian 'crossing, 'crossroads, one-way 'street, 'roundabout.*

• Encourage the use of /ə/ in weak forms, in *to* /tə/ + consonant, in *of* /əv/ and in the word *opposite* /'ɒpəzɪt/.

• Prepositions of place will not be new at this level, but SS have difficulty remembering them. Most of them are easy to demonstrate. However, there may be confusion between *opposite* and *in front of*. *In front of* is opposite in meaning to *behind*. We don't use *in front of* for things which are on opposite sides of rooms/roads. *In front of* relates to a person or thing that is nearer to the front line of a queue/room etc. than you are.You could demonstrate by getting one S to stand behind you and one S to stand in front of you as in a queue. Then get a S to stand or sit facing you to illustrate *opposite*.

• Highlight the use of the imperative which can be replaced by the second person form of the

verb. We use both forms when giving directions. See Exercise 2a).

Students' Book (page 78)
Exercise 1a) You could introduce the words with illustrations on the board.

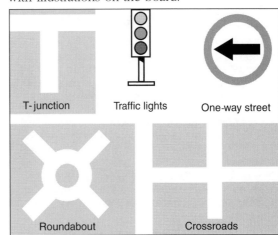

Then use Exercise 1 a) as a check. It is worth taking time to work on pronunciation, particulary word stress. Add other related words *zebra 'crossing, 'dead 'end, 'cul-de-sac.*

1D 2C 3A 4F 5B 6E

Exercise 1b) Check that SS understand prepositions of place before you begin. Be prepared to deal with *opposite* v. *in front of.* (see L). You could extend the activity by including other features on the map.

1 c) 2 e) 3 a) 4 f) 5 d) 6 b)

Exercise 2 Before playing the cassette, check SS understand *turn left/right, go straight on/along/go past.* Note that Penny's directions are not the quickest route, which would be more difficult for a tourist. Your SS may point this out. You could ask them to tell you a quicker route. If your SS can cope with more, include *up/down the hill, take the first/second* etc. *turning.*

[13.1
PENNY: Now listen carefully. When you come out of the station on to Waverley Bridge, turn right and go straight on until you get to Princes Street. Turn left and walk along Princes Street for about fifteen minutes. Go past the Royal Scottish Academy. You'll see the Castle and the Mound on your left. When you get to the end of Princes Street (you'll see the Caledonian Hotel in front of you), turn left again into Lothian Road. Walk straight along Lothian Road and after five minutes you'll see the Usher Hall on your left, opposite the Sheraton Hotel.

The concert hall, the Usher Hall, is opposite the Sheraton Hotel.

Exercise 2b) You may need to stop after each instruction to allow SS time to write.

1 right, go straight on 2 Turn left, along
3 past 4 on the left 5 turn left, into 6 straight along

Exercise 3 You could demonstrate the activity yourself first by asking SS to name the place you direct them to. Point out that all directions start at Waverley Station. Make sure all SS have located this before you begin. If SS are confident enough after they have practised in closed pairs, ask for volunteers to give directions to the whole class. But be careful this doesn't go on too long.

Extra materials and ideas

1 WB page 48, Grammar, Exercise 2.
2 You could introduce the topic by asking questions about SS' countries: *What side of the road do you drive on? Are there problems with too many cars? Where do people cross the road? Are there many accidents? Are there traffic lights? Are they above the road, at the side of the road?*
If SS are studying in England, ask them to talk about the differences between Britain and their countries. If not, give some information about England. People drive on the left. People cross at pedestrian crossings or zebra crossings. Traffic lights are at the side of the road and not above the road as in America.
3 You could begin the lesson by giving directions to somewhere in the school (toilet, canteen) but don't give the name. They tell you where it is. This will tell you how many directions are familiar to SS. SS then give you directions.
P 4 Page 144, 13.1. Give SS a copy of the map. In pairs they agree where the following are on the map: traffic lights; roundabout; zebra crossing; some buildings (school/swimming pool etc). Both maps must look the same. Pairs mark on the map where they live and show each other. Then each marks a restaurant, a cinema, a theatre, a concert hall in another part of town. They don't show their partner. They then invite each other out. Encourage SS to use expressions like *Would you like to ..? Are you free on Saturday?*
One S gives directions to the restaurant, cinema, theatre or concert hall but doesn't give the exact location. The other follows on the map and marks or says where the restaurant etc. is.

SKILLS

- Listening for detail and inferring.
- Speaking: rhyming.
- Reading as a stimulus to speaking activity.
- Writing: anaphoric reference.

Listening

L • Colloquial language should mostly be familiar. Check the meaning of *My mind's made up* and *to depend on someone*.

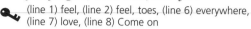

Students' Book (page 79)

Exercise 1a) Write the title on the board. Ask SS if they know the song. Ask why the words are wrong. Then highlight collocations: *smell/nose, feel/fingers, hear/ears, see/eyes.*

 (line 1) feel, (line 2) feel, toes, (line 6) everywhere, (line 7) love, (line 8) Come on

Exercise 2
 (line 10) always, (line 12) feel, (line 14) end, (line 18) bed, (line 20) said, (line 22) you, (line 24) do

Exercise 3 Make sure SS are clear that the question is asking about how the girl feels. There are no absolute answers, so accept SS' ideas, but ask them why they think that way.

Exercise 4 Play the song again. You could extend this beyond the rhyming words in the song by asking SS to give any words which rhyme: *no, know, so, low* /...əʊ/; *depend, send, lend* /...end/; *bed, head, dead* /...ed/; *you, flew, queue, zoo* /...uː/

 show, end, said, do

Extra material and ideas

1 WB page 51, Pronunciation, Exercise 8, Rhyming words.
2 SS sing the song.
3 SS could bring in their favourite romantic songs.
4 Write out the lyrics and cut them up. SS predict the order. Listen and check. You could still keep the gaps as in SB.

Reading and speaking

L • SS need to understand *monogamy* before they read. You could also check *old-'fashioned, three-'quarters, un'natural, 'late 'twenties.*

Students' Book (page 79)

Exercise 1 Refer to the pictures on the page. Ask SS what the word *romantic* means, and what it means to them. You could cue this by asking them to complete the sentences
A romantic person is someone who ...
A romantic person is someone who never ...
This will preview the grammar which focuses on relative clauses.

Exercise 2 You could ask which cultures are not monogamous, but be careful you don't spend too much time on this – it could also be a sensitive issue in some classes.

 1 older people   2 unromantic

Exercise 3 Ask SS why they think the younger people who were interviewed thought monogamy was all right. Further possible questions: *Is it difficult to be romantic in the modern world? Is it difficult to be romantic after twenty years with the same person? What would be your perfect romantic evening?*

Writing: reference words

L • Unit 5 focused on *he, his, their, there, she, him, them, they* for referencing. This unit focuses on *it, her, that, those, him, them*.

• SS may expect to find subject pronoun *they* in a lot of *they found* ... Highlight we have to use the object pronoun *them*. In this case it's the object of a preposition.

• Also highlight we can't say * *them who are most happily...* We can't use *them* as the subject of the verb.

• At this level, don't expect all the referencing words to appear suddenly in SS' written work. However, it is important that they recognise the function of these words in a text. It will help them to understand more easily what they read and hear.

Students' Book (page 80)

Exercise 1 To remind SS of the principles of referencing, write this on the board *Peter had a great watch, but Peter lost the great watch.* Ask SS if it's a good sentence, and how they can make it better. Then refer them to the text.

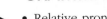
1 monogamy
2 monogamy is old-fashioned
3 people in their late twenties and older
4 people interviewed who didn't have dreams about romantic marriage

Exercise 2 Ask SS to find other examples of the following reference words in the text: *those, they, their* and ask them to find the original reference.

2 it 3 those 4 that 5 him 6 her

GRAMMAR

A • Relative pronouns in defining relative clauses.
• Word order of adjectives.
• *(We) use a ... for.-ing.*

Defining relative clauses: *who, which, what, where*

L • Common mistakes include: **I like people who they laugh a lot. I like the people which live opposite me. That's the shop that I bought the book. That's the shop where sells cheap shoes.*

• The main difficulty is remembering which pronoun is used for people, which for places and which for things. At this level you can expect SS to have problems with the verb form following the relative pronoun because they are concentrating on choosing the correct pronoun.

• Highlight that in defining relative clauses *who* and *that* and *which* and *that* are interchangeable. This is **not** the case in non-defining clauses but don't include this in your analysis for SS.

Students' Book (page 80)

Exercise 1 This is a recognition and fluency activity.

Exercise 2 This shouldn't be a problem as the pronouns are probably familiar and the concept fairly obvious.

1 who 2 which 3 where
1 where 2 who/that 3 which/that 4 who/that 5 which/that

Using your grammar

Exercise 1 This could lead to a class survey and statistical information on the board.

Exercise 2 These are possible answers.

1...loves and understands their child/children.
2...I can relax.
3...organise our work.
4...talks to all his/her guests.

Exercise 3 You could give SS other words and they write definitions to add to the true/false quiz.

1 F 2 T 3 F 4 F 5 T 6 F 7 F 8 T

Adjectives: word order

L • Because the focus is on adjective order: size - shape - colour - material + noun, SS may start to use four adjectives at the same time! (This would be unusual, and should be discouraged.) If SS want to include the age of something in their descriptions explain that like size and shape, age comes before colour. For this level don't try to be any more specific than that.

Students' Book (page 81)

Exercise 1 Write the categories SIZE SHAPE COLOUR MATERIAL on the board and elicit words for each column. Then ask SS to read the sentences in the book.

Exercise 2 You could add more examples: *black hair (short); a tall girl (thin); a small bag (leather); a woollen hat (yellow).*

1 a long grey woollen scarf   2 a large pointed thing
3 a long dark road 4 a big white cat

Extra material and ideas

1 WB page 48, Grammar, Exercise 3. Page 51, Dictation, Exercise 10.
2 On card write sentences which contain several adjectives. The words must be big enough to be read at a distance. Cut the sentences up into individual words. Divide SS into teams. Give each team member a word from that team's sentence. It doesn't matter if there aren't enough word cards for every S in the team as SS without a card can be organisers. Each team tries to be the first to line up holding their cards in the correct order. When a team thinks they are lined up in the correct order they shout *STOP!* The other teams can't make any further moves unless the teacher signals the first team is wrong. That allows all teams to continue until another one shouts *STOP!*

(We) use a ... for ...-ing

L • The structure *(we) use ... for ...-ing* may not seem to be a high frequency item. However, it can be a valuable language tool to access new vocabulary.

📖 Students' Book (page 81)

Exercise 1
1a) 2g) 3d) 4e) 5f) 6b) 7c)

Exercise 2 Avoid complicating matters by using the passive *is used for*. Highlight the use of the *-ing* form of the verb after the preposition *for*.

2 We use a buggy for pushing a small child about.
3 We use a corkscrew for opening wine bottles.
4 We use scissors for cutting things.
5 We use glue for sticking things.
6 We use a blanket for keeping warm in bed.
7 We use a purse for carrying coins.

Extra materials and ideas

1 WB page 49, Grammar, Exercise 4.
2 Roleplay a shop situation. You could supply or elicit the following:
A: *Can I help you?*
B: *Yes, please. I need one of those things you use for ...ing.*
A: *Oh, you mean a ... Yes, we've got some. / I'm sorry I'm afraid we haven't got any.*
SS choose one of the options and complete the conversation. Do some pronunciation practice on the set lines above before SS continue the conversation. Encourage them to begin the sentences with a higher pitch to sound polite.

VOCABULARY

A • To review and extend vocabulary for people's physical appearance and personality.
• To introduce verbs related to relationships.

Describing people

L • Check the following before playing the cassette: *well-'built, beard, bald, 'average build/height, over'weight, plain.* You could use the pictures to illustrate meaning.
• The cassette includes examples of *quite* and *rather* to soften the impact of a negative adjective: *rather short, quite plain. Quite* is also used with *tall,* meaning *not very tall.* You could draw SS' attention to this if you think it won't complicate matters. However, point out that to call someone *fat, small* etc. is often considered impolite.
• With the adjectives describing personality, highlight positive and negative connotation.

📖 Students' Book (page 82)

Exercise 1a) Begin by describing a person in the room and SS guess who it is. Ask SS to look at the pictures and ask them quickly to describe the people. Then play the cassette.

[13.4]
1 A: I met him last night. He works here. He's nearly bald and rather short.
   B: We have a lot of people like that here, sir.
   A: Well, he's got a round face with a pointed nose.
   B: I see.
   A: And a beard.
   B: Well, that could be Mr Page...

2 A: Yes, she's in her mid-twenties and really slim.
   POLICEWOMAN: Fine. Can you give more details? What colour are her eyes?
   A: Let me see. Yes, she's got large green eyes.
   P: Yes, yes I'm sure. You say she's missing.
   A: Yes, she didn't come home...

3 A: Excuse me, I'm looking for my girlfriend.
   B: Oh dear, have you lost her?
   A: Yes, she's...eh...average height, not pretty...quite plain in fact...and a...eh... bit overweight I suppose.
   B: That's not a nice way to talk about your girlfriend!
   A: Sorry...I mean... No... Let me think. She's got short, curly hair with square face, green eyes.
   B: I think I know who you mean. She was the person I saw getting on a plane for Paris with a very good-looking, wonderfully handsome man who looked like a film star...
   A: What?!

4 A: Excuse me. I'm looking for a friend of mine. I said I'd meet him here.
   B: What does he look like?
   A: Um...He's quite tall and well-built. And he's got long black hair. Oh, yes, and he's got a beard and he wears glasses.
   A: Oh, him. Yes. He's in the lounge...

1c) 2b) 3d) 4a)

Exercise 1b) Point out that the two lists refer to the verbs *have got* and *to be.* After you have checked the answers write *?* on the board. Ask if SS know the questions for these answers *She's tall and thin. She's really shy.* Highlight that when we ask *'What's he/she 'like?'* we can describe physical appearance and personality. BUT the question *'What does she 'look 'like?'* only asks for a physical description. Practise these question forms, using a falling intonation pattern. Write the questions on the board and mark the sentence stress.

IS˚	HAS GOT
bald	a round face
short	a beard
in her mid-twenties	large green eyes
really slim	short, curly hair
average height	a square face
not pretty	long, black hair
quite plain	
a bit overweight	
quite tall	
well-built	

Exercise 1d)
1 slim 2 handsome 3 tall, average height

Exercise 2
Possible answers:
Good: clever, tidy, sociable, lively, patient, cheerful
Bad: lazy, bad-tempered, mean
Not good or bad: shy, talkative

Relationships

Students' Book (page 82)

Write the verbs in a column on the left of the board. Ask SS to look at them for a moment and tell them they will need to use them in the next activity. Answer any questions about meaning. Draw pictures on the board like the ones below to help SS.

After SS have read the extract from the letter ask comprehension questions *How long did Matthew and Laura go out together before they got married? When did their problems start? How long were they married?* Do the first gap with the whole class to highlight that SS need to think about the correct form of the verb.

1 was fond of   2 fell in love   3 went out together
4 got married   5 got pregnant   6 got divorced

USE AND REVIEW

• Review of the Second Conditional.
• Vocabulary of crime.

Students' Book (page 83)

Exercise 1 First check the meaning of *'furious* and *'cash register.* While SS are reading, write these questions on the board *What does Suzanne do? What was the thief carrying? Where did he get it from? What did Suzanne do? What did the thief do?*

Exercise 2 Let SS ask you what you would do. You could end the activity by asking *Do you think people should try to stop criminals?*

Exercise 4 Other words from Unit 12: *to burgle, burglar, burglary, to rob, robber, robbery, theft.*

A real fan

Students' Book

General theme: obsession.
Unit topic: fans, entertainment.

USE YOUR ENGLISH: saying the right thing.
SKILLS: reading (two pop fans); vocabulary (guessing meaning from context); writing (adverbials in sentences).
GRAMMAR: *used to*; question tags.
USE AND REVIEW: defining relative clauses; spot the difference between pictures.

Workbook

GRAMMAR: *used to* and *didn't used to* v. the Past Simple; question tags; time expression.
VOCABULARY: entertainment.
SKILLS: listening (having a good time); writing (adverbs).
DICTATION/PRONUNCIATION: sound and spelling: *a*.

USE YOUR ENGLISH
Saying the right thing

- Appropriate responses to situations: congratulating, apologising, receiving and responding to bad news.

- Encourage SS to accept these as holophrases appropriate for certain situations. Avoid detailed analysis or explanations.

- If your SS have little contact with spoken English, this language may seem less urgent. However, the situations are easily identified in any language and are likely to motivate SS.

- Stress, intonation and facial expression are important. They will influence whether the listener perceives the message as genuine or sarcastic. Demonstrate the effect of using flat tones and limited facial expression. You could also demonstrate a situation where we would use these sarcastically, e.g., someone drops and breaks your favourite cup. You could respond with *Well done* (low pitch/probably a sigh/no facial expression unless anger).

- There are times when *Congratulations* and *Well done* are interchangeable, and times when they are not. We are unlikely to say *Well done* when a woman tells us she's pregnant.

Students' Book (page 84)

Exercise 1 Write *Let's watch a video* on the board and ask a S to read it out. Meanwhile you have handed these possible responses to 3 SS on pieces of paper *That's a good idea. I don't care.*

Yes, it's all right. Tell the class that all the sentences are correct English but only one is the right response. Ask SS to listen to the responses and say which is the right one for the situation. You may need to ask the 3 SS to repeat the responses more than once. When you have established which one is correct, practise with SS. Highlight appropriate facial expression and intonation.

You could then mime someone who's extremely nervous and say *I've got an exam at 10 o'clock.* Elicit responses and establish that *Good luck!* is appropriate. You could demonstrate that the British often cross their index and second finger when saying this, and ask SS if they have a similar gesture.

Then ask SS to look at the pictures in the SB and guess what the responses might be before looking at the possibilities. Point out other possible responses for the situations:
1 *Congratulations!* 2 *Oh, I'm sorry about that./What a shame.* 3 *Oh dear, I'm sorry to hear that.*

 1c) 2a) 3b) 4b)

Exercise 2a) Ask SS to compare their answers with another pair of SS before you play the cassette. You could explore other possible responses for each situation: 1 *Oh, fantastic./That's great.* 2. *OK. Just a minute./Just a second/sec.* 3. *No, thanks. It's OK.* How many possibilities you offer SS will depend on how many are completely new. Be careful that you don't overload them. SS practise the sentences.

 1b) 2a)

Exercise 3
 [14.2]
A: Well, it's time to go. We've had a great time. Thanks for everything.
B: Not at all. We've enjoyed having you here.
A: Next time you must come to us.
B: Yes, we'd love to. Have a safe journey. Don't forget to write.
A: Sure. Bye. Look after yourself.

Extra material and ideas

1 To extend the final exercise you could ask SS to write a short thank you note to their friend. Ask SS to include some of these expressions: *Thanks very much for having me/us. Had a great time. Really enjoyed/going for walks/the wonderful food. See you again soon.*

 2 A mingle activity page 144, 14.1. Give half the SS a numbered sentence related to the situations they have used in this section, and the other SS a lettered response. Example: *1 We're getting married. a) Oh, what wonderful news!* They walk around listening to the numbered sentences and respond where they think it's appropriate. Ask them to note the number of the sentences they think their response goes with. In the feedback, ask the SS with the cue sentences to read them for the class. Any SS who thinks their response is appropriate responds. You evaluate the appropriacy. Of course some SS will treat this humourously, (*getting married/hardluck!*). In which case laugh along!

1 a) i) 2 b) c) 3 c) g) 4 d) j) 5 e) f) 6 a) f) 7 g) 8 h) 9 a) i) 10 j) c) g)

3 Gestures used in Britain Mime the gestures for your SS and ask them what they think they mean in Britain.

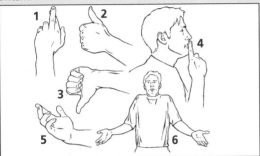

1 I hope/wish   2 Yes/I understand/Good luck
3 No/Not good   4 Be quiet   5 Come here
6 I don't know

You could explore the use of physical gestures across cultures. This is usually well received as one culture often finds another culture's gestures very amusing. If you have a multilingual class, this could take quite some time.

SKILLS

A • Reading: scanning; finding evidence in a text to support a summarising statement; question forms.

• Vocabulary: guessing the meaning of words from context.

• Writing: position of adverbials in sentences.

Reading

L • Preteach, *fan, ob'sessed/ob'session, 'lookalike, to be smart* (as in the way we dress), *office clerk, would rather, worth the money, 'superstars, no one else.* Remember to write them up so SS can recognise them in the texts. Don't accidentally preteach the words which come up in the VOCABULARY on page 86.

• Some of the sentence structures in the texts will be unfamiliar to SS. However, most of the vocabulary is not new and shouldn't worry them unduly, e.g., *No one else can sing like her.*

Students' Book (page 85)

Exercise a) Take in photos of different singers. If you can't find pictures just write the names on the board. Ask the SS *What kind of music do they sing? How old are their fans? Teenagers, adults, elderly people?* Then ask SS *What kind of*

music do you really not like? Who's your favourite singer? Do you play a musical instrument? You may need to remind SS of *jazz, opera, classical, rock, folk music, rap* etc., most of which occurred in Unit 7, USE YOUR ENGLISH. Ask SS to name the singers in the pictures. Do SS know/like their music? Alternatively, take in pictures of ordinary people and get SS to guess what music they like. Read the questions in Exercise 1a) to the class. Encourage SS to read both texts quickly and find the sections in the texts which answer the questions. Then in pairs they discuss their answers.

1 Saf buys every George Michael CD and copies of George Michael's suits. He wants to call his baby 'Michael' if it's a boy. He wants to be a George Michael lookalike.
2 Ruth has spent thousands and thousands of pounds on Barbra. She has been to concerts in California, Las Vegas and London.
3 Saf is more interested in George Michael's appearance. Ruth is more interested in Barbra's feelings.

Exercises b) and c) Put the more confident SS in group B as this is the longer and more challenging text. Don't waste the opportunity for accuracy work, so when SS are in groups walk around and correct the question forms they produce. If one group finishes earlier, they could write other comprehension questions for their text.

(Accept appropriate alternatives here)
GROUP A
1 What does Saf buy?
2 When is Saf's wife expecting a baby?
3 When did Saf's obsession begin?
4 Where is Saf trying to get work?
GROUP B
1 When did Ruth go to Las Vegas?
2 How much has Ruth spent over the years?
3 Does Ruth know Barbra well?
4 What has Barbra done for women?

Extra material and ideas

1 For homework SS could write a paragraph beginning *I'm a fan of _____*. Collect the paragraphs and read them out. The other SS try to guess who wrote the paragraph. Include one you have written. The paragraph could be about sport, art, a political figure, designer wear, e.g. Nike trainers, not just music.

2 As they have the questions and answers for the texts, SS could roleplay a TV/radio interview with Ruth and Saf. Three SS in each group: Saf, Ruth and interviewer. Encourage the S playing the interviewer to think of different questions to ask Saf and Ruth.

Vocabulary

Students' Book (page 86)

Exercise 1 Before the matching exercise ask SS to locate the words in the text, and try to guess the meaning from context. Then move on to the matching exercise.

2a)   3d)   4b)

Exercise 2

1 confident   2 annual   3 spare   4 missed

Extra material and ideas

If there are unfamiliar words that you didn't preteach for the reading, you could do more work on guessing from context. SS could locate their own unknown words in the articles and try to work out the meaning. Then they could feedback to the class. Allow time for them to write any of the words in their vocabulary books/notes.

Writing

L • Remind SS that position of adverbs of frequency was covered in Unit 2 (see SB, page 17, TB, page 25)

• Point out that other time adverbials can go at the beginning or the end of a sentence. However, there are contexts where it sounds odd to put one at the beginning: *When did you see John? *Last night I saw him.* (There is a tendency in English to put the key information at the end of answers to questions.) Consequently, encourage SS to put adverbials at the end, following the *place* before *time* rule.

📖 Students' Book (page 86)

1 He speaks English well.
2 He ran quickly down the road.
3 She went to bed early last night.
4 He always listens to her carefully.

Extra material and ideas

1 WB page 54, Writing, Exercise 9.
2 Write the words from the exercise in SB on cards so they can be seen at a distance. Put SS in groups according to the number of words in each sentence. Each group stands at the front of the class holding up their cards. The other SS get them to stand in the correct order. If they are correct, the SS standing say their part of the sentence. You could ask SS for other possible positions for the adverbs/adverbials. This activity might help some SS to remember word order vividly, because there is a strong visual image and movement.

GRAMMAR

▲ • Presentation of *used to* + base form of the verb.
• Comparison of *used to* and the Present Simple.
• Comparison of *used to* and the Past Simple.
• Question tags.

Used to

L • As SS probably won't know *used to* + base form + *-ing* this common confusion at later levels is unlikely to arise.

• *Used to* has the meaning of either past habit or state now discontinued or changed. *I used to smoke 10 cigarettes a day. Now I only smoke 5. I used to smoke, but I gave up.* By immediately comparing the *used to* form with the Present Simple the concept of habit or state should be reinforced.

• SS may simply register this verb as an alternative for the Past Simple and produce sentences such as *I used to have 10 coffees yesterday.* Highlight the differences early on in the presentation.

• *Used to* is a defective verb which means it has no other time reference than past time. There is no future or present form.

• The more commonly used question form is *Did you use to...? Yes, I did. No, I didn't.* However the original form *Used you to ...?* is sometimes still used.

• Pronunciation. SS often pronounce this structure with strong vowels, /ˈjuːzdtuː/ but it is more commonly pronounced using a weak vowel /ˈjuːstə/, and the final plosive sound /d/ is elided or left out. Note the pronunciation of *to* before a vowel is /tʊ/, but before a consonant it is /tə/. SS may want to pronounce the /s/ in *used to* using a /z/ sound as in the verb *to use* /juːz/.

📖 Students' Book (page 86)

Exercise 1 You could read the passage aloud while SS follow in their books (good listening practice and it ensures everyone finishes at the same time!), or let them read silently. Note that the questions act as both context and concept questions. Write the following on the board *When do we use <u>used to</u>, for the present or the past? Did she do the action once or many times? Finish the rule <u>used to</u> + _____.*
Then ask SS to find three examples of *used to* in the text. Draw the following on the board to give a visual representation of the concept using the example *I used to enjoy staying in with a new novel and a really good apple, and now I enjoy staying in with a new novel and a glass of wine.*

IN THE PAST   BUT   NOW

Ask the SS, *Does she do very different things now?* Then write up **I used to smoke, but I stopped 4 years ago.**

199?   NOW

These two examples will help you to illustrate that the past habit isn't necessarily finished altogether, but *used to* always signals at least a change.

1 She read a new novel and ate an apple.
2 She reads a new novel and drinks a glass of wine.
3 She used to behave badly in her twenties but in her thirties she was too tired.
4 No, she only screamed in Oxford Street once.
5 Yes, it was.
6 No, it isn't.

Exercise 2a)
1 had   2 used to like

Exercise 2b)
1 used to go   2 used to like   3 used to live
4 used to read

Exercise 3 This exercise combines sentence stress recognition and practice of the unexploded plosive /d/ in *used to*. You could use phonemics to highlight the different features (see L).

1 I <u>used</u> to wear <u>short</u> <u>skirts</u>.
/aɪ 'juːs tə 'weə 'ʃɔːt 'skɜːts/

2 He <u>used</u> to drive <u>fast</u> <u>cars</u>.
/hiː 'juːs tə 'draɪv 'faːst 'kaːz/

3 We <u>used</u> to <u>listen</u> to the <u>radio</u>.
/wiː 'juːs tə 'lɪsən tə ðə 'reɪdɪəʊ/

4 I <u>used</u> to be very <u>unhappy</u>.
/aɪ 'juːs tə bi 'veri ʌn'hæpi/

5 She <u>used</u> to eat <u>meat</u> but now she's a <u>vegetarian</u>.
/ʃiː 'juːs tʊ 'iːt 'miːt bət 'naʊ ʃɪz ə vedʒə'teərɪən/

Exercise 4 You could begin or end this exercise by drawing picture cues or supplying word cues to illustrate past habits you had that are now different or have stopped completely. Childhood usually gives us lots to draw on: bedtimes, free time, musical taste etc.

1 I used to live in Rio but now I live in Paris.
2 Pete used to be poor but now he's rich.
3 Angie used to ride a motorbike but now she drives a car.

Extra material and ideas

1 WB page 52, Grammar, Exercises 1 and 2.
2 Spot the difference page 145, 14.2. Give SS copies of the two pictures of Down Cross. They make sentences like *It used to be a tennis court, but now it's a car park*. You could also ask: *Look at the car park. What do people do there now? What did people use to do there 50 years ago?*

Question tags

• Verb forms: *to be* (past and present), Past Simple, Present Simple.
• This area of language is not intrinsically difficult. SS should know the verb forms reasonably well, but question tags can be difficult to manipulate because you have to make the necessary adjustments quickly. If SS leave a long gap between the statement and the tag, it will sound odd. To have an automatic response requires a lot of practice. Don't expect SS to be fluent immediately. Offer frequent opportunities for practice, recognition and production. You could open or close the next few lessons with short practice exercises. If you make up a set of statement prompts, these can be used again and again until SS really don't have to search their memory banks for the tag, and it comes quite naturally. But this will take time and effort on your part as well as theirs.
• Be careful of stating absolute rules about tag questions. It's tempting to give the rules: positive statement → negative tag; negative statement → positive tag. However, positive → positive is used frequently to confirm information which was previously stated or implied. *Oh, you like comedies, do you?* as well as when we wish to be sarcastic. We do not suggest you give this information to SS at this level. However, we recommend you avoid words like *always,* and say instead *We form most question tags by ...'*
• Pronunciation. SS recognise an inverted question form and often automatically use a rising intonation. While this is possible when we use tags as genuine questions, the more common purpose of tag questions is to confirm what we believe to be true when we use a falling intonation.

📖 Students' Book (page 87)

Exercise 1 Begin by asking SS to list the kinds of TV programmes they enjoy. Supply vocabulary as required 'comedies, 'chat shows, the news, 'music 'programmes, 'wildlife etc. The list could be quite extensive so be careful about timing. You could equate *docu'mentary* with *Panorama* when you refer to the SB.

Exercise 2a)

[14.4]
NIKKI: We're not going out tonight, are we?
TOM: No, let's not. I'm too tired. Let's see what's on TV.
NIKKI: Well, there's 'Star Trek' at 6.30. I'm a fan of William Shatner. He's a good actor, isn't he?
TOM: I don't like him very much. Let me have a look. 'Headhunters'. That sounds interesting.
NIKKI: I can't stand Francesca Annis.
TOM: Well, I want to watch it.
NIKKI: OK, we'll watch it if I can watch 'Star Trek'.
TOM: 'Panorama' doesn't sound very interesting this week.
NIKKI: And it wasn't very good last week, was it?

TOM: No. Let's see what else there is. You still like Sting, don't you? He's on.
NIKKI: Yes. I certainly want to watch him.
TOM: I think this wildlife programme's been on before. The one about the elephants. We've seen it, haven't we?
NIKKI: Yes, we have. I don't want to see that again.
TOM: What about Rory Bremner? You liked him last time, didn't you?
NIKKI: All right.
TOM: Yes, let's watch that, shall we?

Nikki likes 'Startrek', 'Later with Jools Holland' and 'Rory Bremner'. Tom likes 'Headhunters' and 'Rory Bremner'.

Exercise 2b) Give an example of positive and negative tag questions. Highlight the necessary changes and practise them using a falling intonation. All the examples on the cassette use a falling intonation.

1 isn't he? 2 was it? 3 don't you? 4 haven't we?
5 didn't you? 6 shall we?

Using your grammar

Used to

You might like to specify a time. Ask SS to close their eyes, sit back and think about their lives 10 years ago. Give them a minute or two, then ask them to tell their partner about the changes. Ask SS to note any really interesting information to feedback to the class. Presumably SS aren't going to mention things they don't want disclosed.

Question tags

Ask SS to look at the picture of Keanu Reeves and elicit any information you can about him. When they do the exercise, make sure they use a falling intonation. If they give repeated examples using a rising intonation, highlight the difference in use. Falling intonation: we expect the other person to agree. Rising intonation is a genuine question: we don't know the answer.

Extra material and ideas

1 WB page 52, Grammar, Exercise 3.
2 Page 145, 14.3. Cut up question tag sentences to be used for:
• **Find your partner** SS have to find the S with the other half of their sentence.
• **Time limit team game** Teams are given up to 20 cut up statements and tags. You set a time limit. When you call STOP! the winning team is the one with the most correct combinations.
• **Match the tags** Statements are placed round the room. Each S has to stick their tag next to the appropriate statement. To practise pronunciation, you could get S to walk around the room in a clockwise direction. When you call a S's name, he/she has to say the tag question nearest to him/her.

Any or all of these could be repeated as quick opening or closing activities for the next few lessons

in an attempt to help SS to manipulate form accurately and quickly. You don't need to change the material. In fact it will help you to gauge how much SS are improving on a daily basis.
Richard bought a new bike, didn't he? I'm meeting you tomorrow, aren't I? I've paid the bill, haven't I? I didn't break it, did I? Nick doesn't smoke, does he? Rachel used to be a nurse, didn't she? Pauline used to wear jeans, didn't she? Mr and Mrs Smith are leaving today, aren't they? Mike can drive, can't he? You can't smoke in here, can you? I'm not working tomorrow, am I? You'll help me, won't you?

VOCABULARY
Entertainment

• Some of the words are compounds. In this section most of them are stressed on the first word: 'video recorder, 'video tape, 'headphones, 'camcorder, 'stereo system BUT loud'speaker. Highlight the stress on all the words presented in this section.

Students' Book (page 88)
Exercise 1 Begin by reviewing the types of TV programmes mentioned in QUESTION TAGS above. You could do this by writing the words up but jumbling the order of the letters: yomced=comedy.
a) video recorder b) TV screen c) video tapes
d) loudspeakers e) stereo system f) headphones g) CDs
h) microphone i) batteries j) cassette

Exercise 2 Repeat that some words can go in more than one list. You could elicit more examples for the lists.
A pop concert: interval, performance, front row, audience, to book, stage, to clap, to buy a programme
An art gallery: exhibition, sculpture, to buy a programme, drawing
A cinema: screen, interval, performance, front row, audience, to book

Exercise 3 Ask SS How do you know?
1c) 2d) 3a) 4b)

Exercise 4 Point out that the first letter is given.
1 actor 2 comedian 3 director 4 musician
5 conductor 6 author 7 artist 8 composer

Using your vocabulary

You could begin by telling SS about something you have seen, heard or watched recently. It might be a good idea to choose something you **didn't** enjoy so SS realise they can give a negative criticism.

Extra material and ideas

1 WB page 53, Vocabulary, Exercises 5, 6 and 7.
2 SS could write a short review of the book, film, TV programme etc. they talked about in USING YOUR ENGLISH. Help them to plan their paragraphs.
Paragraph 1: title/director/author/singer etc.
Paragraph 2: What was it about?

Paragraph 3: Your opinion of it.

3 You could have I RECOMMEND/I DON'T RECOMMEND posters in the classroom where you and SS can make a note of books, music, TV series or current films etc. Initially you may have to keep asking if anyone has anything to add. You can cue this by asking SS what they have done since you last saw them. Have they watched any TV, seen a film, heard any new music etc.? Then ask what they thought of it and ask them to add to the poster just before the end of class. Encourage them to stick any publicity to the poster: theatre programmes, newspaper or magazine advertisements etc. Cinemas will sometimes give you outdated posters to liven up the activity when you first introduce the idea.

USE AND REVIEW

A▶
- Relative clauses.
- Describing people, and what they're doing (Present Continuous).
- Clothes.

Students' Book (page 89)

Exercise 1 Write the following examples on the board to highlight the aim:

A person _____ drives you to places in a car for money is a _____.
Answers: who/taxi driver

A long yellow fruit _____ grows in tropical countries is a _____.
Answers: which/banana

1 where/railway station   2 who/nurse or doctor
3 which/dream   4 who/hairdresser   5 which/snake
6 where/chemist's   7 who/journalist

Exercise 2a) SS must describe their pictures to each other. The focus is on descriptions though you might encourage the use of relatives by giving an example *There's a cup on the table which is next to ...* If it's possible arrange the seats in tango seating (see *Introduction* page 14) or facing one another. Discourage SS from looking at each other's pictures.

In B's picture the woman is wearing sunglasses and a formal dress. She isn't smiling. She's drinking a cup of tea or coffee. She isn't waving to a man in the sea. There's a saucer and a book on the table. Her handbag is different from the one in A's picture. There's a boy with a surfboard behind her.

In A's picture the woman is smiling and waving to a man in the sea. She's wearing a striped T-shirt. She isn't wearing sunglasses. She's drinking a can of drink with a straw. There's a radio on the table and a boy with a ball behind her. Her handbag is different from the one in B's picture.

Exercise 2b)
A's picture
1 She looks relaxed and friendly.
2 She seems sociable and happy.
3 She's at the seaside/on a beach.
4 There's a man in the sea and a boy by the sea with a ball.
B's picture
1 She looks serious and formal.
2 She doesn't look very happy.

3 She's at the seaside/on a beach.
4 There's a boy with a surf board behind her.

School rules

Students' Book

General theme: education.
Unit topic: schools.

USE YOUR ENGLISH: changing money.
SKILLS: listening and speaking (an American girl and a Japanese girl compare schools); vocabulary (informal language); writing (linking words - *although, but, however, too, also*).
GRAMMAR: quantity words (*some-, any-, no-, every-*), *too* v. *very, too much, too many*.
VOCABULARY: education.
USE AND REVIEW: error correction; crossword.

Workbook

GRAMMAR: *someone, anyone, no one, everyone, something, anything, nothing* and *everything, too much* or *too many*?
VOCABULARY: education; British and American English.
SKILLS: reading (first day at school); writing (linking words).
DICTATION/PUNCTUATION: word stress.

USE YOUR ENGLISH
Changing money

L • Numbers. A common mistake is to add a plural -*s* when an exact number is used: **five hundreds, *five thousands*. Highlight that we only add -*s* when we are talking in general terms: *Hundreds of people came to the concert*.

Students' Book (page 90)

Exercise 1 You could use the exchange rate chart in Exercise 3 to introduce this section and ask *What's this? When do we use it? What's the currency in your country/Britain? What's the exchange rate now?* The chart will inevitably be out of date. If you can get an up-to-date one, use that. However, the language is still relevant, and you can compare the exchange rates between 1995 and now. Then get SS to answer the questions in the SB which revise numbers and money words.

1 £89.85 2 He can change a traveller's cheque.

Exercise 2 You could take the role of the bank clerk and invite SS to roleplay the conversation with you.

[15.1]
BANK CLERK: Yes, sir?
CARLOS: Can I *change* a traveller's cheque for $100?
BANK CLERK: Sure. *Sign* at the top, please. Can I see your passport?

CARLOS: What's the *exchange* rate at the moment?
BANK CLERK: $1.41 to the pound. So that's £70. How would you *like* the money?
CARLOS: Three twenties and a ten, please.

Exercise 3 Be prepared to do some on the spot remedial work on saying numbers. You could ask more confident SS to roleplay the conversations for the class after they have had time to practise.

75 Cyprus pounds = £102.73; 1,500 Yen = £9.56; 300 Swiss francs = £152.28; 500 Austrian schillings = £30.49; 200 Brazilian reals = £147.06

Exercise 4 Ask SS *How can we pay for things in a shop?* Highlight prepositions: **by** *cheque,* **by/with** *a credit card, but* **in/with** *cash*. You could introduce *Do you take credit cards? Can I pay by/with/in ...?*

You might ask SS to stick their conversations round the room. They walk round checking and correcting each other's work. When you signal stop, in pairs, they read the conversation nearest them. The same idea is possible with SS passing the papers round the class. You could also do this as a whole class activity by eliciting, shaping (doing work on pronunciation, correcting or improving their suggested lines) and practising the same conversation.

(This is a suggested answer but accept appropriate alternatives.)
CARLOS: How much is this coat?
SHOP ASSISTANT: It's £300.
CARLOS: Do you take credit cards?
SHOP ASSISTANT: No, I'm afraid we don't. We only take cash or cheques.
CARLOS: I'm afraid I haven't got any cash.
SHOP ASSISTANT: I'm very sorry.

Extra material and ideas

1 Number dictations
• You dictate numbers to SS, including fractions, decimals, hundreds, thousands, millions, dates, years etc.
• PW. You give SS a set of numbers to dictate to their partner. This is a self-checking activity as SS have to make themselves understood.
• You say a mathematical sum and SS write down the answer: *Two hundred and six minus/take away/subtract a hundred and four.* SS write down 102. In the feedback SS dictate the numbers they have written to you, and you write them on the board, but only if SS say them correctly and the answer to the sum is correct. This is an opportunity to introduce *times/multiply, add/plus* and *divided by* etc.
• Divide the class into three or four teams, depending on how big the board is. SS line up in their teams in front of the board. You whisper a number to the person at the back of each team. They whisper this down the line and the person at

the front writes it on the board. This person then comes to the back of the line and hears the next number from you and passes it down the line to the front and so on. Each round should produce the same number from each team, but it often doesn't! Remember to keep a record of the numbers you have dictated so you can check!

2 Get SS to work out the prices of things in sterling or their currency. You need magazines, catalogues, brochures with prices listed. If the prices are in their currency ask them to change them to sterling. If the prices are in sterling, ask them to change them into their currency. This could be an interesting comparison of the cost of living.

SKILLS

▶**A**

• Reading and speaking: introduces the topic.

• Listening and speaking: listening for detail.

• Speaking: exchanging information from different listening passages and talking about education, personal experience and opinions.

• Vocabulary: to encourage SS to use dictionaries, and continue to point out the different kinds of information they can find in a good dictionary.

• Writing: linkers to highlight the concept of formal v. informal language.

Reading and speaking

L

• The text is short and fairly simple. Check that SS understand 'timetable, 'punishments, 'pupils, 'classes.

• Check the concept of different routines, i.e. having the same classroom all day and different Ts coming to the SS' room, or SS going to different rooms for different lessons.

Students' Book (page 91)

Exercise 1 Begin by asking what the rules are for your school. If there aren't any, you could ask SS if they think there should be rules. If there are rules, you could ask them for their opinion.

Listening and speaking

L

• There are examples of informal language in the listening passages, but these are highlighted in the vocabulary exercise. Check understanding of 'modern and tra'ditional. SS may need time to tune in to the American and Japanese accents.

• Revision of modals of permission and prohibition: have to, must(n't), can, can't.

Students' Book (page 91)

The following information was volunteered by the Japanese and American girls who were interviewed, but because of length it has had to

be cut from the cassette. You could feed the facts into the discussions which will arise. However, be careful not to divulge too much too soon, as this will remove the need for SS to listen.

America: Many schools have police patrolling the school with guns. Some schools have a weapons search at the door. SS can say what they like to Ts. Ts are not allowed to hit SS. Drugs, guns and crime are the biggest problems.

Japan: Ts are allowed to hit SS. SS must remain silent unless asked a question. Classes are large.

Exercise 1 This is a prediction exercise, so avoid going into too much detail.

Exercise 2 The two short extracts focus on routines.

[15.2]

KAREN: Well, the day starts at eight o'clock. You stop for lunch at twelve and then you leave school in the middle of the afternoon. Then you go home or do some sport.

RIE: School starts at half-past eight and we have to be there at about eight o'clock. It finishes at four o'clock in the afternoon but we have many different activities so we have to stay at school until seven o'clock every evening.

In Japan.

Exercise 3 Divide the class into two groups. Tell SS to listen once then check with others in the same group. If they disagree, they could listen again and try and reach agreement. Try to avoid one group taking much longer than the other.

If you don't have two tape recorders available, do it as a whole class exercise.

[15.3]
GROUP A

KAREN: We don't have very many rules at our school back in the States. The main rules are: no drugs, no smoking and no fighting, but there are crazy rules too like no wearing hats.

INTERVIEWER: What happens if someone breaks the rules?

K: Then you have to stay in the classroom at lunch time which is crazy because you just spend your time talking to your friends. If you do something serious, like drugs, they call the cops.

I: Do you have to wear a uniform?

K: No, you can wear what you want to but everybody wants to wear the latest fashions, which is crazy in school.

I: And are the teachers very strict?

K: No, not really. You can do what you want in class, talk in class, even when the teachers are talking. They don't really mind.

I: How does your school in America compare with your school in Britain?

K: In the States, you can do what you want when you want. You can miss classes - they don't really care - but here in England it's very strict and you have a lot more rules, a uniform and things like that.

[15.4]
GROUP B

INTERVIEWER: Are there many rules in your school in Japan?

RIE: Yes, a lot. For example, we have to wear a school uniform but we mustn't go to town in a uniform. We have to go home first and change into our normal clothes.

I: What's the uniform like?

R: The traditional Japanese school uniform is navy blue with a long skirt. Sometimes it's quite pretty but no one likes it. The modern uniform with a short skirt is quite popular.

ɪ: Do you have to work hard in your school?

ʀ: Yes, very. And our teachers are very strict. If we don't study hard they punish us.

ɪ: What kind of punishments do they give you?

ʀ: We have to stay late after school and study. Sometimes the teachers phone our parents and our parents have to come to school.

ɪ: Rie, how does your school in Japan compare with your school in Britain?

ʀ: My school in Japan is a girls' school but here it is a mixed school. In Japan we have fifty students in one class and we stay in the same room all day. Here there are only twenty students and we have to move each lesson.

 In the USA students mustn't take drugs, fight or wear hats. The teachers call the police.
In Japan students have to wear school uniform and study very hard. They mustn't wear school uniform to go to town. The teachers ask students to stay after school and sometimes they phone the pupils' parents.

Exercise 4a) SS exchange information. You could play both recordings as a final check, but only if there has been a problem or SS have indicated they would like to listen to them again.

1 The Japanese school has more rules.
2 They talk to their friends.
3 Karen's school in America is not as strict as the school in England where there are a lot more rules. Rie's school in Japan is stricter than the school in England. It is only for girls but the school in England is mixed, girls and boys. There are fifty students in a class in Japan but only 20 students in a class in England. In Japan, students stay in the same class all day. In England, they move for each lesson.
4 The modern skirt is shorter.

Exercise 4b) Supply or elicit example questions *Do/did you like school? Why/Why not? What was your first day at school like? How old were you when you started? Tell us about 3 good and 3 bad things. Did you have a lot of homework? Did you have tests? Did you have to buy your books? Was it a mixed school?* etc. You could let SS practise these questions by asking you about your experience at school, before interviewing their partner.

Extra material and ideas

1 WB page 57, Reading, Exercise 6.

2 In a multilingual class, Exercise 4 could be a cultural information exchange tabulated on a poster or board. If SS are confident, ask them to give a 2 minute information talk to the whole class about education in their country. They could organise the talk according to questions you have set. Other SS could ask further questions if they wish to. Don't have too many talks at once. If enough SS want to do it, you could have one or two talks at the beginning and/or end of the next few lessons.

3 Ask SS to draw up a list of ways to improve either your school or education in general in their country to include revision of *should*.

4 If SS are interested give them some cultural information and tell them about the different types of schools in Britain: *primary (infant/junior), secondary, boarding school, public v. state school.* Education is compulsory in Britain between the ages of 5 and 16. However, children can go to play/nursery school from the age of three, but these are mainly private and parents have to pay. Between the ages of 5 and 11, children go to primary schools. Infant school lasts from 5–7, junior school from 7–11. From 11 to 16 they go to secondary schools. If pupils want to go to university, they have to stay at school for another 2 years until they are 18.

5 You could get SS to write a report for themselves. You could give them guidelines as to what to include.

Vocabulary

🅛 • The intention is to highlight informal style, and its appropriate use: *boss, fancy, kids, hang on, great.*

📖 Students' Book (page 92)

 1 children 2 want 3 wait 4 employer 5 very good

Extra material and ideas

WB, page 56, Vocabulary, Exercise 5, has an exercise on American v. British English. It includes a listening exercise to check answers, which also compares accents.

Writing: linking words

🅛 • Do some quick revision of meaning and position of linkers from earlier units *and, so, but, because*. Highlight *so/but* (reason/result). The new linkers are *although, however* (compared with *but*), *too, also.*

• The position of the linker and the punctuation need to be highlighted.

📖 Students' Book (page 92)

You could begin by writing a base sentence on the board *She lost her money.* Ask SS to use *so, but, because* and *and* with this sentence so they have 4 new sentences, each one using one of the linkers. Then get SS to read the explanation of *although, however, but* and continue with the base sentence but this time they should use *however* and *although*. Do the same for *too* and *also*. Highlight the punctuation throughout this section. Then do the exercise from SB.

1 The actors were very good, **but** I didn't like the film very much.
Although the actors were very good, I didn't like the film very much.
I didn't like the film very much, **although** the actors were very good.
The actors were very good. **However,** I didn't like the film much.
2 I'll buy this bag. I'll **also** buy these shoes.
I'll buy this bag. I'll buy these shoes, **too.**
3 My car is old, **but it** runs very well.
Although my car is old, it runs very well.
My car runs very well, **although** it's old.
My car is old. **However,** it runs very well.

You might want to do further checks using these

sentences. *Betty's working late today./Betty's working late tomorrow.*
I need some new shoes./I haven't got enough money.
Julia doesn't feel well./She has gone to work.

Extra material and ideas

1 WB page 58, Writing, Exercise 7.
2 Cut up sentences on card which include the linkers and punctuation. The punctuation should be on separate cards. Stick the cards on the board, putting the punctuation cards up first and then jumbling the other words. In pairs SS work out the order and write the sentence down. One pair of SS could rearrange the cards on the board. Other SS say if they agree or not e.g.,

, . . WENT I TO OFFICE
HOWEVER THERE HE JOHN'S WASN'T

(I went to John's office. However, he wasn't there.)
  Obviously, you don't have to use cards. It could all just be written on the board. However, you will need to plan it before you begin, to ensure that you don't miss out words and/or punctuation.

GRAMMAR
Quantity

Describing quantity: *some-, any-, no-, every-* words.

L • This section builds on the grammar in Unit 6. You might ask SS to look back at the *Language reference* on page 41 for homework before you begin this section.
• The quantifiers are: *someone, anyone, no one, everyone something, anything, nothing, everything, too much, too many.*
• *Someone* refers to a single person (cf *some people*).
• Questions can be a conceptual nightmare. Compare *Is anyone there? Is someone there? Is everyone there? Is no one there?* At this level it's perhaps better not to explore these unless SS raise questions.
• *Too* and *very* are often confused. SS equate them both with the idea of *a lot*, and fail to grasp the concept that *too* expresses excess. And even if they do grasp this idea, they attempt to collocate *too* with adjectives such as *happy* or *hungry. I'm too hungry/too happy.*
• However, there is an underlying sense that there can't be an excess of happiness, and hunger is in itself an excess. To express a strengthening for these types of adjectives we can only add an intensifier, *really, very* etc.
• Closely related to this area of grammar is *not enough.* It can be quickly equated with *too* + a negative adjective: *too small* = not big enough. You could draw the following to illustrate this.

There is an example of this in Exercise 1a), but only draw attention to it if you think SS can cope with it.

📖 **Students' Book** (page 92)

Some-, any-, no-, every- **words**

Exercise 1a) A deductive approach is probably the most efficient presentation for this grammar. Begin by writing on the board:

every + one = everyone = (every person)
no + one = no one = (no person)

You could illustrate this visually on a cline.

0% ├────────────────────┤ 100%
no one   everyone

Everyone wants coffee.
No one wants tea.
some + one = someone (one person not named)
Someone wants sugar in their coffee.
Does anyone want milk?

🔑 everyone, anything, no one

🔑 **Exercise 1c)**
no one, everyone

🔑 **Exercise 1d)**
anything

Exercise 2 Go over the grammar box with SS. If you think it won't overload your SS, mention that for people we can say either *someone* or *somebody, everyone* or *everybody* etc.

🔑 2 anyone 3 nothing 4 no one/everyone
5 anything/everything 6 anyone 7 someone
8 everyone

Too and *very*

Exercise 3) This exercise hopes to anticipate the common confusion between *too* and *very*. *too* = more than is good/wanted/right/necessary /enough/possible etc. It would be advisable to keep repeating this idea as you check each answer.

🔑 very, too, very, too

Exercise 4 Ask a S to read out the last sentence from Exercise 3a) *I'm too old to live in a big house*. Use boxes/colour/underlining to highlight the structure **too + adjective + to + base form of verb** before they begin the next exercise.

🔑 1 It's too cold to go swimming. 2 He's too tired to go out. 3 He's too ill to get up. 4 It's too expensive to buy.

🔑 **Exercise 5**

1 He's too young to get married. 2 It's too dark to see the road. 3 This programme is very interesting for children. 4 My coffee is too hot to drink.

Too much and *too many*

Exercise 6 If you asked SS to read *Language reference* Unit 6, page 41 for homework, get them to tell you when we use *much* and *many*. Do a quick review of countable and uncountable nouns. Name a letter of the alphabet and SS try to think of a countable and an uncountable noun beginning with that letter: A *air, apple*, B *butter, banana* etc.

🔑 too many people/houses/trees
too much time/salt/money

Exercise 7 Highlight that we are putting the idea of *too* with *much* and *many*. We're joining them to express excessive quantity. Note *too much to do*. It's probably better to teach this as a fixed phrase rather than trying to explain the concept of uncountable.

🔑 too much, too many.

🔑 **Exercise 8**

1 We can't buy that house. It costs too much money.
2 You've got too much furniture and too many clothes. You should sell some.
3 I can't see. There are too many people in front of me.
4 You spend too much time watching TV.
5 I can't eat this cake. There's too much sugar in it.

Extra material and ideas

WB page 55, Grammar, Exercises 1 to 3.

VOCABULARY
Education

L •The names of subjects usually cause pronunciation problems for SS, particularly if they have a similar word in their L1 which is stressed and/or pronounced differently. Highlight the stress and check pronunciation of each word; '*languages*, '*science*, *I'T* (*Infor'mation Tech'nology*), '*literature, eco'nomics,*

P E ('*Physical Edu'cation*), '*history*.
• Noun/verb collocation: *pass and fail, study for/exam, attend/class, go/university, have/lessons, take/break, get/degree, do/homework*.
• Obvious problems with *no* v. *not very good at*. The cline should illustrate the conceptual difference, but use check questions to highlight that *no good at* is worse than *not very good at*. Also, you need to point out the use of NO v. NOT. A common mistake would be *no very good*. The preposition *at* comes as a surprise to many SS who expect *with* to follow the adjectives.

📖 **Students' Book** (page 94)

Exercise 1 Remind SS to use dictionaries to help with stress and pronunciation. Mark the stressed syllables, and practise the words. You could draw the cline on the board. Highlight the difference between *no good* and *not very good* (see L above) and the use of *at* after the adjectives. Then tell SS about yourself at school, e.g., *I wasn't very good at X. I was useless at Y, but I was good at Z*. You could invite them to tell the class about themselves or they could work in pairs.

🔑 a) science b) IT (information technology) c) art d) languages

Exercise 2 You could add *to make/correct a mistake*.

🔑 1 take 2 do 3 taking/fail/study/pass 4 got 5 go 6 have 7 attend

Using your vocabulary

Exercise 1 If SS find the ranking too difficult, this could easily be changed to agree or disagree, give a mark out of 3 (1=very important, 2=quite important, 3=not important), or complete these sentences with *because* ...

Exercise 2 This could turn into a useful discussion on ways to make learning easier, useful study habits/hints.

Extra material and ideas

1 WB page 56, Vocabulary, Exercise 4.
P **2** Page 146, 15.1. In a multilingual class you could do a survey on education across the world. Give SS copies of the questionnaire for them to interview as many people as they can. You could tabulate the results or some of the results on the board or a poster to stimulate further discussion.

Country	free	SS in class	age begin	etc.
France				
Austria				
UK	✓	30+	5	
etc.				

3 Before you begin VOCABULARY you could find out what subjects SS already know. Write the letters of the alphabet on the board. In groups they try to find a subject for each letter. One person in the group is the runner responsible for writing the words on the board. You can expect quite a lot of spelling mistakes even if they know the words. It can be a team game. Points scored for correct word and correct spelling.

4 The following day's lesson could begin with a word stress exercise which will act as a vocabulary review. Here are some words and patterns:
Ooo beautiful, happily, chemistry, stereo, uniform, possible
ooO engineer, mountaineer
oO begin, address, report, CD
ooOo politician, electrician, economics, television, education
oOo professor, delicious, potato
Oo concert, headphones, carpet, children, student, history
oOoo economist, geography, political, impossible, psychology
Oooo regularly
Below are some activities:
• **Find your partner.** Give some SS word stress patterns, give other SS words. They have to match the word and the pattern, e.g. oOoo ge'ography;
Oo 'history   Ooo 'languages   Oo 'science
Ooo 'literature   ooOo eco'nomics.
• In groups of four give SS three word stress patterns and 8 – 10 word cards. Some words will go with patterns they have, some will not. The idea is to get rid of any words that don't belong to the group's patterns. Two people from each group should act as runners. Runners try to find where the words belong. However, if the other groups don't think the word matches their patterns, they don't have to accept it. The groups all have different patterns and words. E.g. one group has these word stress patterns: Oo, oOoo, oOo and these word cards: *economics, potato, concert, botany, CD, stereo, chemistry, headphones* and *geography*. The group keeps *potato, concert, headphones* and *geography* and the runners try to get rid of *economics, botany, CD, stereo* and *chemistry*.

Word Stress Patterns	Word Cards
Oo	economics potato ✓ concert ✓
oOoo	botany CD stereo
oOo	chemistry headphones ✓ geography ✓

They keep the 4 ticked cards and the runners get rid of the others.

• PW. Give each S words with the stress pattern marked. They say their words to their partner who draws the stress pattern on a piece of paper. When both SS have said all their words, they exchange the cards and check their answers.

USE AND REVIEW

• Revision of question tags.
• *Used to.*
• Vocabulary.

 Students' Book (page 95)

Exercise 1
1 Carly *went* to a Thai restaurant last night.
2 These days I *(usually) catch* a bus at six o'clock every morning.
3 When he was younger he used to *spend* every Saturday in bed.
4 You haven't seen her, *have* you?
5 David likes tennis, *does/doesn't* he?

Exercise 2a) Allow SS to choose whether they want to work alone or with others.

1	→	author
1	↓	audience
2	↓	ter
3	↓	right
4	←	annual
5	→	ircus
6	←	hang
7	→	useu
8	↓	fan
9	↓	ar
10	→	zoo
11	→	earns

Exercise 2b)
used to

TEST

There is a progress test for Units 11-15 on pages 154 and 155 of this book for you to photocopy for your students. See page 159 for the Key.

Have you heard the news?

Students' Book

General theme: apologising.
Unit topic: saying sorry.

USE YOUR ENGLISH: saying sorry.
SKILLS: reading and speaking (two strange stories); vocabulary (negatives with *un-, in-, dis-, non-*); writing (improving a paragraph).
GRAMMAR: the passive, Present and Past Simple.
VOCABULARY: news stories.
USE AND REVIEW: quantity words from a picture; *some, any, no one.*

Workbook

GRAMMAR: the passive.
VOCABULARY: negatives with *dis-, un-* and *in-;* same sound, different spelling and meaning.
SKILLS: listening (three news stories); writing (punctuation).
DICTATION/PRONUNCIATION: the passive.

USE YOUR ENGLISH
Saying sorry

- Apologising and giving reasons and excuses.
- Responding to an apology.
- Asking someone to repeat.

- Apologies using *(I'm) very/awfully sorry.* The pronoun and verb can be omitted and intensifiers added such as *so sorry/really sorry.*
- Fixed phrases to respond to an apology. *It doesn't matter. That's all right. Don't worry,* which are interchangeable or said in quick succession. *It's not your fault* is used when we blame someone/thing other than the person who's apologising.
- *Sorry* is also used to ask the speaker to repeat what they've just said. This is often said with a noticeable rise in intonation which signals a question. Intonation is important. Said with a high fall or rise fall *sorry* can sound sarcastic. Although there isn't one way to say *sorry* and mean it, it's safer to use a low rise.

 Students' Book (page 96)

Exercise 1a) Begin the lesson with a bit of amateur dramatics. Set up situations where you keep having to apologise to SS. Knock books off desks, bang into SS, drop pens on them, hand them something but let go before they take it etc. Then say, *The lesson today is about ..?* leave a gap and see if SS can fill it with *saying sorry.*

You could write **to apologise** on the board and say this means *saying sorry.* Explain that the British say *Sorry* in many situations and they think it's impolite not to apologise in these situations. Then ask SS to look at the pictures and elicit the situations.

1 Sorry, but my watch stopped.
2 I'm awfully sorry. I didn't see you there.

Exercise 1b) Highlight possible excuses we would use.

1 Oh, yes. You always say that.
2 That's all right. Don't worry.

Exercise 1c) When SS have checked their answers against the cassette get them to practise the dialogues. Focus attention on how the speaker says *Sorry.* Demonstrate an impolite/sarcastic apology so SS can hear the difference.

[16.1]
A: Where have you been?
B: Sorry, but my watch stopped.
A: Oh, yes. You always say that.
A: For heaven's sake. Look what you are doing!
B: I'm awfully sorry. I didn't see you there.
A: That's all right. Don't worry.

Exercise 2 Highlight other functions of *Sorry:* when we want to get past someone; refusing an invitation; asking someone to repeat what they've said. *Excuse me* is equally appropriate in all these situations but British people are more likely to say *Sorry.*

 1 c 2 a 3 b

[16.2]
1 ANDREW: You didn't *ring* me last night.
  NICOLA: *Sorry*?
  A: I said you didn't ring me last night.
  N: I know. I went back to work.
  A: What was the problem?
  PASSENGER: Sorry.
2 N: Oh, *sorry.* Are you trying to *get off*?
  P: Yes.
  N: I had to phone America.
  A: Oh yes?
  N: Yes. I had to talk to our American director. Why don't we meet tonight?
  A: No, I don't think so.
  N: Oh, damn! Why won't this work?
3 OFFICIAL: Can I have a look at your ticket? *Sorry* but this is *out of* date. Would you come with me?
  N: Oh, no. Did I forget to buy a ticket?

Exercise 3 You could change the pace here by getting SS to write the conversations first. Then SS pass them round the class for others to check. When you signal stop, SS practise the dialogues they have. Ask SS to add some actions and make it more of a roleplay, e.g., a phone conversation for the invitation, calling the waiter over to tell him about the broken glass etc. Ask the more confident SS to say the dialogues during feedback.

(These are suggested conversations but accept appropriate alternatives)

1 A: I'm awfully sorry. I've just broken a glass.
  B: That's all right. Don't worry. I'll clear up the pieces.
2 A: Would you like to come to Roger's party on Saturday evening?
  B: I'm very sorry, I'm afraid I can't. I'm going to stay with my grandparents in York.
3 A: I'm very cold.
  B: Sorry. I can't hear you. What did you say?

Extra material and ideas

1 Page 146, 16.1. Give SS copies of the conversations, get them to add *Sorry* in the correct place and then practise saying them. SS can listen and check against 📼 16.3 on Class Cassette B.

1 A: Mum's not very well.
  B: [Sorry] What did you say?
  A: I said Mum's not very well.
2 A: [Sorry] Can I get past?
  B: Sure.
  A: Thanks a lot.
3 A: [Sorry] You can't come in.
  B: Why not?
  A: Because you're too young.
4 A: Ouch! my foot!
  B: [Sorry] I didn't know you were there.
  A: It's all right. Don't worry.

2 Writing a note to apologise You are staying with a British friend. It's your last day and your friend has gone to work. You broke a cup at breakfast. Leave some money for a new cup and write a note of apology.

Dear ...

Once again, many thanks for everything. I had a lovely time.

However, I've got some bad news...

SKILLS

- Reading for gist and detail.
- Speaking: an information exchange/fluency activity when SS summarise short texts for each other.
- Vocabulary: negative prefixes.
- Writing: improving a piece of written work.

Reading and speaking

- Both texts are humorous and quite short. The vocabulary in Group B's text is more difficult but the text is shorter. This may influence how you arrange your groups. Unfamiliar vocabulary includes: 'razor blades, 'light bulbs, 'breathing and 'breathalyse. Vocabulary in Group A's text should be familiar, apart from *to wave*.

Students' Book (page 97)

Exercise 1 Use the pictures to elicit guesses about the story and perhaps introduce *to breathalyse* and *razor blades*. However, don't do too much at this stage as there's a danger that you'll remove the need to read the texts.

a), c) and e) tell a story about a man who eats light bulbs and razor blades. The other story is about an old lady who cons two strangers in a restaurant to pay her bill.

Exercise 2 At this level SS feel more secure and less frustrated if they know they can ask you to explain vocabulary while they're reading. If you think this is appropriate for your class, tell them they can ask you. If it isn't appropriate for your class to do a jigsaw activity, then do it as a whole class activity. If you do the jigsaw activity, set a reasonable time limit to encourage SS finish at roughly the same time. Let the members of each group compare and check their answers with you before they summarise the text for a member of the other group.

Group A: 1 a) c) 2 a) d)
Group B: 1 2 4 5 7

Exercise 3 Remind SS to use the pictures when they retell the story and explain any vocabulary their partner doesn't understand.

Extra material and ideas

1 When SS have finished summarising the texts for each other, divide the class into their original groups again. In a light-hearted way say you're going to test how well they told each other about the texts. Ask Group A questions about text B. Ask Group B questions about text A. As you ask the questions you will probably find the opposite team trying to add information they forgot to give in their summaries. This is where the humour creeps in.

2 A roleplay based on the texts. In groups of four assign the following roles: the romantic couple in the restaurant; Jim Rose; a radio interviewer. Tell the couple and Jim Rose to reread the texts to make sure they have all the details ready for the interview. The interviewer prepares his/her questions. Tell them they are going to make 2 short news items for the end of a news programme. Record the SS if possible. Highlight positive things as well as mistakes.

Vocabulary: negatives

- SS often ask for rules about which prefix to use, but they are very unlikely to help. At this level it's better to help SS just to learn the prefixes by reviewing them regularly until they become known. You could point out that the most common prefix used with adjectives, verbs and adverbs is *un-*. Therefore if they don't know which prefix to use, this would be a good first guess. It's still being added to new words, whereas many of the others are no longer productive.

- The problem associated with prefixes and word stress is that because the prefixes *un-*, *in-*, and *dis-* usually take a secondary stress SS often hear and/or produce them as primary stresses. They are only likely to be primary stresses if used as a contrast *No, he doesn't like it. He*

DIS*likes it*. Normally the stress will stay on the main word, the verb, adjective, noun or adverb. However, this is less clear with the prefix *non-*. In the word *nonsense, non-* is the primary stress. In words like *nonstop, non-smoking , non-fiction* there seems to be equal stress but the pitch is higher on the second stress.

Students' Book (page 98)

Exercise 1 SS should look up the prefix part of the word. If you want them to discover the stress from the dictionary, ask them to do this as they look up the word to save time. Get SS to practise saying the words which will help them commit them to memory.

1 un'happy 2 'nonsense 3 disa'gree 4 un'luckily
5 dis'honest 6 'non'stop 7 inco'rrect 8 un'kind

Extra material and ideas

1 WB page 60, Vocabulary, Exercise 5.
2 To help SS learn these negative prefixes, recycle them as often as possible in the next few lessons. You could include them in teacher to SS dictations, S to S dictations, matching exercises, spot the mistake exercises etc. When you think SS are reasonably accurate, stop reviewing them for the next couple of lessons, then check again. Continue like this until SS know them. It really needn't take more than a minute or two at the beginning or end of a lesson. It could be as simple as spotting a prefix in a text and asking SS how many others they can remember from the lesson they did on prefixes.

Writing: improving a paragraph

 • The text is improved by: using more descriptive adjectives and adverbs, linkers and referencing.
• Negative prefixes are recycled in this exercise.

Students' Book (page 98)

Exercise a) Adding adverbs and adjectives. Tell SS you're going to read a text to them and you want them to think about the way it's written. Read the text and ask them to comment. Then get them to look at the text and elicit other problems: very short sentences, not enough adjectives and adverbs, same words repeated.

Exercise b) Linkers. Do the first one as an example. Ask SS to put the first three sentences together using linkers from the box. Then let them continue individually or in pairs.

Exercise c) Referencing. Point out that *Fred* is used sixteen times and *policemen* is used four times.

Last night Fred was very unhappy but he decided to go to an inexpensive restaurant. He went alone because he didn't want to go with the unpleasant people who were staying with him. He was very tired and he had an argument with an unfriendly waiter so he decided to go home. He wanted to drive nonstop

all the way. However, he nearly fell asleep so he decided to stop. Unluckily some policemen saw him and they asked him what he was doing. Fred was angry and shouted at them. They were angry too and (they) took him to the police station.

GRAMMAR
The passive

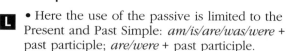 • Here the use of the passive is limited to the Present and Past Simple: *am/is/are/was/were* + past participle; *are/were* + past participle.
• The passive is used when:
  a) The subject is unknowable: *Those mountains were formed millions of years ago.*
  b) The subject is an unknown group: *The city was rebuilt after the war.*
  c) The subject is unknown though it is perhaps possible to find out: *She was murdered last night.*
  d) The subject is of less interest to the speaker/writer: *Jon was fired yesterday.*
  e) Responsibility is shifted away from the speaker: *You're working week will be cut by two days.*
• The passive is mainly used in situations or texts where information is given. It occurs much less in imaginative and literary works.
• The active voice is far more common.
• In 4 out of 5 instances the agent is not mentioned. However, there are times when the agent must be referred to: *This was painted by Janet Woolley. This was painted by one of Britain's finest illustrators.*
• Problems for SS include the past participle form of irregular verbs, and the fact that they're usually still grappling with the past of the verb *to be.*
• Pronunciation. Encourage SS to use the weak and contracted forms of the verb *to be*, past and present. The problem of *-ed* endings in regular past participles is likely. In connected speech the difference between /t/ and /d/ pronunciation of *-ed* endings is often indistinguishable unless a vowel follows. However, overuse of /ɪd/ needs constant attention.

Students' Book (page 98)

Exercise 1 SS are asked to think about why the focus is on what happened rather than who did it.

1 The young man.
2 No, we don't. No, they aren't.

Exercise 2 The focus is on the form. It would help to add visual clues as you ask the questions.
Use the same approach as in the SB with present active and passive sentences. You could make it look like a newspaper item:

Someone pays a woman £200 a week to take his dog for a walk.

A woman is paid £200 a week to take a dog for a walk.

1a) 2b) 3a) 4b)

Exercise 3 Do this with the whole class as it's the first time you're asking them to produce the form.

1 My gloves were stolen yesterday.
2 Pat was hit last night

Exercise 4 The focus is on *by* used to introduce the agent. You could ask SS to transform this into an active sentence and then ask why this wasn't used in the newspaper. (The man is more important than the dog.) This will reinforce *why* and *when* we use the passive. If you *only* give transformation exercises, active ➜ passive, passive ➜ active, there is a danger that SS won't perceive a difference in use.

The postman was attacked by a dog.

Exercise 5
2 are eaten   3 was met   4 was drunk   5 was built
6 are made   7 was sold

Exercise 6
3 What is she called?
4 We weren't given the right tickets.

Exercise 7 All the sentences require the past form of either the active or the passive voice.

1 was created, was printed   2 ate, were made
3 was destroyed, were killed, found
4 was hit, jumped, crashed, was found

Using your grammar

Exercise 1 Make sure the SS have formed the questions correctly before they ask each other. Answers on page 127 of SB.

Group A
4   Who was television invented by?
5   What is the Japanese drink sake made from?
6   Where were the Winter Olympics held in 1994?

Group B
4   Where was Martin Luther King assassinated?
5   Who was the play *Hamlet* written by?
6   In which country is champagne produced?

Extra material and ideas

1 WB pages 59 and 60, Grammar, Exercise 1 to 4 and page 61, Dictation, Exercise 9.

2 Past participle tennis page 147, 16.2. PW. Give each S one of the lists of verbs. Before the match begins SS fill in the past participles on their lists. The idea is to keep serving to get through his/her list first. SS toss a coin to see who starts. A gives B the first base form on their list. If B gives the correct past participle, he/she 'serves' his/her first base form. When a S fails to give the correct past participle the opponent serves again. The winner is the first to get to the end of the list.

VOCABULARY
News stories

- Naming parts of a newspaper.
- Homophones leading into the use of puns.
- Common collocations in news stories.

- SS may be familiar with the American word stress for *adver'tisement*. It's not a problem if SS use the American pronunciation, but point out they will hear a different pronunciation from a British speaker.
- SS may find it hard to work out and therefore appreciate the humour created by the homophones in the headlines. However, it continues to highlight the very real problem of sound and spelling that SS face.
- Common collocations found in news stories: *'car crash, 'bomb explosion, world 'record, 'tennis champion, 'road block.*

Students' Book (page 100)

Exercise 1 Take in one newspaper (it doesn't have to be a British newspaper). Use this to introduce the theme. If you take in a lot of newspapers and hand them round, SS will understandably be drawn into reading what they can, so time things accordingly. Ask questions *What's this? Do you read newspapers often? Which part do you always read first? What kind do you like/read? Do you read all the paper? Do many people buy newspapers in your country? How much do they cost?* etc. Point out that in headlines the passive voice is often shortened to just the past participle as in the example, *Killer shot dead.*

1c)   2a)   3e)   4d)   5b)

Exercise 2 Introduce the idea of homophones by saying you're going to dictate some words. Then say 1 *I* 2 *eye*. Initially SS will look puzzled but someone usually catches on. If someone does, let them explain to the others and then continue. If no one does get it immediately, just continue. They'll catch on after a couple of examples.
3 *sail* 4 *sale* 5 *hear* 6 *here* 7 *there* 8 *their*
9 *they're*. The last examples should be 10 *meet*
11 *meat*.
Get SS to compare notes. Although they don't often have them all individually, they usually have all the alternatives between them. Get them to spell them and write them on the board. The last examples then lead into Exercise 2. Ask SS to tell you the meanings of *meat* and *meet*, then see if they can work out the pun in the headline.

Exercise 3 PW. If SS really find this difficult, help them and try to keep it light-hearted.

🔑 a) too, weight, (good)bye, piece, right

🔑 b) 1 Write and wrong   2 Den's wait problem

Exercise 4 Highlight the stress patterns of the collocations but don't spend time practising pronunciation as they are mainly for recognition not production.

🔑 car crash, bomb explosion, world record/champion, tennis champion, road block
Good news: world record/champion, tennis champion
Bad news: car crash, bomb explosion, road block

Using your vocabulary

Exercise 1 Check SS understand the meanings of the words, can produce them and recognise the pronunciation. The different groups are responsible for telling different parts of the same story. You could conduct this as a whole class activity if it's more appropriate to your situation.

🔑 (These are suggested answers but accept any appropriate alternatives.)
In Group B's picture (the first of the two) the policeman has thrown away his baton. He isn't directing the traffic, he's dancing. The drivers are confused and there is going to be a big traffic jam.
In Group A's picture the policeman is very tired. His dancing has caused a big traffic jam. A lorry has run into a gun shop and the owner is furious. He is going to shoot the policeman!

Extra material and ideas

1 WB page 60, Vocabulary, Exercise 6, and Listening, Exercise 7.
2 SS write sentences with the wrong spelling of a homophone. They exchange with a partner who tries to find the mistakes.
3 SS write the story they produced in USING YOUR VOCABULARY as a newspaper article, with a headline and visuals.

USE AND REVIEW

- Crime-related vocabulary.
- Quantifiers: *some, a few, a lot of, someone, anyone*, etc.

 Students' Book (page 101)

Exercise 1 Read the article to SS and let them follow in their books. Ask a few basic comprehension questions to guide them to the humour of the article.

🔑 Because one man committed a lot of crimes (17% of all the crimes in the area).

Exercise 2 Get SS to name all the things in the picture and write them in two columns, A and B, on the board. One half of the class talks about *how much* and *how many things* the man stole of things listed in column A. The other SS do the same for column B. As they listen to each other they should check if they agree with their partner's description of *how much/many.*

A: He stole some cameras.
B: *Yes, he did. He stole a few.* or *No, he didn't. He stole a lot of cameras.*

🔑 They found a little jewellery, a little money, a lot of CDs, a few bottles of Coke and a few TVs.

Exercise 3 Ask SS to do this exercise alone first. Then check with another S. When they agree on the answers they practise saying the conversation. Confident SS could say it for the class if they've had enough time to practise it.

🔑 someone, No one, anyone, too many, anything, Everyone, too

Exercise 4 When SS have had some time to form an opinion, ask questions to the whole class, as a survey *How many of you think ten years in prison is too little for murder?* Tabulate the numbers on the board or ask a S to put the numbers up for you, e.g.

murder = 10 years

too little	right	too much
15	4	3

The majority says too little. It should be …

Then ask why and what would be better etc. Keep adding the results to the board so the information can be compared. By asking questions in this way everyone can be involved at some point without having to say very much.

Celebration

Students' Book

General theme: celebration.
Unit topic: special occasions.

USE YOUR ENGLISH: special occasions.
SKILLS: reading (Chinese New Year); vocabulary (guessing meaning from context); writing (paragraph construction).
GRAMMAR: Present Perfect Continuous and Past Perfect Simple (the unfinished past); *for* and *since*.
VOCABULARY: having a party.
USE AND REVIEW: Information gap about past participles, passives, headlines and stories.

Workbook

GRAMMAR: Present Perfect Simple and Continuous.
VOCABULARY: word families.
SKILLS: listening (Christmas); writing (paragraphs and improving a letter).
DICTATION/PUNCTUATION: contrastive stress.

USE YOUR ENGLISH
Special occasions

- Revision of days and dates.
- Fixed phrases for special occasions and congratulating someone (see also Unit 14 SB page 84).
- Cultural information exchange about public holidays and festivals.

- Fixed phrases *Happy 'Birthday, Happy New 'Year, Merry 'Christmas, Have a good 'time, 'Good 'luck, Congratu'lations. Good luck* refers to a future event and *Congratulations* to something already achieved.
- The vocabulary load here is quite heavy but SS only need to recognise many of the items not use them.
- Background information:

Hallowe'en, 31 October
This is all about witches and ghosts. It's mainly a children's event. Children dress up as witches and monsters and visit houses in the neighbourhood saying, 'Trick or treat!' This means 'Give us some sweets or we'll play a trick on you.' People usually give them sweets, but a trick might be ringing their doorbell and then running away. Hallowe'en is not a public holiday. The events happen in the evening.

Bonfire Night, 5 November
This festival remembers a rebel called Guy Fawkes who tried to blow up the King and the Houses of Parliament in 1605. He put gunpowder in the cellars but he was caught before he could blow them up. Before 5 November children make a figure of Guy Fawkes. They take it into the street and ask people to give money for the Guy. With this money they buy fireworks. On 5 November there are fireworks and bonfires to burn the figure of Guy Fawkes. It's not a public holiday.

Christmas, 25 December
A Christian holiday celebrating the birth of Jesus Christ. The Christmas holiday can be up to a week for some working people, though others only get Christmas Day and the day after, called Boxing Day. Traditionally, people put Christmas trees in their houses which are decorated. On Christmas Eve (24 December) when the children are in bed, Father Christmas (Santa Claus in the USA) brings presents. People also send cards to friends and family at this time. The traditional meal includes turkey, roast potatoes, vegetables and a dessert of plum pudding – Christmas pudding.

New Year's Eve, 31 December
This is often celebrated by having parties. At midnight everyone holds hands in a circle and sings a special song 'Auld Lang Syne' to celebrate the passing of the old year and the coming of the new year. Everyone kisses each other. By tradition, many British people celebrate the new year in Trafalgar Square in London, by kissing policemen and climbing into the fountain. The following day is a public holiday for most people who are often recovering from a little too much alcohol and not enough sleep! In Scotland this is a very important celebration. It's given a special name – Hogmanay. New Year's Eve is also the time when we make resolutions about what we hope to do in the next year, to stop smoking or study harder or take more exercise.

Saint Valentine's Day, 14 February
This is a day when lovers show their love for each other or when we send anonymous cards to those we love but daren't tell. The main image is a red heart. Husbands and wives, boyfriends and girlfriends exchange small gifts and cards. This is not a public holiday.

 Students' Book (page 102)

Exercise 1 Ask two SS to write the dates on the board while the others practise saying them. Check that both the written and spoken forms are correct (see also Unit 4 page 24). Then

establish what the dates represent. Give SS information (see L), about each event, or write short descriptions for SS to read as homework the night before. There is a lot of information to absorb so don't be surprised if they can't retain very much. As long as they have an idea of what each event represents, the details aren't important. You could draw the following as prompts:

🔑 31 October is Hallowe'en; 5 November is Bonfire Night or Guy Fawkes' Night; 14 February is Saint Valentine's Day; 1 January is New Year's Day; 25 December is Christmas Day; 31 December is New Year's Eve.

Exercise 2a) The events are not referred to in the dialogues. SS should be able to deduce the answers if you have given them some cultural background. However, if they can't get it from context, don't wait long before telling them. You could ask them to listen for background noises which will give them clues, e.g. fireworks going off.

📼 [17.1]
```
1  A:  Put this present under the tree.
   B:  Oh, thanks!
   A:  You mustn't open it until the morning.
   B:  OK.
   B:  And don't eat too much tomorrow.
   B:  Impossible! I always do.
2  A:  I want to see the fireworks.
   B:  Oh, I'll come with you.
   C:  Have a good time, you two! and be careful! Don't
       get too near the bonfire.
3  A:  Have you made your resolutions yet?
   B:  Yes, I'm going to give up smoking.
   A:  What, again?!
4  A:  Oh, what a horrible sight! Here take these sweets.
   B:  Thanks very much. Thank you.
   A:  Not at all. Now go away!
5  A:  Darling.
   B:  Yes?
   A:  Who was that card from?
   B:  I don't know. There's no name on it.
   H:  You went very red when the postman came.
   W:  Did I?
   H:  Yes. It's not from your new boss, is it?
```

🔑 1 Christmas 2 5 November 3 New Year 4 Hallowe'en
5 Saint Valentine's Day

Exercise 2b
a 31 October b,c 25 December d 5 November
e 31 December f 14 February

Exercise 3 Highlight the stress on the fixed phrases (see L). Different intonation patterns are possible but a medium fall on the main stress would be appropriate on all of the phrases. It isn't just the intonation that carries attitude/mood of the speaker. It's important that SS give the right signals with facial expression, too.

🔑 Merry Christmas! Happy Christmas/New Year/birthday! Have a good time!

Exercise 4a) Highlight the difference in use between *Good luck* and *Congratulations* (see L). Possible situations for *Good luck*: taking an exam, a driving test, first day at school, going to a job interview, just before a wedding etc. For *Congratulations*: announcing a wedding, a birth, a wedding anniversary, passing an exam, getting a job, winning a prize etc.

Exercise 4b) As you monitor SS note any particularly good conversations. Make sure they are completely correct, then ask the SS to say their conversation to the class. Try to get at least one conversation to illustrate the use of *Good luck* and one for *Congratulations*. You could also point out that when British people wish someone *Good luck* they sometimes cross index and middle finger.

Exercise 5 In a multilingual class ask SS how many public holidays they have a year, what these days celebrate and how people celebrate these days. This can take quite a lot of time so plan accordingly, and perhaps set time limits. You could collate information on the board about how many public holidays each nationality has. The difference can be quite surprising to SS. Britain has 8. In a monolingual class ask if SS know how many public holidays there are in the year. Then SS could tell their partner which is their favourite event and why. Get some SS to feedback to the class.

SKILLS

▲ • Reading: prediction, reading for gist, reading for detail.
• Vocabulary: guessing meaning from context.
• Writing: ordering information in a paragraph.

Reading

L This is a fairly long text but if SS have completed USE YOUR ENGLISH, the topic area will be familiar and the text shouldn't present too many problems. There will be unfamiliar vocabulary items but DO NOT preteach 'lanterns, 'lasted, banned, safe, 'injured, close to and grow up, as they form the basis of the vocabulary exercise. Check *'faithful, super'stition, 'zodiac* and *to 'kneel* before the SS read the text.

📖 Students' Book (page 103)

Exercise 1 Any discussion in USE YOUR ENGLISH will have served as a general prediction. However, the picture of different aspects of Chinese New Year celebrations allows SS to make more specific predictions. If you have Chinese, Taiwanese or Hong Kong SS they can read the article to see if it's a correct description of what happened in the past and what happens now.

Exercise 2 You may want to preteach some of the vocabulary not included in VOCABULARY (see L). Before SS read, go over the questions and make sure they realise they only have to find the paragraph where the information can be found. They don't have to answer the questions. Tell them you are going to ask everyone to stop at the same time, and they should try to find the right paragraph as quickly as possible. A reasonable time guide is if you read it through twice at an average speed.

🔑 2 E 3 A 4 D 5 B

Exercise 3a) SS read the text again to find more detailed information. This time don't place a time limit on the reading as the exercise asks them to make notes too. The notes shouldn't be corrected. They are only a stimulus to Exercise 3b).

> **Extra material and ideas**
>
> **1** WB page 63, Listening Exercise 7 is one person's view of Christmas.
> **2** If your SS enjoy being read to, read the passage to them after they have completed Exercises 1–3. They should have their books closed. They then have the advantage of knowing the content and can check to see how good they are at associating the written and the spoken word, i.e., can they understand it when they hear it as well as when they read it?

Vocabulary

🅛 Be careful that with the words *lantern* and *banned* you show their collocational limits. It's easy to lead SS into making mistakes because we give a quick and simple synonym.

Ban is an official stoppage of something, a formal word. You couldn't say **I banned my friend from telling my secret. A lantern* is more commonly used outside, it has a naked flame which is protected by a container usually made of glass. So you couldn't use *lantern* to mean *a light.* You can't say **Switch on the lantern.*

📖 Students' Book (page 103)

Exercise 1 This should be a teaching rather than testing activity. You are trying to build SS' confidence about tackling texts with SOME unfamiliar vocabulary in it. Therefore, perhaps it's better to do the first two with the whole class. Allow time for everyone to locate the word and stop the quicker SS from shouting the answers out. Ask them to say why they chose the meaning they did and if necessary show them where the clues to the meaning are. Let them do the last one on their own, and ask them to find the clues in the text which helped them to guess the meaning.

🔑 1 b) 2 a) 3 b)

Exercise 2 A reversal of the previous activity but it requires a similar process. Let SS work alone then check their answers with a partner.

🔑 1 close 2 grew up 3 injured 4 safe

Writing: paragraphs

🅛 • Stressing simple paragraph construction is important for SS at this level. They are still fairly limited in terms of language so the need to order information is vital. A basic model might be:
statement (topic sentence) → explanation/development → conclusion. You could simplify this for SS by writing on the board:
say what it is → explain →
give examples → finish

• In the exercise the topic sentence and the conclusion are given. Sentence 2 is a development sentence, 1, 3 and 4 are examples of what happens. These need to be sorted into chronological order.

📖 Students' Book (page 104)

Exercise 1 There is a reasonably obvious logical order for the information about Christmas, so let SS try this on their own after you have established the objective and given guidance (see L above). If your SS are capable, ask them to say why they ordered it the way they did.

🔑 2 1 (or 1 2) 4 3

Exercise 2 Ask SS to say which festivals they are going to write about and list them on the board. In monolingual classes this might discourage SS from all writing about the same festival and in multilingual classes the list might stimulate curiosity and motivation.

Exercise 4 SS could put their paragraphs around the room and walk around reading each other's descriptions. They should take a piece of paper and a pen with them so they can make a note of any questions they want to ask other SS about their descriptions. You could do the same.

GRAMMAR

- Present Perfect Continuous: the unfinished past.
- *For* and *since*.

Present Perfect Continuous: the unfinished part

- It will take SS considerable time to assimilate this area of grammar. You are simply beginning to expose them to the Present Perfect Continuous aspect. The problem is compounded by its apparent similarity to the Present Perfect Simple. The aims should be for SS to recognise the form; understand the general time reference and meaning (not all the subtleties); be aware of pronunciation; and make some initial attempts to use it in context.
- Use/Meaning: it relates past time to present time. It describes an action or state which began in the past and is probably still continuing in the speaker's idea of present time even if it isn't happening right now *I've been working for them for 6 months*. However, it's possible the action or state has just come, or is about to come, to an end *I've been waiting for you for ages!* Clearly the waiting is over in this example.
- Present Perfect Continuous v. Present Perfect Simple:

  a) Sometimes the difference is very subtle and is influenced by whether the speaker feels the situation is permanent or temporary, complete or incomplete: *I've been staying with Metin for four weeks* (a temporary situation). *My aunt's lived in London all her life* (a permanent situation). *I've been reading New York Stories* (I haven't finished it). *I've read that* (I've finished it).

  b) A clearer difference can be seen when we compare duration v. quantity. *She's been reading for hours* (duration). *She's read 100 pages* (quantity).

  c) When a **verb** is used to mean a **state** it is less likely to take the continuous form. We can't say **I've been having this cold for a week. *I've been knowing Lynne since 1994.* It might be helpful to ask SS not to use the following verbs

in the continuous form. Don't say they can **never** take it just say it's safer not to use the continuous. Write on the board:
Don't use -ing with:
like, hate, love, prefer, want, think, feel, understand, need

- Pronunciation : contracted forms and weak forms need to be highlighted.
  Betty's been driving since ...
    (has) /bɪn/
  How long have you been living ...?
    /g(h)əv/   /bɪn/

Students' Book (page 104)

Exercise 1a) Use the picture to elicit the situation to lead in to the dialogue: He's a writer. It's his birthday. He's working. SS could practise saying the dialogue when you have highlighted the general meaning of *unfinished*. Point out that we can't use a present form to talk about past to present duration. Compare *I'm living here for two months* which has a future not a past reference, and *I've been living here for two months* which has a past to present reference.

🔑 1 At Christmas.   2 Yes, he is.

Exercise 1b) Again elicit relevant information from the pictures before asking SS to form sentences using the Present Perfect Continuous.

🔑 1 Jon's been working on a novel since Christmas.
2 She's been playing computer games all morning.
3 I've been learning Spanish since February.

Exercise 2 This exercise begins the long task of highlighting the differences between the Past Simple, Present Perfect Simple and Present Perfect Continuous. Use the concept questions more than once. Write the answers on the board and use colour, large writing, boxes, anything to highlight differences in meaning:
He's written two short stories since then.
(Both finished.)
  I've been working on it for the last week.
(He began a week ago and it isn't finished.)

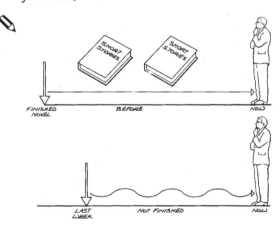

(See also *Language reference*, SB page 107.)

You could introduce the idea of verbs that can't always take the continuous form. However, rather than going into whether the use of a verb is stative or dynamic (see L) give SS the suggested list and say it's better not to use the continuous with these verbs.

1 Two short stories. 2 Yes, they are. 3 Last week. 4 Yes, he is. 5 The Present Perfect Continuous.

Exercise 3a) Be prepared to keep going back and using the concept questions to check that SS understand the use and meaning of the correct form. In 3 the verb *know* is highlighted. When checking ask them why the continuous isn't good here. Point back to the list of verbs which can't usually take -*ing*.

1 Have you read   2 have you been cleaning/Haven't you finished   3 have you known   4 has been living   5 has liked   6 have you been waiting   7 I've played   8 's been raining

Exercise 4
has /z/ or /həz/;   have /əv/;   been /bɪn/

For* and *since

For and *since* can be used with both the simple and continuous form of the Present Perfect. *For* refers to how long a situation has been happening. *Since* refers to the point when the situation began.

Students' Book (page 105)

Exercise a) Ask a S *How long have you been learning English?* Use the S's name and add the information to these sentences on the board:
X's been studying English since Y.
X's been studying English for Z.

Then ask *Which tells me when X began? Which one tells me about the number of days/months/years?* Then ask SS to look at the SB.

for: six weeks, a year, a few days, three minutes
since: March, yesterday, we met, my birthday, 14 June, the end of the lesson, 6.45

Exercise b)
1 He's been watching television for three hours.
2 She hasn't seen him for a long time.
3 He's been talking on the phone since lunch time.
4 They've been playing football since three o'clock.
5 We've been married for ten years.

Using your grammar

Demonstrate the activity. Write information on the board about yourself, following the cues in the SB. Then invite SS to ask you questions beginning with *How long have... ?/ How long have you been ...?* Watch out for the common mistake *How long have you been having that skirt?*

Extra material and ideas

1 WB pages 62 and 63, Grammar, Exercises 1-4.
2 Have you met my friend? In pairs the SS create a new identity for themselves and give this information to their partners. They can be any nationality (though they'll probably stay loyal), have any name, live anywhere, have any job, be married to anyone they want etc. They should add details such as when they got married/when they began their job/when they began living where they live. The SS should write their new names on a label and wear it so others can read it. You could have a straight mingle activity or try to create more of a party atmosphere by taking in music etc. SS walk around with their partners and introduce them to the other pairs of SS.

A: *Hello X and Y. Have you met my friend Z. She's an architect and she's married to Keanu Reeves.*

X and Y then try to find out more information. *Oh, how long have you been married? Where do you live? How long have you been living there?* etc. You could conduct feedback as someone who didn't go to the party. You want to find out who was there and any gossip SS can tell you.

VOCABULARY
Having a party

• Exercise 3 focuses on:
a visitor someone visiting a person or place v. *a guest* someone who's staying at your house or is at your party because you invited them.
a cooker equipment to cook food v. *a cook* a person who cooks.
strangers people we don't know v. *foreign* (adj) from another country.
a tour to go round a place or country v. *a trip* to go to a place.
learn is what SS do v. *teach* is what teachers do.
lend you give something to another person but you want it back v. *borrow* you get something from another person but you return it later.
passed past form of verb, *I passed my exam* v. *past* a noun, adjective, preposition or adverb *It's about the past. I've known about it for the past week or so. He walked past the door. The girl ran past.*

Students' Book (page 106)
Exercise 1 Get SS to practise the dialogues.
1 enjoying yourself   2 celebrating   3 soft

Exercise 2
1 boring 2 live 3 drunk

Exercise 3
(See L.) 1 visitors   2 cook   3 foreign students
4 tour   5 teach 6 lent   7 passed

Using your vocabulary

Exercise 1 As a lead in with a multilingual class you could begin by asking SS why people have parties in their countries. In a monolingual class ask SS to talk about the very best party they have ever been to, explaining why it was so good. Do some feedback at the end of the discussion and encourage SS to say why they have a particular opinion.

Exercise 2 It goes without saying that it would be lovely if this could be a plan for a real event.

Extra material and ideas

WB page 63, Vocabulary Exercise 5 focuses on words that are often confused, Exercise 6 on word families.

Extra material and ideas

GW x 3. SS could make a short news programme based on the headlines. Ask each group to choose 3 headlines and for each write 1-3 sentences about the story. E.g., *Last night Kennedy Airport was closed because of bad weather. No planes could leave. Passengers had to wait for 6 hours.* Each S should then practise saying one of the stories. Then the group presents their programme to the class. The first S in each group should begin: *Good evening. This is the evening news.* The third S should end: *That is the end of the news. Thank you. Good night.* If possible record the SS on audio or video cassette and let them hear themselves.

USE AND REVIEW

 Revision of the Present and Past Simple Passive form.

 Students' Book (page 107)

Exercise 1 It might be worth beginning by asking SS to make a list of regular verbs. Sometimes we are so concerned with irregular verbs that we forget SS need to recognise which verbs are regular.

 Student A's list: written, seen, been, bought, shut, taught, read, done, caught, eaten
Student B's list: heard, sold, worn, broken, understood, put, thought, said, spoken

Exercise 2
1 The tickets are sold out.
2 It was broken by a child.
3 It was drunk last week.
4 He was taken to hospital yesterday evening.
5 He was assassinated in 1994 by someone from another country.

Exercise 3 You could ask SS to turn the headlines into complete sentences. Three will be passive sentences and three will be active.
A film star's had a new baby.
An ice-skater broke her/his leg.
A train crashed in Sweden.
A missing sculpture was found.
More CDs were sold last year.
An airport was closed because of bad weather.

Good news: More CDs sold last year; Films star's new baby; Missing sculpture found
Bad news: Airport closed by bad weather; Ice-skater breaks leg; Train crash in Sweden

Love your neighbour

Students' Book

General theme: manners.
Unit topic: politeness.

USE YOUR ENGLISH: being polite.
SKILLS: listening and speaking (noisy neighbours); vocabulary (phrasal verbs); writing (phrasal verbs).
GRAMMAR: sentence patterns 1(verb + person+ *to* + base form); sentence patterns 2 (reported sentences); *say* and *tell*.
VOCABULARY: doing things in the house; *do* or *make?*
USE AND REVIEW: easily confused words; job application.

Workbook

GRAMMAR: sentence patterns 1 and 2.
VOCABULARY: phrasal verbs; *Do* or *make?*
SKILLS: reading (a strange story); writing stories.
DICTATION/PRONUNCIATION: sentence completion; sound and spelling: *u*.

USE YOUR ENGLISH
Being polite

- Polite requests using the correct register/style.
- Agreeing or not agreeing to a request.

- Which form we choose depends on how well we know the person, and how big, difficult or inconvenient we think the request is. Even if the person is a close friend, we could move into a more formal tone if we feel tentative about the request. Often the more tentative we feel, the more words we use. Although in this area it's difficult to draw clear lines between formal and informal a guide for SS might be:

Less formal *Can you... / Could you...?* More formal/tentative *I'm sorry to trouble you but do you think you could ...? Would you mind... -ing...?*

Point out the effect of using *please*. It would be acceptable for SS to use shorter, less formal structures in more formal situations as long as they use *please*.

- Pronunciation. Help SS to identify the main stress in each request to discourage them from stressing too many syllables. All the structures will sound polite if SS use a fall rise pitch movement on the main stress:

Can you_open the window, please?
/wəʊpən/

Could_you_open_the window, please?
/djʊwəʊpən/

I'm sorry to trouble you but do_you think you could_open the window, please?
/djʊ/
/dəʊpən/

Do_you think you could_open the window, please?
/djʊ/ /dəʊpən/

Would_you mind_opening the window, please?
/djʊ/

Show SS where simple consonant vowel links occur. This can really make a difference to their sense of rhythm as well as helping them to recognise sounds in natural speech.

 Students' Book (page 108)

Exercise 1a) Use the pictures to elicit the situations and some of the key areas such as the relationship between speakers and how big the request is. Ask SS what they think the people are saying. This will give you some idea of how much they know.

Exercise b)

[18.1]
1 A: Are you all right?
  B: Oh, *could you* give me a hand with these, please?
  A: Sure. Where do you want them?
  B: I'm trying to get them to my car.
  A: OK.
2 A: I'm going into town. Shall I post those for you?
  B: No thanks, I'm not quite ready yet. Oh *but can you* get me some stamps, please?
  A: Sure.
3 A: Damn! I need two fifty ps. *I'm sorry to trouble you* but have you got any change?
  B: I don't know. Let me have a look. Sorry. No. I've only got a five pound note.
4 A: Tom. Excuse me. *Could you* give me a push?
  B: Sorry?
  A: I said do you think you could give me a push?
  B: OK.
5 HUSBAND: Hello. Oh, little Oscar.
  NEIGHBOUR: Hello.
  WIFE: I hear you're going away.
  N: Yes, I am. *Would you mind* looking after Oscar for a few days?
  W: Ah! I'm afraid we're going away too. Sorry.

 1c) 2e) 3d) 4a) 5b)

Exercise 1c) Play the cassette again stopping at the appropriate place to allow SS time to complete the sentences. Ask SS to dictate the examples to you and write them on the board. Focus on the form and pronunciation (see L).
See tapescript above.

Exercise 1d) Focus on appropriacy.

Highlight the fact that by using *please* and appropriate intonation SS could use less formal exponents even in formal situations. If your SS were familiar with most of the examples, you could extend to other expressions. *Will you ..., please?* (less formal) *I was wondering if you could...?* (more formal) *Could you possibly ...?* (more formal)

1 I'm sorry to trouble you.
2 Excuse me. Would you mind ...-ing?

Exercise 1e) You could extend into other possible replies *Certainly / Of course / No problem. I'd like to but ... I'm afraid I can't because ...* To be polite, we usually give a reason why we can't comply with the request, even if it isn't exactly true !

1 Sure. OK.
2 Sorry

Exercise 2 Keep this light-hearted. It offers SS opportunity the practise the forms they want to, so don't treat it like a drill.

(These are suggested answers but accept appropriate alternatives.) Would you mind closing the window, please? Could you lend me £5, please? Can you lend me a pencil, please? I'm sorry to trouble you but could you clean the board for me, please? etc.

Exercise 3 This written activity offers a change of pace and focus. The exercise could be done as a speaking activity though SS will need time to think it through. You could help them to decide on the appropriate form by establishing what the relationship is in each situation or how difficult the request is.

Suggested answers:
1 Would you mind driving me to Edinburgh?
2 Excuse me. I ordered a salad but you brought me a steak. Could you change it?
3 Could you help me get into my flat, please?
4 Would you mind taking a photograph of me?
5 Could you wake me at five?

Extra material and ideas

P **An action chain** page 147, 18.1. You and the SS stand in a circle. Tell them they are going to make requests and agree to do them. Photocopy the picture cues and cut them up. Take the first picture cue, turn to the S on your right and make an appropriate request. The S agrees to do it and takes the picture. Then that S turns to the S on his/her right and makes a request which the next S agrees to do and takes the card etc. Meanwhile you have fed in more cards at various points in the circle so that S aren't left waiting too long. Then return to your original place in the circle and keep feeding in more pictures.

Repeat the activity but instruct SS not to agree and give an excuse. In the first round SS have to think about the request and agreeing doesn't cause much of a problem. They can just say *Sure* or *OK*. In the second round the requests have been established so they can now concentrate on the refusal and excuse.

SKILLS

• Listening and speaking: prediction; listening for detail; reacting to a text by stating opinions.
• Vocabulary: phrasal verbs from the texts.
• Writing: stylistics, raising awareness of formal v. informal vocabulary; writing a note.

Listening and speaking

L • Both recordings are quite short and include mainly familiar vocabulary. However, they're monologues so SS will probably experience some difficulty in understanding because they are being asked to process the language and information at a speed they can't control, unlike reading a text. Consequently, based on your knowledge of your SS, you should give as much support as is necessary. Suggestions are given in Exercise 1 below.

• Potentially difficult words: Recording A - *loud, to lie 'down, to be 'off 'work, a 'limit;* Recording B - *loud, com'plain, 'bothered, 'shouting, drums, 'cellar.*

Students' Book (page 109)

Exercise 1a) The situation is noisy neighbours. Use the picture to elicit information to help SS to predict content. Be careful not to elicit information which corresponds to the text exactly as this removes the need to listen in Exercise 2. Elicit alternative possibilities so SS listen for which one, if any, is correct. This way you have established a need to listen. You could join in by completing the sentences.

Exercise 2 Offer SS as much support as they need (see *Introduction* page 11). If you haven't got access to two cassette recorders, do the exercise as a whole class activity.

 [18.2]
Group A
HENRY: The music's so loud - thump, thump, thump, nearly every night. It gives me headaches and I have to lie down. I've been off work because of the noise. You can't imagine having a headache and hearing that noise. Sometimes I get really angry. The other night I went into the garden and shouted 'Shut up'. I phoned the police but they said they couldn't do anything. A lot of young people come and go. Sometimes they come into my garden and move my pot plants. Or knock on my front door. I don't mind if they have a good time but there has to be a limit. If they're going to have a party, at least they could tell me and I'd go out. It used to be very quiet round here.

[18.3]
Group B
TIM: It's sad that we are annoying this man next door. We had no idea. Sure we like music in the day and we sometimes have loud parties. But we've never had any trouble. If anyone wants to complain they can always come round. We're not going to get into a fight. I play loud music to wake myself up. About ten in the morning that's when it's the loudest. Yes, another person here plays very loud music but not all the time. Me I play music quietly when I'm up. I haven't had a party for six months. I'm surprised Mr Skitt is

bothered. Perhaps he doesn't like the kind of music. Heavy metal or rap. I hear Mr Skitt's TV all the time and I hear him shouting at his cats but that's what you get if you live close to people. We obviously have a different way of life. I play the drums but I try not to be too loud. That's why I play them in the cellar.

Group A
1 He doesn't like it.
2 Nothing. They couldn't do anything.
3 He's had a lot of headaches.
4 They move his plant pots.
5 He'd go out.

Group B
1 Tim didn't know he was annoying Henry.
2 In the morning(s) to wake himself up.
3 Six months ago.
4 He hears the TV and him shouting at his cats.
5 So they aren't too loud.

Exercise 4 SS give personal opinions and exchange information about similar problems. You may have SS who don't have neighbours but this shouldn't exclude them from the activity. Try to involve as many SS as possible in the feedback but be sensitive to when they have had enough of the subject.

Extra material and ideas

1 Page 148, 18.2. Read the following text about noise and neighbours to the class.
Neighbours, Noise and Death
In the last six years seventeen people have died because of problems caused by noisy neighbours. Some of these were murders and some were suicides. In the UK there are now more than 88,000 complaints a year. If you're found guilty of making too much noise and you don't stop, you can be fined up to £5,000. However, only about 3% of the complaints end with the people being taken to court.
Then give each S a photocopy of a different incident to read for homework. Next lesson, write the names of the victims on the board and the questions *Who was ... and what happened to her/him?* Invite SS to ask about the people they didn't read about for homework. A good opportunity for you to monitor SS' use of language and do error correction.
2 Blank out parts of the text in 1 and use as a dictation.
3 Give each S one complete and one incomplete case history. In pairs they have to ask and answer questions to complete the case histories.

Vocabulary: phrasal verbs

The context related meanings of these phrasal verbs are quite easy to illustrate/explain: *lie down:* demonstrate/draw the meaning; *to be off:* not to go to work, usually because you're ill; *to come round:* to visit someone at their home; *to get into a fight:* began to fight someone; *to wake up:* mime – but this is probably familiar anyway.

Students' Book (page 110)
Write the phrasal verbs on the board and ask SS to find them in the *Tapescripts* on SB page 143.

Check meaning (see L) before doing the gap exercise.

1 come round 2 lie down, wake me up 3 get into
4 be off

Writing: phrasal verbs

Students' Book (page 110)
We tend to use more phrasal verbs in informal letters, notes, cards etc. than we do in formal writing. However, this doesn't mean we never use phrasal verbs in formal writing. It's just less common.

1 turn off, turn up   2 give up, broke down
3 take out, stay up

Extra material and ideas

WB page 66, Exercise 4.

GRAMMAR

- Sentence patterns: verb + person.
- The beginnings of reported speech, some examples of simple back shifting and the use of *say* and *tell*.

Sentence patterns (1): verb + person

- SS already know *tell* and so the main focus is on the form not the meaning of the infinitive structure which follows *ask/tell someone to do/not to do something.*

Students' Book (page 110)
Exercise 1 Ask if SS know the author Roald Dahl. Explain he is a very popular writer with children because he often makes parents and other adults the bad people in his stories while the children are the heroes! Read the story and then ask comprehension questions to reinforce the pattern *What does George's mother want him to do? What does she not want him to do?* On the board write
(told George) be a good boy
(asked George) don't forget to give Grandma her medicine
  Ask SS to use the words in the brackets to complete the sentences and highlight the use of the base form in the sentence pattern with colour or boxes. Then elicit the rule and write it up.
ASK/TELL SOMEONE + TO DO SOMETHING
ASK/TELL SOMEONE + NOT TO DO SOMETHING

Exercise 2 Read the continuation of the story. The exercise is a simple reinforcement of the above.

1 Grandma told/asked George not to forget her medicine.
2 Grandma told/asked George to behave well.

Exercise 3 Read the next section of the story and ask comprehension questions to show the humour of the passage and how Roald Dahl makes the grandmother into a fussy person who demands a lot and who is very strict. This is not the usual image of a grandmother in children's stories. *What kind of person is Grandmother? How do you know that? Does George like her?* The exercise is more demanding as SS have to piece sentences together from cues.

1 She told/asked George to put in one spoon of sugar.
2 She told/asked George not to put any milk in.
3 She told/asked George to put more sugar in.

Sentence patterns (2): reported sentences

Say or *tell?*

• The main focus is on the different uses of *tell* v. *say*, but this section includes simple reported sentences where the main verb back shifts. Highlight that *tell* has to be followed by a person whereas *say* is usually not. The back shifting is restricted to present tense → past tense. The use of *that* is optional:
He told me (that) he was ill.
He said (that) he was ill.

• The most significant pronunciation feature with this area of grammar is the use of weak forms for pronouns.
He told me... . She said she... .
/hi/   /mi/   /ʃi/   /ʃi/
SS needn't produce these forms but they will need to recognise them when they hear them. If *that* is used, then it too is pronounced as a weak form /ðət/.

Exercise a) Write SAID TOLD on the board. Then write: *George _____ he was only a boy. George _____ his Grandma he was only a boy.*

Ask SS which verb goes in which sentence. Write whatever the majority says. Then ask them to look in the SB to check. If it's correct, ask why. If it's incorrect, correct it and ask why it was wrong. Don't highlight the back shifting at this point. The exercise only asks them to fill a gap with *said* or *told.*

1 told   2 said   3 told   4 said   5 told

Exercise b) Point out the back shift effect of reported speech used in the exercise. However, remember this isn't the main issue here and don't labour the point. Indeed, the present tense can be used with the reporting verbs in the present *They say they want to* .... So avoid overcorrecting and remember the focus is on the sentence pattern caused by the use of *say* or *tell.*

1 Sally and Peter said they wanted to see the film.
2 Tony said he was watching television later.
3 Emma told her they liked Disneyland.

4 Mary said she was very happy.
5 Tina told Sonia that Greg was hungry.

Using your grammar

Two SS are members of a family, the third is a go-between. If your class isn't a multiple of 3, you could have two go-betweens so that all the SS are involved at the same time. However, if you think the SS playing the family members need more time to think of their responses, then groups of three are better. You could set the roles so the same family members are involved. This allows the option of letting all the same family members think of problems together initially and gives you time to talk to the go-betweens so they understand that their objective is to bring peace to the situation. The activity will work better if the family members are in different parts of the room. Don't worry if back shifting isn't being used, but monitor the sentence patterns and remind SS if necessary. Try to find some humorous examples of problems for feedback. Ask the go-betweens if they were successful in getting peace.

Extra material and ideas

1 WB page 65 and 66, Grammar, Exercises 1, 2 and 3.

2 Think of some advice about love and life that you have been given and tell the SS, e.g., 'My mother told me to enjoy life as much as possible. She always says, "You're a long time dead!"' Ask SS if they can think of any good advice they may have received from family or friends about love or life. If your SS are imaginative, you could ask them to think of two pieces of advice for love and life.

3 Agony Aunt situation page 148, 18.3. Divide the class into Agony Aunts/Uncles and people with problems. Give one of the photocopied problems to each of the people with problems who then try to see as many Agony Aunts/Uncles as possible. They should make a note of the advice each one gives them. The Agony Aunts/ Uncles should note the problem and the advice they give to each SS. The objective is to find the best Agony Aunt/Uncle. The feedback should be full of *I think X is the best/worst because he/she told me to .... He said I should ...*

VOCABULARY

• Collocation of *make* and *do.*
• Vocabulary of housework: verbs and verbal nouns.

Doing things in the house

• Pronunciation. Highlight the silent *r* in *iron* /'aɪən/; that in the phrasal verbs *wash up* and *tidy up* the particle takes more stress than the verb; the pronunciation of *dust* /dʌst/.

Students' Book (page 112)

Exercise a) You could mime the actions first and elicit/supply the vocabulary. Then SS use the matching exercise to check/consolidate.

a) iron b) dust c) wash up d) hoover e) tidy up
f) decorate

Exercise b) Focus on + -*ing* to form a noun from the verb.

b) She's dusting.
c) He's washing up.
d) She's hoovering.
e) She's tidying up.
f) He's decorating.

Exercise c) Other jobs in the house: '*washing,* '*polishing,* '*painting,* '*cleaning* '*windows.*

Do or make?

• Collocation of *make* and *do*: all the verbal nouns here take *do*. *Do* also collocates with *do the washing/dusting/ironing/cleaning/housework, right, one's best. Make* collocates with *a mistake, a cup of, a mess, the bed, a noise.*

There are guidelines for when to use *make* and *do* in the SB. However, with many examples it's difficult to see how they fit in with the guidelines. Highlight the potential problem and encourage SS to keep lists of the collocations.

1 A: do   B: doing
2 A: made/made   B: made/do   A: do   B: do/make
3 A: make   B: do/'m doing

Using your vocabulary

Exercise a-c) You could discuss the concept of the 'new man'. Ask SS if they think things are changing in this area. You could also extend the discussion into what children/ young people are asked to do in the home.

Extra material and ideas

WB page 66, Vocabulary, Exercise 5.

USE AND REVIEW

• Vocabulary revision.
• Present Perfect Simple and Continuous.
• Use of *for* and *since* with the Present Perfect.

Students' Book (page 113)
Exercise 1
1 A stranger is someone we don't know. A foreigner is someone from another country.
2 Soft
3 A cook is the person who cooks. A cooker is the equipment we use to cook food.
4 Not recorded.

5 (These are suggested answers but accept appropriate alternatives.)
Please lend me some money. I'll pay you back tomorrow.
If you want to borrow some money, here's £10. Pay me back when you can.

Exercise 2 You could ensure greater accuracy by eliciting the possible questions and listing them on the board.

Extra material and ideas

You could set up the job interview by having three or four SS form interview panels for each job. While the applicants fill in the forms, the interview panels could work out questions they want to ask to get more information about each person. The interview panel have a few minutes to read the application forms. Then each panel interviews four applicants at the same time. To accommodate larger classes, you can set it up so that you have more than one panel interviewing for the same job. Ask the panels to choose the best applicant and say why. The other applicants are allowed to ask why they failed the interview.

Unit 19

Team spirit

Students' Book

General theme: sports.
Unit topic: sports fans.

USE YOUR ENGLISH: talking about different cultures.
SKILLS: reading and speaking (an unusual football fan); vocabulary (guessing meaning from context); writing (punctuation in direct speech).
GRAMMAR: verb patterns (1) (*if, when, as soon as, unless*); verb patterns (2) (verb and two objects - *give it to him, give him the present*).
VOCABULARY: sports.
USE AND REVIEW: *true or false; do or make?*

Workbook

GRAMMAR: *if or unless?*; verb patterns (1); verb patterns (2).
VOCABULARY: sport.
SKILLS: listening (a skiing accident); writing (punctuation).
DICTATION/PRONUNCIATION: rhythm and sentence stress.

USE YOUR ENGLISH
Talking about different cultures

L • A variety of functional exponents to give advice: Imperative *Always order at the bar;* Negative imperative *Don't forget to ...;* Present Simple *Usually you have drinks before...;* if + present + imperative *If you .... make sure you ...* None of these should present a problem as structures and vocabulary are familiar. However, SS may not be aware that these structures can be used to advise.

Students' Book (page 114)

Exercise 1a) The guessing will only work if SS have knowledge of British habits. If they don't, help them to predict content by asking them about their own customs. *Do you kiss people when you first meet them? What time do you arrive if someone invites you to dinner at 9 pm? If you stay in someone's flat or house, would you have to ask permission to have a shower? How do you call a waiter to come to your table?*

Exercise 1b)
[19.1]
1 ZOE: In a formal situation you should shake hands and say 'Nice to meet you' or 'How do you do.' We don't usually kiss people when we first meet them.
2 Always order at the bar. Take your drinks and sit down where you can find a seat. Here people sometimes share a table. To get food you usually order at the bar, too. There aren't usually any waiters although sometimes they will bring you your food.
3 Don't forget to ask before you have a bath or a shower. And try not to spend too long in the bathroom!
4 Never clap your hands or hit your glass with a knife. Say 'Excuse me!' or try to catch the waiter's eye.
5 People normally expect you to be a few minutes late. Never arrive early. Usually you have drinks before the meal. After you eat, you usually sit around chatting for a while. If you want to leave soon after the meal, make sure you say you've had a lovely evening and the food was delicious and then make an excuse.

1d) 2a) 3e) 4c) 5b)

Exercise 1c) You could get SS to underline the pieces of advice on the tapescript on page 143 and compare their answers with another S. If necessary, elicit the examples by asking *What does X say about calling a waiter?* etc.

Exercise 1d) If you teach a multilingual class, allow extra time. Point out that if we don't know these things, it is easy to upset someone from a different culture or even make them angry.

Exercise 2 A whole class activity. Check understanding of '*dropping 'litter, 'crossing the 'road.*

Exercise 3 PW in a monolingual class. SS could be asked to say what they think about their country's customs, are customs changing, do they do these things etc. GW in a multilingual class, different nationalities working together. Encourage SS to ask each other questions. You may need to elicit examples. (*In your country do people give tips, kiss when they meet* etc?) Ask SS if they learned anything that surprised them.

Exercise 4 This could be a speaking or writing activity but a change of skills focus can be valuable. Let SS show their lists to each other. Tell them they can use structures other than the imperative.

Extra material and ideas

1 For Exercise 4 you could ask SS to write DOs and DON'Ts inside an outline of their country. Prepare one for Britain as an example.

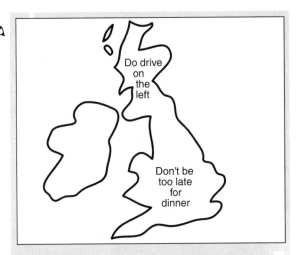

Do drive on the left

Don't be too late for dinner

2 SS look back over the SB and find as many examples of British culture as they can and write a tourist's guide to Britain.

SKILLS

• Reading: prechecking vocabulary to facilitate comprehension and enable SS to predict content; reading for gist and more detailed information; forming questions about the text.
• Vocabulary: guessing meaning from context.
• Writing: punctuation.

Reading

• There is quite a lot of difficult vocabulary in this text. Don't preteach *crowds*, *'punches*, *'covers*, *'passion*, *pale* as they form the basis of the vocabulary exercise. You could preteach the following if your SS have problems tolerating unfamiliar vocabulary: *cheat*, *well-'known*, *a 'studio*, *at'tending 'Mass*.
• *Beat* and *win* are often used incorrectly by SS. We can't say *Liverpool won Chelsea*. We have to say either *Liverpool won* or *Liverpool beat Chelsea*. However, we can say *Liverpool won the match*.

Students' Book (page 115)

Exercise 1 GW x4. Hand out copies of pictures of various sports from magazines etc. Ask SS to name the sports. Meanwhile write this on the board
What kind of person does these sports?
Women/men/the rich/everybody/children/young people/any age
Then elicit the names of the sports and list them on the board. In a multilingual class ask *Could you do all of these sports in your country?*
Name one of the sports on the board and ask SS to think about the question and discuss what kind of person would do this in their country. Get feedback and then choose another and let

them discuss it briefly, get feedback then choose another. This way you can pace the activity to good effect. Then ask SS to focus on the picture in the book and elicit/supply the vocabulary. Remember they should see the written form so they can recognise it when they read it. Ask SS *What do you think the passage is going to be about?*

1 Two: Manchester United and Chelsea.
2 The place where the game/match is played and people sit or stand to watch.
3 The person in black who makes sure the players follow the rules.
4 The people who are watching the match.
5 Maybe the man in red on the left who is waving with his right hand.
6 It's a home match for Manchester United, an away match for Chelsea.
7 Manchester United won.
8 No, they didn't. Manchester beat Chelsea.

Exercise 2 Preteach more vocabulary if you think your SS need it (see L). Check *nun - a woman who has a simple religious life*. Read the gist questions out while SS follow in their book. Then encourage them to read the text quickly to find the answers. Reassure them they will read it again later. Ask them what they thought of the text. Was it funny or strange?

2 C 3 D 4 E

Exercise 3 These are more detailed questions. Allow SS to refer to the text. They could compare answers with a partner.

1 Lazio are playing AC Milan.
2 Because he didn't allow Lazio's goal.
3 When Lazio score a goal and she is happy.
4 For twenty years.
5 She talks about their problems and says prayers with them.

Exercise 4 This also checks SS' comprehension. If they haven't understood the reference they are unlikely to form the right question.

1 When did Sister Paola become a Lazio supporter?
2 Did Lazio beat AC Milan?
3 What does Sister Paola do during the week?

Extra material and ideas

1 Ask SS which sports are: dangerous, fast; which sports are best in cold/ hot countries; which sports they like/don't like; who are their favourite teams/sports personalities.
2 As an alternative to Exercises 3 and 4, divide the class into two groups. SS in Group 1 read paragraphs A and B and then write questions for Group 2. SS in Group 2 read paragraphs C, D, E and F and write questions for Group 1. They can work out the questions together in their groups but every SS should write them down so they can exchange papers with a person from the opposite group.

Vocabulary

Students' Book (page 116)

SS should now be familiar with this kind of

vocabulary skill development exercise to guess meaning from context.

1 crowds 2 punches 3 covers 4 passion 5 pale

Writing

L Punctuation : speech marks and commas are used when writing direct quotes but not in reported speech. Speech marks (' ') reading open and   close direct speech. Any relevant punctuation, e.g. commas and questions marks, usually come before the closing speech marks.

Exercise 1 The questions guide SS to the rules of punctuation related to direct speech.

1 The referee is a cheat.
2 ' and '
3 Before the closing speech marks.

Exercise 2 These are all examples of direct speech. Highlight that item two is a question and that SS need to think about contracted forms when they rewrite the sentences.

1 'I'm going out,' she said.
2 'What are you thinking?' he asked her.
3 'I won't do it,' I told him.

Exercise 3 SS have to discriminate between direct and reported speech and punctuate accordingly.

She told me about her husband. 'He's a Chelsea supporter.' 'Really?' I said. 'How could you live with him?' She saw the look on my face. 'Why don't you tell him to support Manchester United or you'll divorce him?' She laughed. 'You're crazy, you know. Really crazy,' she said.

> **Extra material and ideas**
>
> WB page 72, Writing, Exercise 7.

GRAMMAR

A Two common verb patterns:

• *If, when, unless, as soon as* followed by a present tense but referring to a future time.
• Verb + two objects: *I gave the pen to Angela. I gave Angela the pen.*

Verb patterns (1): the future

If, when, as soon as, unless

L • SS are familiar with *if* clauses (Units 9 and 12) so the idea of a present tense having a future reference is not new. *If* clauses suggest the speaker is unsure of the result. *When* signals a certainty. *As soon as* is similar in meaning to *when* but the idea of immediacy is added. *Unless* is potentially more difficult for SS even when the concept is limited to meaning *if not. I'll walk if it doesn't rain. I'll walk unless it rains.* Highlight that in these cases the idea is the same. Both sentences mean that the walk will only happen if it isn't stopped by the rain. We can't use

unless in sentences like *I'll be pleased if he doesn't come* because the meaning would change.
• Highlight the weak forms and linkage that occurs in *as soon as* /əzsuːnəz/.

Students' Book (page 116)

Exercise 1a) Highlight the focus by writing the following on the board and telling SS to look at what happens to the verb after these words.

Talking about future time using:

If + ?   As soon as + ?
When + ?   Unless + ?

Then get SS to look at the pictures in the SB and ask what they think the parents are like. (*They're worriers.*) Gap fill from the cassette to establish the use of the present tense. You could ask SS to predict the gaps before you play the cassette.

[19.1]

FATHER: What are you going to do when you *get there*?
TIM: I'll go straight to the hotel. I'll probably be very tired.
MOTHER: How will we know that you're all right?
TIM: Oh, Mum. Don't worry. I'll call you as soon as I *can*.
FATHER: Then make sure you phone your uncle. Have you got your traveller's cheques?
TIM: Yes, Dad.
MOTHER: What will you do if he's not there when you *phone*? He won't know you're at the hotel.
TIM: I'll try again later. It'll be OK.
FATHER: He won't come and pick you up unless you *phone*.
TIM: I know. Please don't worry.
MOTHER: Have you got everything? Have you packed your woollen socks and your big jumper?
TIM: Yes.
MOTHER: And your uncle's present. Don't forget. Give it to him as soon as you see him.
TIM: Yes.

Exercise 1b) When you have checked the answers rub out the ?s on the board and write: **the present form of the verb**. Remind them that the time reference is FUTURE.

Exercise 1c) Put a box round *If* and *When* on the board and try to elicit the different meanings. Ask SS to look at the sentences in the SB and answer the questions.

1 When you see him, give him our love.
2 If you see him, give him our love.

Exercise 1d) Check comprehension of the difference between *if* and *when*.

1 If 2 When

Exercise 1e) Draw a box round *Unless* on the board and introduce the concept (see L). It sometimes reinforces the concept if you ask SS to rewrite the *unless* sentences using *if + not*. Keep the explanation as simple as possible. If necessary give more examples and ask SS to transform them into sentences using *if*.
She won't come unless I ask her.
Unless I see him this morning, will you give this to Pete?

Unless you study more, you won't pass the exam.
Unless he apologises, I won't speak to him ever
again.

1 If   2 Unless

Exercise 2 Draw a box around **As soon as**
and tell SS the meaning is similar to *when* but
the idea is immediate. *As soon as I see him =*
immediately I see him.

1 get up   2 study   3 don't tell   4 opens   5 'll be   6 'll invite
7 miss   8 'll go

Before you close this section ask SS to complete
each of the examples on the board using
she/come/I/go
If *she comes, I'll go.*
When *she comes, I'll go.*
As soon as *she comes I'll go.*
Unless *she comes soon I'll go.* (Add *soon* to
this example to make it sound natural.) Ask SS
to tell you in their own words what they mean.
Then highlight again the form and time
reference. Allow SS time to copy this from the
board and encourage them to use their own
words to explain the meaning and grammar as
they write it in their personal grammar.

If your SS have had difficulty with the Verb
patterns (1) leave Verb patterns (2) until another
lesson and move on to the USING YOUR GRAMMAR
which is an activity designed to reinforce Verb
patterns (1).

Verb patterns (2)

Verb + 2 objects

L • Conceptually this shouldn't present any
problem for this level. However, SS may still be
uncertain about the pattern difference created by
the positioning of the direct and indirect object.

Students' Book (page 117)

Exercise 1 Give 7 SS a word card with one of
the following words on it. Hand them out in a
jumbled order: **I gave the book to your sister.**

Ask the SS to come to the front of the class and
face the other SS, holding their cards so the
others can see them. The SS who are not
holding the cards direct the others so they stand
in the right order to form the sentence. The SS
with the cards then stick or write their words up
in the correct order on the board.

Do the same with: **I gave your sister the book.**
I gave it to your sister.

If necessary correct any mistakes of word order.
Then ask SS to look at the word *to*. Try to elicit
a rule but don't say whether it's right or not. Tell
the SS to read the grammar box on page 117
and check if their rule is correct. Again give
visual reinforcement by adding colour and /or
boxes to highlight form.

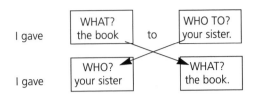

Then do Exercise 1 in the SB.

1 The camera.
2 His brother.
3 Give the <u>camera</u> to your brother.
Give <u>it</u> to your brother.
Give your brother <u>the camera</u>.
4 Give the camera to <u>your brother</u>.
Give it to <u>your brother</u>.
Give <u>your brother</u> the camera.
5 to

Exercise 2a)
read, show, pass, bring, send, lend, pay, sell, take

Exercise 2b)
1 Please give him the message./Please give the message to
him.
2 Please give it to her later.
3 Please take him the book./Please take the book to him.
4 Please read the children a story./Please read a story to
the children.
5 Please show me the way./ Please show the way to me.
6 Please lend me the money./Please lend the money to me.

Exercise 3 Use the pictures to elicit what each
person wants. Then ask SS to make sentences
using this information with the verb patterns
above. Ask some confident SS to work at the
board so you have an immediate reference point
for efficient checking.

1 Please pass me the sugar./Please pass the sugar to me.
2 Please bring me a magazine./Please bring a magazine to
me.
3 Please send my mother some flowers./Please send some
flowers to my mother.
4 Please show me the photographs./Please show the
photographs to me.

Using your grammar

Establish the context of secret agents. Refer to
any films that SS might know and elicit what the
agent's mission was. SS are asked to write the
instructions for the agent but this could also be a
speaking activity.

Extra material and ideas

1 WB pages 69 and 70, Grammar, Exercises 1, 2 and
3.
2 Get the SS to personalise examples using Verb
patterns (1). Ask them *What will happen to your life*
in the next few years? Get them to talk about things
like: money, school or work, relationships, jobs,
health, travel, homes. Write these words on the
board to help them.
1 I'll ———— as soon as I ————
2 When I ————, I ————
3 If I ————, I ————
4 Unless I ————, I ————

VOCABULARY

L • Regular verbs: *kick, bounce, punch*. Highlight that none of these are pronounced with an /ɪd/ ending in the Past Simple or Past Participle.
• Irregular verbs: *hit, run, throw*.
• Collocation with verbs *to go* and *to play*. *Go* is usually with activities we do alone (and take an *-ing* form) and *play* when there is an opponent or an opposing team involved.

Students' Book (page 118)

Exercise 1 Begin by eliciting the sport associated with the picture then match equipment and venue with pictures.

1 tennis racket/court/ball 2 golf club/course/ball
3 athletics shorts/track 4 swimming costume/pool
5 football ball/pitch 6 boxing gloves/ring

Exercise 2 Collocation of *go* v. *play a sport* (see L). If SS can't identify a pattern ask *Do you need other people to play tennis? Do you need other people to go jogging?*

go: jogging, windsurfing, skiing, ice-skating
play: basketball, squash, baseball, football

Exercise 3a) Highlight regular and irregular verbs. (see L).

1f) 2d) 3c) 4e) 5a) 6b)

Exercise 3b)

2 golf/tennis/squash 3 athletics 4 basketball/baseball
5 tennis/basketball/squash 6 boxing

Using your vocabulary

Exercise 1 Lead in by asking SS to write down any exercise or sport they did last week. You could join in here, too. Ask them to count and see who did the most that week. Then go to the SB.

Exercise 2 You could, alternatively, ask SS to find someone who is very different from themselves.

Extra material and ideas

1 WB page 70, Vocabulary, Exercise 4. Page 71, Listening, Exercise 5.
2 You could extend the vocabulary in terms of:

Sport/Exercise	Equipment	Place
riding	bridle, reins	riding school
ice hockey	puck, hockey stick	ice-rink
tennis	racket, ball	court
etc.		

3 You could conduct a class survey about sports, or try to interview SS in another class.
4 Ask SS where they would hear these:
Good shot! (a cricket/tennis match/ a game of golf)
A hole in one. (a game of golf)
They've scored again! (a football/rugby/hockey match)
What a great match! (a football/rugby/hockey match)
She's won! What a close race. (athletics/swimming race)

USE AND REVIEW

A • Reporting verbs in reported speech.
• Vocabulary: types of housework.
• Collocation of *do* v. *make*.

Students' Book (page 119)

Exercise 1 Highlight that SS should use the verbs *say* and *tell* when they feedback to the class. Remind them of the sentence patterns for each and tell them to use the back shift rule if they use *say* and *tell* in the Past Simple. If you have an odd number in the class, you could join in the activity of making True and False sentences about yourself.

Exercise 2
Upstairs
A man is ironing. A woman is making the bed. A man is washing/cleaning the bathroom floor.
Downstairs
A man is cleaning the windows. A woman is hoovering. A man is dusting. A woman is sewing. A woman is washing up. A man is cooking.

Going away

USE YOUR ENGLISH
Booking in

L
• Most of the vocabulary will be familiar but *re'ception, 'porter, to check 'in* may need checking.
• Functional exponents for making requests and offers should now be familiar *Could you/I ...? Would you like ...?*

Students' Book (page 120)

Exercise 1a) Use the pictures to elicit vocabulary. Remind SS of collocations, *catch/take a bus, give a tip.* Highlight the difference between *to give* and *to leave a tip. Leave a tip* if we don't give it directly into the hand of the person, e.g. in a restaurant where you might leave the money on the table for the waitress. Remind SS to use the Past Simple to sequence the events.

b) d) c) a)

Exercise 1b) Ask SS to guess what might be in the gaps before they listen. Let SS practise the dialogue to prepare them for the roleplay.

[20.1]
RECEPTIONIST: Good afternoon. Can I *help you*?
ANNA: Yes, I've *booked* a room for two nights.
R: *Could you tell me* your name?
A: Anna Escobar.
R: Single or *double*?
A: Single.

R: Do you want a room with a *bath* or a shower?
A: A shower, please.
R: Just *fill in* this form, please.
A: Certainly. How much *is it* a night?
R: Sixty eight pounds with breakfast. How *would you like to pay*?
A: With American Express. Is that OK?
R: Fine. How much *luggage have you got*?
A: Just these two suitcases.
R: *Your room number* is two twenty. Breakfast *is from* seven to nine thirty. *Would you like* an evening meal?
A: No, thanks. *Could I change* a traveller's cheque later?
R: Of course, here's your key. Enjoy your stay.

Exercise 2 The S taking the role of the hotel guest will need time to work out the questions he/she wants to ask the receptionist. Meanwhile the receptionist should spend time making sure he/she understands all the written information about the hotel and should think of questions they will need to ask the guest. Encourage SS to commit the information about the hotel to memory rather than just reading it. Check understanding of *resi'dential 'area/ 'family 'atmosphere/over'looking/en-'suite*. SS playing the same roles could work together during the preparation phase to share ideas. Tell SS that because they are at the end of the book your expectations are high to inspire them to aim for greater accuracy. Also remind them to use intonation and facial expression to sound and appear polite.

Extra material and ideas

P
1 Page 149, 20.1. A ranking exercise: what SS dislike about hotels. Give SS a copy of the list. They should choose 5 things and put them in order (1-5) (1 = the things they dislike the most.)

P
2 The hotel receptionist game page 149, 20.2. Guests have problems but they don't speak a language that the receptionists can understand. Divide the class into teams, maximum 6 per team. Give each team a photocopied set of situations cut up, face down on a desk. In turn, each S takes one of the cards and mimes the problem to the other SS who have to guess what the problem is.

SKILLS

A
• Reading and speaking: prediction and reading for detail; summarising a short passage and telling other SS about it.
• Listening: prediction and listening for detail.
• Writing: linking and sequencing words.

Reading and speaking

L
• The passages are fairly short humorous pieces.

Students' Book (page 121)

Exercise 1 SS should be able to guess the meaning of the unfamiliar words. Use the pictures in the SB to help SS to predict the content.

Exercise 2 When SS have read their text and answered the questions, let them check their answers with others who read the same text. They could then send one of the pair/group to check their answers with you and report back.

Group A
a) c)
b) 1 typhoons   2 it rained for two weeks
3 the first person to get her bags at the airport
4 the wrong bag/someone else's suitcase

Group B
a) a)
b) 1 the train to Boulogne   2 sleeper part
3 said he was too late   4 to Milan

Group C
a) b)
b) 1 comfortable   2 the plughole in the washbasin and the swimming pool   3 wouldn't go faster than 5 mph
4 wanted to leave

Exercise 3 Ask SS to regroup so that each group has at least one SS who has read texts A, B and C. They then summarise their texts for the other members of the group. When each SS has finished giving a summary, other SS should try to answer the questions about that text from the SB. If they can't answer a question, they should ask for further clarification from the S who gave the original summary. If the jigsaw activity is impractical, the retelling could be done with the whole class. However, make sure you either ask for volunteers or choose more confident SS to do the retelling for the whole class. It could be quite threatening for SS at this level.

Exercise 4 GW or whole class activity or if you feel SS need a change of skills focus, set this for homework. Ask SS to make notes and begin the following class by exchanging stories. Some SS may be excluded from this either because they haven't had a holiday as such or they have only experienced good ones!

Extra material and ideas

WB page 75, Exercise 7 Listening, is about a positive holiday experience. You could use this in class as a comparison. If you have set SB Exercise 4 for homework, then SS could write notes on either a good or a bad holiday experience.

Listening

L • SS will find this passage challenging because it is based on detailed results of a survey. The information seems demanding but SS are only asked to process numerical information and the subject matter related to these figures is written in the questionnaire which they will refer to

before and during the listening.

• It is essential they can recognise percentages when they hear them.

Students' Book (page 122)

Exercise 1 Ask SS to read the questionnaire and look for any vocabulary they don't understand. As SS to identify vocabulary problems and write them on the board so other SS can find them, too. When all the unknown items have been identified, clarify the meanings. This should build confidence. You're letting SS become familiar with the different items on the survey and removing potential barriers caused by unknown vocabulary.

Exercise 2a) Do a class survey as feedback. Elicit SS' predictions about the British response to the survey and write the numbers which refer to these predictions on the board for reference later. If SS think drinking a lot, which is number three on the list, is important, you write 3 on the board. SS are only asked to choose one from each list, the one they think most British people said they liked or disliked.

Exercise 2c)-d) [20.2]

ANOUNCER: According to the latest survey the British still like their holidays. These are the results. 90% enjoy the beauties of nature and the countryside and 89% like being away from home and the daily routine. The same number - 89% like spending more time with the family and friends. This was surprising. In fact, according to the survey, family holidays seem to be good for family relationships. These are the other figures about what the British like. 88% of the British people we asked like meeting new people and 87% like seeing life in different countries. A lot of people think the British don't like meeting new people but according to this survey this is not true. New kinds of food interested 79% of the people and 60% were mainly interested in lying on the beach and getting a suntan. Most people admit to putting on weight on holiday. Going to museums and art galleries interested only 58% and even fewer - a surprising 35% - just like drinking a lot. On the other hand what people most dislike about their holidays is the journey. In particular not having information about why they have been delayed - 76% - while 72% hate any kind of waiting at the airport. The same number - 72% - hate traffic jams. The journey is often the most difficult part of the holiday. These are the other figures about what the British dislike. 58% of people hate paying too much for something and 56% hate noisy or rude people. However, 46% of the people we asked complain about getting lost and arguing with each other and 37% say they hate fighting to get a place by the swimming pool. At the bottom of the list only 32% worry about not speaking the language - we think this would be different for other nationalities - and 27% hate packing. The survey suggests that the British like being with other people more than we think. Interestingly, more than a quarter arrive home as tired as or more tired than when they went.

c)

LIKE	British people said	d) %
1	7	58%
2	2	89%
3	8	35%
4	4	87%
5	1	90%
6	5	79%
7	3	88%
8	6	60%
9	2	89%

DISLIKE	British people said	%
1	4	56%
2	8	27%
3	6	37%
4	1	76%
5	2	72%
6	7	32%
7	2	72%
8	5	46%
9	3	58%

Extra material and ideas

It might be advisable to do a number dictation before beginning this section. Include quite a few percentages. You could get SS to dictate given numbers or numbers they think of to each other. This then checks production as well as understanding.

Writing: linking words

📖 Students' Book (page 122)

You could convey the drama of the story by reading it aloud to the SS, pausing where the gaps are. Ask them to check for unfamiliar vocabulary before they try the gap filling.

when, and, Then, because, after, Finally, but, so

REVISION UNITS 11-19

A
• Grammar from Units 11-19: the Second Conditional; comparatives and superlatives; question tags.
• Pronunciation: weak forms and contractions.
• Vocabulary: phrasal verbs.
• Fixed expressions covered in Units 11-19, USE YOUR ENGLISH.
• Correcting a piece of written work which reviews Units 11-19, WRITING.

Grammar

📖 Students' Book (page 123-125)

You could do this section as a test though, there are specific tests on pages 156 and 157, and it

might be more productive to get SS to work together on these exercises. If you choose to do them as a co-operative exercise, think about the grouping. You may want to put weaker SS together so that you can work with them and give them some undivided attention.

Exercise 1 Ask SS to read through the conversation first and check they have understood the context.

[20.3]
PAT: How long *have you been* a fan of Picasso?
BILL: A long time. But I *haven't seen* any of his paintings *since* the Paris exhibition in 1966. In those days I *used to find* it difficult to understand his work.
P: I *went* to an exhibition of his in New York, in 1973, the year he died. I *have been* waiting for an exhibition like this to come to London *for* years.
B: Me too.
P: Look at this sculpture of Jacqueline. It says in the programme that it *was made* by Picasso's assistants from a paper model.
B: Yes, it's *very* interesting. I like things *which* are a bit different.
P: I *told* Louise to come when she *has* the time. I want *her to see* some of these paintings.
B: Yes, Louise is *someone* who would like Picasso.

Exercise 2 could be a self-checking task. SS work in groups. When they have finished and agreed on the answers, one or two members of the group look at the answers which you have posted somewhere in the room. These SS return to the group and if there are any mistakes they say which numbers were wrong but they don't give the correct answers before the others have had a chance to correct the mistakes.

1 If I knew her address, I'd write to her.
2 If she worked, she would have some money.
3 If I went swimming, I'd be fit.
4 I'd invite you to the theatre if I had another ticket.
5 If it wasn't/weren't snowing, we could go out.

Exercise 3 could also be a self-checking task.

ADJECTIVE	COMPARATIVE	SUPERLATIVE
good	better	best
bad	worse	the worst
hard-working	more hard-working	the most hard-working
happy	happier	the happiest
comfortable	more comfortable	the most comfortable
big	bigger	the biggest

Exercise 4 When the answers have been checked against the cassette, get SS to focus on the pitch movements before and on the tag. Ask SS to practise saying them.

[20.4]
1 There's something wrong, *isn't there*?
2 He liks jazz, *doesn't he*?
3 She didn't try, *did she*?
4 It wasn't very nice, *was it*?
5 Tom's very attractive, *isn't he*?

Extra material and ideas

WB pages 73 and 74, Grammar, Exercises 1-3.

Pronunciation

[20.5]
1 He's *bigger and quicker than* you. (7)
2 If *I knew his* address, *I'd write to him.* (10)
3 *I used to be very* rich. (6)
4 He *was given a* watch *for his* birthday. (8)
5 How long *have you lived in* London? (7)
6 Give *it to him as soon as you see him.* (10)

Vocabulary

Exercise 1a) You could begin by asking SS to shout out as many phrasal verbs as they can think of. List them on the board. Point to one and ask SS to make a sentence using that verb. The sentence should illustrate the meaning in some way. Then move to the exercise in the SB.

1 fill in   2 split up   3 hang on   4 sold out   5 look after
6 take off   7 grow up   8 broken down   9 stayed up

Exercise 1b)
2 stay up   3 broke down   4 hang on   5 look after
6 grow up

Exercise 2 Check first whether any SS will be offended by the betting involved in the activity. Establish the rules for the exercise. SS could work alone, in pairs or small groups. Whatever you decide, to set this up you will need to devise a way of scoring. It's easier in groups because you're recording fewer bets. If SS are working individually, you could ask them to place their bets with another S so the monitoring is seen to be fair. Once you have identified all the incorrect sentences, offer bonus marks for correcting the sentences.

3x 4x 5✓ 6✓ 7x 8x 9✓ 10x 11x 12✓
1 Have you **done** your homework?
3 She **took/did** a degree at university.
4 He **beat** him at tennis.
7 I **enjoyed** the party.
8 Did you **go** jogging yesterday?
10 He's very **dishonest**.
11 She's a very good **cyclist**.

Extra material and ideas

1 WB pages 74 and 75, Vocabulary, Exercises 4-6.
2 You could review all the lexical areas in the book:
• **The vocabulary box** (see *Introduction* page 12).
• **A game of Outburst** (see TB Unit 10 page 70). It's better if you assign the lexical areas to the different teams.
• **Back to the board** Divide the class into two teams. Each team sends a representative to sit in front of the board facing the group. You then write a word on the board behind each representative. The team have to help their representative to guess the word on the board by taking it in turns to give a clue. You could give two related words (e.g. *scarf, gloves*) or completely unrelated words (e.g. *toaster, flu*). The objective is for each team to guide their S to guessing the word on the board first. Extra points could be awarded if the representative can also spell it correctly.

3 Give SS 6 - 8 items of unrelated vocabulary from any unit. In pairs they write a story including all the words. They pass the story to another pair who try to guess which the 6-8 words were. The objective is to include such a rich selection of vocabulary that the opposition won't be able to guess. Put a time limit on the story writing. Ten minutes is usually sufficient.

Use your English

Use the pictures to elicit the different situations and then use the first picture to elicit different possibilities so that SS realise there isn't only one: *I'm terribly sorry. I'm so sorry* etc. SS could write the dialogues and pass them around for other SS to check for mistakes. If you ask SS to act the dialogues out, go round and help them to identify main stresses and allow them time to practise.

(These are suggested answers but accept any appropriate alternatives.)
1 I'm terribly sorry.
2 Hello, how lovely to see you.
3 Congratulations! What a beautiful baby!
4 May/Could I change this money into sterling?
5 Excuse me. May/Could I have the bill, please?

Writing

Get a pair of SS to work at the board so you have an efficient means of checking. Ask the others if they agree with what's on the board, and correct where necessary. Make sure you choose SS who are reasonably confident and whose handwriting is legible.

I usually go to the USA every summer. However, this year I went to Greece because I wanted to see my friend Andreas. Andreas looked very well. "It's great to see you," he said. "Are you coming to the Acropolis this evening? It's beautiful at night."
However, I told him I was a little tired. "Let's go tomorrow," I said.
Andreas looked disappointed so I changed my mind. We went out and had a very happy evening.

LEARNING REVIEW

• To get SS to reflect on the way they learn.
• Ways of consolidating what they have covered in the book.
• Ways of continuing to develop outside the classroom.

Students' Book (page 125)

The questions could be discussed in groups. Unless you have very dedicated SS, the answer to many of these will be *No*. Nevertheless, keep it light-hearted. The object isn't to embarrass SS but to remind and encourage them to employ useful strategies to ensure progress. Learning seems to be a process of review and extend, review and extend etc.

If possible, get SS to reread earlier passages in the book which at the time they found difficult. It can be quite a boost to morale that a once difficult passage now presents no problem. Similarly, if you have any cassettes of them from earlier on in the course, it's often revealing to record them doing the same task at the end of the course and let them compare their performances. Indeed, any opportunity to help SS acknowledge that they have made progress should be seized upon.

TEST

There is a progress test for Units 16-20 on pages 156 and 157 of this book for you to photocopy for your SS. See page 160 for the Key.

Photocopiable material

P 1.1

Student A	Student B
Lucy lives in London .... Her boyfriend's got blue eyes, ... buy a house and have three children.	.... and works in a bank near Green Park. .... and brown hair and he's very tall. They want to get married, perhaps next summer, ...

✂ •

P 1.2

```
A R Z G U S T M N O Y O
Q R P R B A Y U Z E E Q
R U G E R M A N K N I X
X S W E O E N R C G R S
A S P C N I U E D L E W
D I S E T T F C H I L E
F A N L O A I G H S A D
E N B D U L J N I H N I
G Y W Z I Y K L A N D S
V H X C D A F R E N C H
```

P 1.3

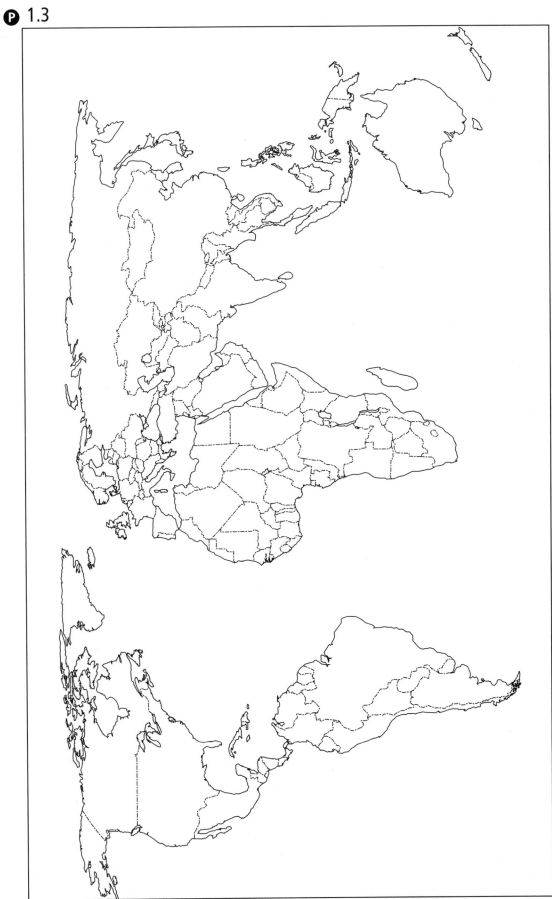

℗ 1.4

'Your Song' by Elton John

It's a little bit funny this feeling inside,
I'm not one of those who can easily hide,
I don't have much money, but, boy if I did,
I'd buy a big house where we both could live.

If I was a sculptor but then again no,
or a man who makes potions in a travelin' show,
I know it's not much but it's the best I can do.
My gift is my song and this one's for you.

And you can tell ev'rybody
This is your song.
It may be quite simple but now that it's done,
I hope you don't mind, I hope you don't mind that
  I put down in words.
How wonderful life is while you're in the world.

I sat on the roof and kicked off the moss,
Well a few of the verses well they've got me
  quite cross,
But the sun's been quite kind while I wrote
  this song,
It's for people like you that keep it turned on.

So excuse me for forgetting but these things I do,
You see I've forgotten if they're green or they're
  blue,
Anyway the thing is what I really mean,
Yours are the sweetest eyes I've ever seen.

'Your Song' by Elton John

It's a little bit funny this feeling inside,
.... not one of those who can easily hide,
I don't have much money, but, boy if .... did,
I'd buy a big house where .... both could live.

If .... was a sculptor but then again no,
or a man who makes potions in a travelin' show,
I know it's not much but it's the best .... can do.
.... gift is .... and this one's for you.

And you can tell ev'rybody
This is .... song.
.... may be quite simple but now that it's done,
I hope .... don't mind, I hope .... don't mind that I put down in words.
How wonderful life is while .... in the world.

.... sat on the roof and kicked off the moss,
Well a few of the verses well .... got me quite cross,
But the sun's been quite kind while .... wrote this song,
It's for people like .... that keep it turned on.

So excuse .... for forgetting but these things .... do,
You see I've forgotten if .... green or they're blue,
Anyway the thing is what .... really mean,
.... are the sweetest eyes I've ever seen.

ⓟ 2.1

℗ 2.2

Shopping Questionnaire

Name ....

Country ....

● In your country:

1 When do shops open and close?

    ....

2 Do you have open air markets?

    ....

3 Do you have big supermarkets?

    ....

4 Do you have shops that only sell one thing? For example, a shop that only sells bread ?

    ....

5 Do people usually shop for food every day or do they do one big shop every week?

    ....

    ....

6 Do you have shopping malls ?

    ....

7 Can you buy food from England in your shops?

    ....

8 Do shops sell food from many different countries?

    ....

9 What food is a) cheap b) expensive?
    a) ....
    b) ....

10 Who usually does the food shopping, men or women?

    ....

P 2.3

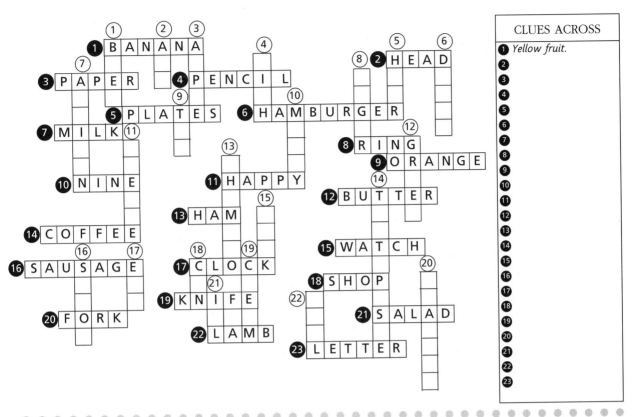

CLUES ACROSS

1 *Yellow fruit.*
2
3
4
5
6
7
8
9
10
11
12
13
14
15
16
17
18
19
20
21
22
23

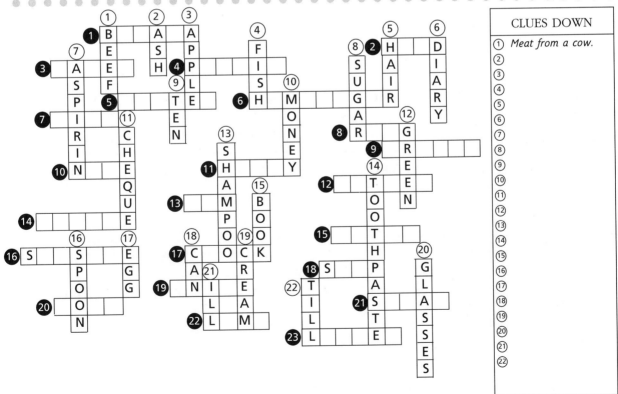

CLUES DOWN

1 *Meat from a cow.*
2
3
4
5
6
7
8
9
10
11
12
13
14
15
16
17
18
19
20
21
22

℗ 3.1

went	caught	thought
came	bought	drank
brought	took	spent

found	broke	fell
left	woke	slept
became	wrote	was

caught	ate	took
drank	said	found
rang	woke	swam

went	fell	had
read	rang	was
wrote	met	began

bought	told	fell
paid	woke	lost
said	spent	broke

sent	came	sold
rang	put	read
heard	was	flew

hit	came	drove
put	lost	sat
saw	thought	wrote

sat	lost	told
wrote	slept	gave
had	spent	rang

read	wrote	got
flew	paid	swam
stood	hit	sold

woke	flew	stood
got	sold	drove
rang	became	taught

P 3.2

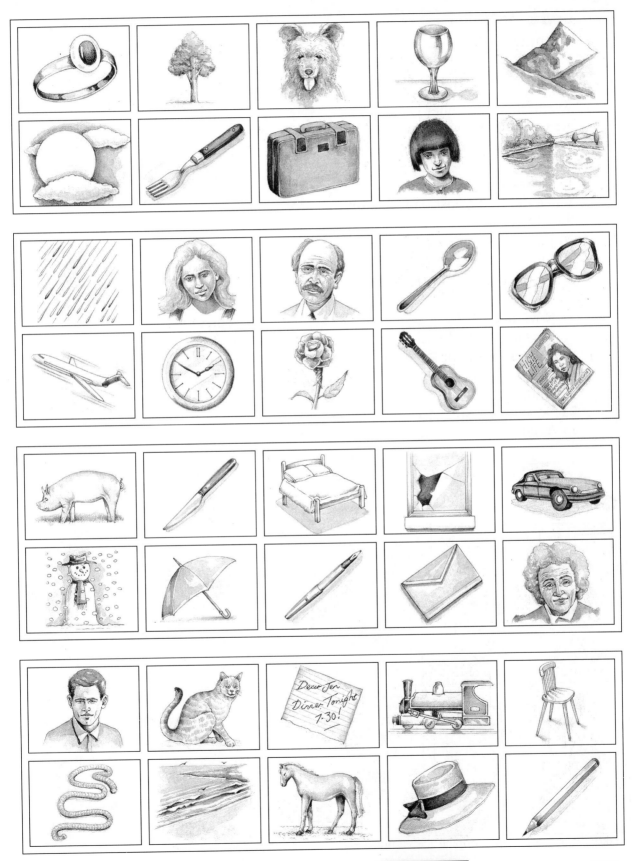

P 4.1

History quiz

How many history dates
do you know?
Tick the correct box.

1 When did Christopher Columbus
   arrive in the Bahamas ?

   12 November, 1498 ☐
   14 October, 1502 ☐
   12 October, 1492 ☐

2 When did Neil Armstrong walk on
   the Moon ?

   20 June, 1969 ☐ 20 July, 1969 ☐
   20 June, 1968 ☐

3 When did the First World War end ?

   13 November, 1916 ☐
   11 November, 1918 ☐
   11 December, 1917 ☐

4 When was President Kennedy
   killed ?

   20 January, 1962 ☐
   22 November, 1963 ☐
   14 August, 1964 ☐

5 When did Alexander Bell make the
   first telephone ?

   1876 ☐   1878 ☐   1880 ☐

6 When did Edmund Hillary climb
   Mount Everest ?

   1954 ☐   1953 ☐   1952 ☐

7 When was the Sony Company
   started in Japan?

   1949 ☐   1947 ☐   1946 ☐

8 When was penicillin discovered ?

   1928 ☐   1938 ☐   1958 ☐

9 When did Magellan begin his
   voyage round the world?

   22 September, 1518 ☐
   20 September, 1519 ☐
   24 September, 1520 ☐

10 When did Magellan return to Spain
   after his world voyage ?

   6 September, 1521 ☐
   6 September, 1522 ☐
   16 September, 1521 ☐

P 4.2

open/door

cup of tea

lend/money

get/doctor

take/dog/walk

close/window

take/station

help/shopping

find/boot

open/window

buy/stamps

get/plaster

℗ 4.3

> You sleep for 12 hours every night but you still feel tired in the day.
>
> Your boyfriend/girlfriend left you and you're very depressed.
>
> You're not eating more than usual but you're getting fat.
>
> You are losing weight but you're eating the same as you usually do.
>
> You can't sleep more than two hours a night.
>
> You can hear strange noises all the time.

℗ 4.4

P 5.1

Baby it's cold outside

I really can't stay.
Baby, it's cold outside.
I've got to go away.
Baby, it's cold outside.
This evening has been...
Been hoping that you'd drop in.
So very nice.
I'll hold your hands, they're just like
ice.
My mother will start to worry.
Beautiful, what's your hurry?
My father will be pacing the floor.
Listen to that fireplace roar.
So really I'd better scurry.
Beautiful, please don't hurry.
Well, maybe just half a drink more.
Why don't you put some records on
while I pour?
The neighbours might think...
But baby it's bad out there.
Say what's in this drink?
No cabs to be had out there.
I wish I knew how...
Your eyes are like starlight now.
to break the spell.
I'll take your hat, your hair looks
swell.
I ought to say no, no, no.
Mind if I move in closer?
At least I'm going to say that I tried.
What's the sense of hurting my
pride?
I really can't stay.
Baby, don't hold out.
Baby, it's cold outside.

I simply must go.
Baby, it's cold outside.
The answer is no.
Baby, it's cold outside.
The welcome has been...
How lucky that you dropped in.
so nice and warm.
Look out the window at that storm.
My sister will be suspicious.
Gosh your lips look delicious.
My brother will be there at the door.
Waves up on a tropical shore.
My maiden aunt's mind is vicious.
Gosh your lips are delicious.
Well, maybe just a cigarette more.
Never such a blizzard before.
I've got to get home.
But baby you'll freeze out there.
Say, lend me a coat.
It's up to your knees out there.
You've really been grand.
I thrill when you touch my hand.
But don't you see?
How can you do this thing to me?
There's bound to be talk tomorrow.
Think of my lifelong sorrow.
At least there would be plenty
implied,
If you caught pneumonia and died.
I really can't stay.
Get over that old doubt.
Baby it's cold outside.

P 5.2

WHAT can I do? I was looking after my friend's pet mouse and it escaped. She loved it very much, and I can't tell her it's gone! She'll never forgive me.

A MAN I really fancy has finally invited me out. The problem is that he has got two tickets to an opera and I hate opera. I'm worried because maybe I'll fall asleep. What shall I do?

I ALWAYS seem to get terrible headaches at the end of the week. They're so bad that I have to lie down in a dark room. I sometimes feel sick, too, and can't eat anything. Why do you think that is, and what should I do?

P 6.1

• *International Eating Habits* •	QUESTIONNAIRE

Name: ....

Country: ....

1   What time do you have lunch and dinner?

   ....

2   Which is the main meal of the day ?

   ....

3   Do you eat with a fork, knife and spoon or chopsticks ?

   ....

4   Is it OK to eat food with your hands at the table?

   ....

5   Is it OK to eat food in the street?

   ....

6   Is it rude to put your elbows on the table?

   ....

7   When you go to someone's house for a meal, should the host or the guest start eating first?

   ....

8   Is it OK to belch at the table?

   ....

9   Is it OK to eat with your mouth open?

   ....

10   Is it OK to smoke at the table when people are eating?

   ....

11   Is it polite to leave some food on the plate ?

   ....

℗ 7.1

℗ 7.2

You've just broken a vase.	You've just fallen down the stairs.
You've just seen a ghost.	You've just seen a really sad film.
You've just cut your finger on a broken glass.	You've just had a nightmare.
You've just missed your train.	You've just woken up.
You've just spilt a cup of coffee on your leg.	You've just ripped your coat.
You've just bought a sports car.	You've just had an argument with your husband/wife.
You've just fallen off your bike.	You've just bought a new hat.

P 8.1

	beautiful	boring
drunk	sunny	simple
sober	cloudy	difficult
boiling	light	happy
freezing	dark	depressed
fantastic	expensive	cooked
awful	cheap	raw
enormous	funny	long
tiny	serious	short
ugly	interesting	

P 8.2

Jack bought Sam a green and white hat yesterday.

No, he bought him a blue and white hat yesterday.

Jack bought Sam a green and white hat yesterday.

No, he bought him a green and white hat last week.

Jack bought Sam a green and white hat yesterday.

No, he bought me a green and white hat yesterday.

Did you order a large coca cola?

No, I ordered a small coca cola.

Did you order a large coca cola?

No, I ordered a large orange juice.

Did you order a large coca cola?

No, Sam ordered a large coca cola.

Rosie got a beautiful cat for her birthday.

No, she got an ugly cat for her birthday.

Rosie got a beautiful cat for her birthday.

No, she got a beautiful dog for her birthday.

Rosie got a beautiful cat for her birthday.

No, Linda got a beautiful cat for her birthday.

Ⓟ 9.1

A B C D E

F G H I

Ⓟ 9.2

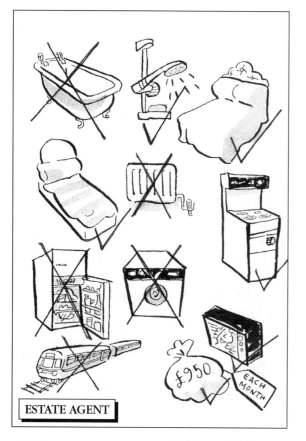

ESTATE AGENT

TENANT

℗ 9.3

In the middle of the night Sandy woke up sudden. She heard a noise loudly outside her window. She got out of bed quick and walked quiet to the window. Careful she opened the curtains a little, but she couldn't see anything because dark it was outside. She fell asleep again quick. She didn't sleep very good because she had some dreams terrible.

• •

℗ 9.4

Jazz chant **1**

A:	I **think** I'll **have** a **par**ty.
B:	**Great!**
A:	I **think** I'll **have** it in **June**.
B:	**So soon?**
A:	And if it **doesn't rain**, we'll **drink** cham**pagne**, and **dance** by the **light** of the **moon**.
B:	Are you **go**ing to in**vite** your **mo**ther?
A:	**No!**
B:	Are you **go**ing to **ask** your **Dad?**
A:	You're **mad!** I'm **not go**ing to in**vite** **people** I don't **like**. **They can't come.**
B:	Well, **that's too bad**. But I'm **glad** that you're **hav**ing a **par**ty.
A:	**Me too!**
B:	I'm **sure** that it's **go**ing to be **great**.
A:	**I can't wait**.
B:	But you'll **have** to **make sure** that it isn't a **bore**.
A:	**That's easy.** **You** won't **know** the **date!**

Jazz chant **2**

A:	I think I'll have a **par**ty.
B:	**Great!**
A:	I think I'll have it in **June**.
B:	So **soon?**
A:	And if it doesn't **rain**, we'll drink cham**pagne**, and dance by the light of the **moon**.
B:	Are you going to invite your **mo**ther?
A:	**No!**
B:	Are you going to ask your **Dad?**
A:	You're **mad!** I'm not going to in**vite** people I don't **like.** **They** can't come.
B:	Well, that's too **bad**. But I'm **glad** that you're having a **par**ty.
A:	Me **too!**
B:	I'm **sure** that it's going to be **great**.
A:	I can't **wait**.
B:	But you'll have to make **sure** that it isn't a **bore**.
A:	That's **easy**. You won't know the **date!**

℗ 11.1

A

1 The most popular country for tourism is France. In 1991 there were 55,731,000 foreign visitors to France.

2 The country with the most post offices is India. In 1988 there were 144,829 post offices in India.

3 The city with the highest population is Mexico City. In 1990 Mexico City had a population of 20,200,000 people. By the year 2000 they think the population will be 25,000,000.

4 The smallest planet in our solar system is Pluto. Its diameter is 3430 miles.

5 The most spoken language is Chinese. 1 billion people speak this language.

6 The Chinese invented the first paper money in AD 812 but the earliest banknote was made in Stockholm in Sweden in 1661.

7 The earliest steam train was built in 1812 in Leeds in England.

8 The longest film is a German film *Die Zweite Heimat*. It is 25 hours and 32 minutes long. It was first shown in 1992 in Munich.

9 The world's most dangerous animal (not including humans) is the mosquito which carries dangerous parasites. Not including wars, mosquitoes have killed 50% of all the people who have died since the Stone Age.

10 The country with the most boundaries with other countries is China. It has borders with 16 other countries.

11 The country with the most dentists is America. In 1992 the USA had 139,625 dentists.

12 The longest attack of hiccupping was 69 years and 5 months. Charles Osborne began when he was killing a pig in 1922 and he hiccupped every 1½ seconds until one morning in February 1990. He had two wives and eight children, and he died in 1991.

B

1 The country with the most hospitals is China. In 1989 there were 6,929 hospitals.

2 The language with the most irregular verbs is English. There are 283 irregular verbs.

3 The most expensive jewellery was a ruby and diamond necklace which was sold at Sotheby's in Switzerland for $50 million.

4 The longest walk in space was 8 hours 29 minutes in May 1992. The three astronauts were Pierre Thuot, Rich Hieb and Tom Akers.

5 The longest attack of sneezing happened to Donna Griffiths of Britain. She started sneezing on 13 January 1981 and the first day she had without sneezing was 16 September 1983. She sneezed about 1,000,000 times.

6 The most expensive wedding dress ever made is worth $ 7,301,587. It has diamonds and platinum on it. The public first saw it in Paris, France on 23 March 1989.

7 The longest poem ever written in English is 129,807 lines and it took 40 years to write it. It was called *King Alfred* by John Fichett.

8 The brightest planet in our solar system is Venus.

9 The earliest restaurant opened in 1725 in Calle de Cuchilleros 17, Madrid, Spain.

10 The driest place on earth is Death Valley, California, USA.

11 The word most often used in English is 'the'.

12 The highest price ever paid for a car is $15 million for an Italian Bugatti. A Japanese company bought it.

P 11.2

A

B

C

P 12.1

Can I have a word with you, please?	Ah. There you are!
I'm sorry. I'm busy at the moment.	I'm sorry I'm late. I got lost.
I was sorry to hear about your exam results.	What's the matter?
Thanks, but I didn't expect to pass.	I can't find my keys.
Are you free tonight?	Have a seat. How can I help you?
Yes. Do you want to go out somewhere?	I've got a really sore throat.
Do you fancy a drink?	Lovely weather, isn't it?
Yes, please. A white wine.	Yes. It's usually very cold in December.

P 13.1

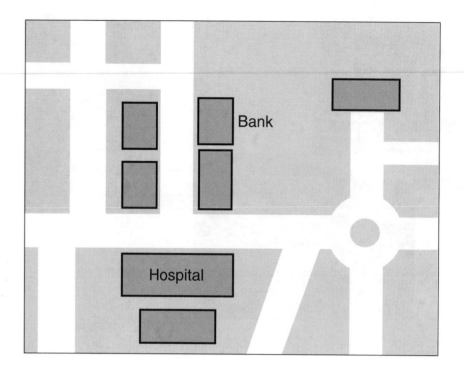

P 14.1

1 We're getting married.	a) Oh, what wonderful news!
2 My pet bird died.	b) Oh, how sad. I'm sorry.
3 I have to have an operation.	c) Oh, I'm sorry to hear that.
4 My computer won't work.	d) Hang on a minute, I'll get John. He's knows all about these machines.
5 It's my birthday today.	
6 I'm going to Jamaica for six months.	e) Oh, many happy returns.
	f) Lucky you.
7 I'm sorry I can't help you.	g) Never mind, don't worry.
8 Thank you for helping me.	h) Not at all.
9 I passed my driving test.	i) Congratulations.
10 I didn't pass my driving test.	j) Oh, hard luck.

P 14.2

Down Cross, 1955

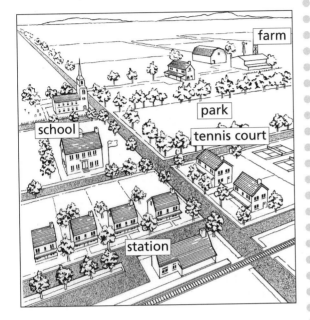

Down Cross, today

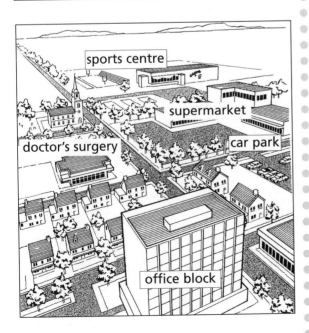

P 14.3

| Richard bought a new bike |
| I'm meeting you tomorrow |
| I've paid this bill |
| I didn't break it |
| Nick doesn't smoke |
| Rachel used to be a nurse |
| Pauline didn't use to wear jeans |
| Mr and Mrs Smith are leaving today |
| Mike can drive |
| You can't smoke in here |
| I'm not working tomorrow |
| You'll help me? |

, didn't he?	, aren't I?
, haven't I?	, did I?
, does he?	, didn't she?
, did she?	, aren't they?
, can't he?	, can you?
, am I?	, won't you?

P 15.1

SCHOOL QUESTIONNAIRE

Name ....

Country ....

1   Do you have to go to school?
....

2   How many years do you have to
stay at school?
....

3   What age do children start school?
....

4   How many students are usually in a
class?
....

5   When does the first lesson start?
....

6   When does the school day finish?
....

7   How many days a week do you go
to school?
....

8   Is education free?
....

9   Do students have to pay for books?
....

10 Do students study art, music,
dance, drama and sport at school?
....

11 Do students have to learn another
language?
....

12 Do students have school meals at
lunchtime?
....

P 16.1

Sorry!

1
A: Mum's not very well.
B: What did you say?
A: I said Mum's not very well.

2
A: Can I get past?
B: Sure.
A: Thanks a lot.

3
A: You can't come in.
B: Why not?
A: Because you're too young.

4
A: Ouch! My foot!
B: I didn't know you were there.
A: It's all right. Don't worry.

ⓟ 16.2

A

eat	wake ....
think	sleep ....
ask	die ....
buy	hear ....
take	ran ....
begin	write ....
swim	fly ....
put	work ....
drive	make ....
know	cut ....

B

drink	break ....
hit	leave ....
speak	live ....
say	see ....
talk	come ....
understand	bring ....
go	choose ....
sing	play ....
sell	do ....
feel	go ....

ⓟ 18.1

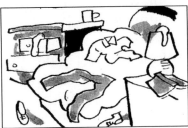

℗ 18.2

VALERIE JONES, aged 45, died of pneumonia after she sat in a park for a few nights in the cold and rain. Mrs Jones went to the park because her neighbour played loud music all the time. Mrs Jones' husband complained 25 times in the 18 months before his wife died.

Jack Hake, 57, killed himself with whisky and pills after noise from a teenage neighbour and her friends drove him crazy.

HARRYCLARK, aged 48, was stabbed 22 times by his neighbour Chris Neal. Neal used to make a lot of noise. When the people in his street decided to get together to try to stop him, Neal went crazy. He stabbed four other people before he killed Mr Clark.

Victor Chester, 65, was killed by his neighbour Michael Lancing. Lancing killed Mr Chester because he made a lot of noise when he was putting new cupboards in his kitchen. The noise kept Mr Lancing's children awake. Lancing was put in prison for 12 months.

Pat O'Mahoney, aged 29, was murdered outside his home after he had a fight with his neighbour. His neighbour, Derek Cross, used to play loud music a lot. Cross was sent to prison for life.

DOREEN BURKE, 43, died in a house fire which was started by her neighbour, Lillian Romney, 36. In court Romney said that Doreen Burke's dog kept her children awake all night.

℗ 18.3

You have a younger brother and every time your girl/boyfriend comes to visit, your brother won't leave you alone.

Your parents want you to study law but you want to be a rock'n' roll singer.

Your new girlfriend/boyfriend has a motorbike. They love this machine and want you to ride on it with them. You're frightened of motorbikes.

You have fallen in love with your boss but she/he doesn't know this. It's very difficult to work with her/him every day but you really like your job and you don't want to leave.

Your daughter/son is going out with someone who has just come out of prison. He/She robbed a bank and has been in prison for five years.

You bought a house from a lovely old lady last month. Then you lost your job. Last weekend you found £100,000 in the attic.

Two really good-looking men/women have asked you to go out with them. You really like them both.

Your teacher gave your homework back and inside your book there was a copy of the exam you are taking next week.

℗ 20.1

What do you dislike about hotels?

noise ☐	long way from the town centre ☐	dirty ☐
bad service ☐	rude/unhelpful staff ☐	no restaurant ☐
too cold ☐	a long way to walk to your room ☐	small rooms ☐
too hot ☐	no room service after 10 pm ☐	no parking ☐
no porters ☐	no mini bar in the room ☐	no view ☐
no lifts ☐	no TV in the rooms ☐	expensive ☐
no swimming pool ☐		bad food ☐

℗ 20.2

Your shower only has cold water.	Your husband/wife is coming tomorrow so you want a room with a double bed.
You dropped your ring down the plughole in the washbasin.	You want to change your room because you want a view of the sea.
There's a stranger in your bed asleep.	You want breakfast in your room at 8 am tomorrow.

Test 1 Units 1-5

GRAMMAR

A Question forms (10 marks)

Write questions for these answers. Use the Present Simple, the Present Continuous or the Past Simple.

1 A: _____any children?

  B: Yes, they've got two boys.

2 A: _____ bed?

  B: She usually goes at half past seven during the week.

3 A: _____ ?

  B: I'm a teacher.

4 A: _____ to the doctor's yesterday?

  B: Yes, I did. He gave me some medicine.

5 A: _____ that dress?

  B: Because I'm going to a wedding.

B The present (10 marks)

Complete these sentences. Use the Present Simple or the Present Continuous.

1 He (wash) _____ his car once a week.

2 Oh, no! It (rain) _____again!

3 Remember that we (meet) _____ Tim at five o'clock.

4 Ssh. Mum (speak) _____ on the phone.

5 I (not/play) _____ the piano, but I would like to learn.

C The past (15 marks)

Ruth Turner saw a bank robbery yesterday when she was doing her shopping in town. A policewoman is questioning her. Change the verbs in brackets to the Past Simple or the Past Continuous.

POLICEWOMAN: So you actually saw the robbery, Mrs Turner? What exactly (you/do) (1) _____ at the time?

RUTH: I (come) (2) _____ out of the supermarket in the High Street when suddenly two men (run) (3) _____ out of the bank. They (carry) (4) _____ guns!

P: (you/see) (5) _____ the men's faces?

R: No, they (wear) (6) _____ masks.

P: What (you/do) (7) _____ next?

R: I (shout) (8) _____ at them. 'Drop your guns!' I said. They were very surprised. They stopped and looked at me. While they (look) (9) _____ at me, I (go) (10) _____ up to one of them and I (hit) (11) _____ him on the head with a big bag of potatoes.

P: What (happen) (12) _____ then?

R: He (fall) (13) _____ over and the other man (run) (14) _____ away.

P: Well, Mrs Turner, thanks to you we (catch) (15) _____ one of the robbers yesterday.

D The future (10 marks)

Complete these sentences with *will* or *going to* or the Present Continuous.

1 I'm sorry I can't see you this afternoon. I (go)_____ out to lunch.

2 A: I'm going home.

  B: That's a good idea. I think I (come) _____ with you.

3 A: Have you decided what job you want to do?

  B: Yes, I (be) _____ a doctor.

4 A: Let's go out this afternoon.

  B: Sorry, I can't. I (play) _____ tennis at 2.30.

5 Oh, no, the door's locked. Wait a minute and I (find) _____ my key.

E Modals (5 marks)

Andy has got flu. The doctor is talking to him. Complete the following sentences. Use each of the modal verbs once:

© Longman Group Limited 1995 Photocopiable

mustn't, can, don't have to, should, have to.

You (1)_____ take this medicine twice a day, as the instructions say. It makes you sleepy so you (2)_____ drive your car. It's dangerous. You (3)_____ stay in bed if you don't want to, but I think you (4)_____ stay inside. You (5)_____ go back to work when all the medicine is finished, but only if your temperature is normal again.

F Mixed verb forms (20 marks)

Correct the underlined verb forms.

1 The President <u>was arriving</u> at 3.30 yesterday.

_____

2 He <u>is always wearing</u> a tie for work.

_____

3 <u>Do you open</u> the window, please?

_____

4 He <u>goes</u> to Italy for his holidays last year.

_____

5 They <u>aren't usually liking</u> that kind of film.

_____

6 We <u>watched</u> television when he arrived.

_____

7 I think I <u>stay</u> at home this evening. I'm tired.

_____

8 <u>Do they enjoy</u> the dinner party last night?

_____

9 <u>Do you come</u> to Julie's party tonight?

_____

10 He <u>was going</u> to the park last week.

_____

VOCABULARY

G Words and expressions (15 marks)

Can you remember these words and expressions? The first letter is done for you.

1 In Portugal they speak P_____ .

2 You can buy meat at a b_____ .

3 A jacket and trousers is sometimes called a s_____ .

4 If something is too big, it doesn't f_____ .

5 Your brother or sister's daughter is your n_____ .

6 I t_____ a_____ my mother. I have the same nose.

7 An a_____ person wants to get a good job and earn a lot of money.

8 Someone who tells the truth is h_____ .

9 The doctor says I have to g_____ u_____ smoking because I have a bad cough.

10 I hate diets, but I must l_____ w_____ before I can wear my shorts.

11 I've got a really sore t_____ and it hurts to speak.

12 Can you r_____ a horse?

13 I live very near the office so I go to work o_____ f_____ .

14 My mother thinks skiing is d_____ , but none of the sports I like are safe!

15 Travelling by bus is quite cheap but not very r_____ . They're often late.

WRITING

H Punctuation (10 marks)

Write this paragraph on a separate piece of paper and put in the correct punctuation. Make five sentences.

kate and nick moss are both models they are english but kate works a lot in the united states she is very famous there i think have you ever seen photos of her in magazines their mothers got dark hair a nice face and dark brown eyes

I Linking words (5 marks)

Complete each of the sentences below with *and*, *but*, *because* or *so*.

1 I really enjoy Spielberg's films _____ they are so exciting.

2 They wanted to get up early _____ they set the alarm clock for five o'clock.

3 I like spring and summer _____ I really hate the English winter.

4 She was very clever at school _____ she was a fantastic sportswoman, too.

5 He felt ill _____ he made an appointment to see the doctor.

Test 2 Units 6-10

GRAMMAR

A Quantity expressions (10 marks)

Complete the sentences, using these words at least once: *a, some, any, a few, a little, a lot, much, many*. Sometimes more than one answer is possible.

JILL: Tom, have we got (1)_____ eggs? I

want to bake (2)_____ cakes.

TOM: Yes, I think there are (3)_____ in the

fridge. Have a look.

JILL: Oh, yes. Oh dear, there aren't (4)_____

eggs left – only three!

TOM: Well, there might be (5)_____ box in

the cupboard.

JILL: No, I've already looked. There's only

(6)_____ sugar left, too. I'll have to go and

buy (7)_____ more things.

TOM: Well, you don't need (8)_____ flour,

there's (9)_____ . But there isn't

(10)_____ butter. If you give me a list, I'll

go and do the shopping.

JILL: OK. Thanks, Tom.

B Present Perfect and Past Simple (10 marks)

Put the verbs in brackets into the Present Perfect Simple or the Past Simple.

1 We (*see*) _____ this film before. I can't remember when.

2 I think they (*arrive*) _____ . There's a car outside.

3 Your husband (*call*) _____ earlier and left a message.

4 I (*meet*) _____ him at a conference last year.

5 It (*not rain*) _____ yet this week.

C Time expressions with the Present Perfect (10 marks)

Put one of these words in the correct place in each sentence. Use one word twice: *yet, just, ever, never*.

1 I've been to Paris but I'd love to go one day.
2 She's left. If you run, you'll catch her.
3 I haven't had breakfast. Can you wait five minutes?
4 Artichokes are delicious. Have you eaten them?
5 No more coffee, thanks. I've had some.

D Opinions about the future (10 marks)

Change the verbs in brackets to opinions about the future. Use *will / won't* or *might*.

1 I'm sure it (*be*) _____ sunny later. The clouds have nearly gone.

2 They (*go*) _____ to Cyprus for their holidays. They're not sure.

3 I promise I (*forget*) _____ your birthday.

4 You (*hurt*) _____ yourself. Be careful.

5 Yes, it's possible. They (*win*) _____ the match – they're playing quite well today.

E First Conditional (10 marks)

Complete the sentences with the correct form of the verbs in brackets.

1 If you (*work*) _____ hard, you (*pass*) _____ your exams easily.

2 I (*leave*) _____ the country if Labour (*win*) _____ the election again.

3 I am sure he (*have*) _____ a crash if he (*continue*) _____ to drive so fast.

4 They (*not/be*) _____ late if they (*run*) _____ .

5 If the weather (*stay*) _____ good, we (*probably have*)_____ a picnic.

F *-ing* or *to*? (5 marks)

Underline the correct word or words in these sentences.

1 I've decided *to change / changing* my job.
2 He would like *to meet / meeting* us next week.
3 She's worried about *to take / taking* the exam.
4 Do you enjoy *to learn / learning* English?
5 We're really excited *to see / seeing* you.

VOCABULARY

G *-ing* or *-ed* adjectives (5 marks)

Underline the correct adjective in these sentences.

1 The story of the film was really *interested / interesting*.
2 That was the most *boring / bored* evening I have ever had!
3 I was very *frightened / frightening* when I saw the man take out a gun.
4 It's *depressed / depressing* that there are still wars in the world.
5 I invited my friends to dinner but then I forgot. I felt really *embarrassed / embarrassing*!

H Phrasal verbs (10 marks)

Complete the sentences with the correct form of these phrasal verbs: *get on with, hang on, give up, try on, pick up.*

1 She'll be back in a minute. Would you like to _____ or shall I ask her to call you back?
2 We _____ them _____ from the airport early this morning. They're in bed now.
3 Have you _____ the next size? That dress looks a bit small.
4 They didn't _____ each other when they were children, but they're good friends now.
5 I hope he _____ smoking soon. His cough is terrible!

I Adjectives (5 marks)

Use these adjectives to complete the sentences: *safe, cheap, dirty, mean, difficult.*

1 The clothes in that sale are really _____ . Some of them are half-price!
2 She never spends any money but she has a lot. I think she's a bit _____ .

3 Flying is quite _____ compared with driving. More people die on the roads.
4 It's a _____ language to learn. The alphabet is different from ours.
5 The streets in this town are really _____ . Nobody ever cleans them.

J Mixed vocabulary (15 marks)

Wordsearch. Find fifteen words in the puzzle (across or down) connected with restaurants / food; the house (kitchen / bathroom); and jobs.

T	O	W	E	L	P	C	D	B	I	L	L
I	A	C	B	R	E	N	S	F	Z	W	O
P	B	L	A	R	A	R	T	V	W	T	E
G	S	A	B	F	R	I	D	G	E	S	Q
C	E	N	M	U	X	N	R	O	P	O	P
Q	N	L	A	M	B	B	A	N	Q	A	I
S	G	R	I	L	L	W	O	T	A	P	L
M	I	F	U	Y	V	T	N	V	T	B	O
U	N	Q	A	R	C	H	I	T	E	C	T
L	E	V	B	T	Y	O	O	I	T	V	Q
S	E	R	V	I	C	E	N	P	Y	B	L
U	R	S	A	U	C	E	P	A	N	T	U

WRITING

K *The* (5 marks)

Read these sentences. Cross out *the* if it isn't necessary.

1 I've always enjoyed listening to the country music.
2 I have finished reading the book I bought last week.
3 She doesn't like the weather in this country.
4 Many British people have the rabbits as pets.
5 Do you like watching the horror films?

L Adjectives and adverbs (5 marks)

Underline the correct words in these sentences.

1 The party was really *well / good*.
2 She speaks English *well / good*.
3 How *fast / fastly* can you run?
4 We have to work *hard / hardly* with that teacher.
5 She won the race *easy / easily*.

Test 3 Units 11-15

GRAMMAR

A Making comparisons (15 marks)

Make sentences using the comparative or superlative form of the adjective in brackets, or (*not*) *as....as.*

1 I like cats. They / snakes (nice).

_____

2 Everest / mountain in the world (high).

_____

3 My dog can hear everything. I can't. His hearing / mine (good).

_____

4 Don't eat hamburgers! They/for your health / fruit (good).

_____

5 Jo is growing very fast. He and his father are the same height. He's / his father (tall).

_____

B Second Conditional (10 marks)

Complete these sentences with the correct form of the verb in brackets.

1 If I (win) _____ £1 million, I (travel) _____ round the world.

2 I (stay) _____ a long time in a place if it (be) _____ interesting.

3 If I (like) _____ the local food, I (learn) _____ how to cook the dishes.

4 If I (speak) _____ the local language, I (communicate) _____ with the people.

5 I (keep) _____ a diary if I (want) _____ a record of my trip.

C Adjective word order (10 marks)

Put the underlined words in the correct order.

1 I'll take my <u>grey large leather</u> suitcase.

_____

2 She wore a <u>cotton black short</u> dress.

_____

3 They made a <u>round big pink</u> cake.

_____

4 The boat was a <u>wooden small brown</u> one.

_____

5 We bought them a <u>china white tall</u> vase.

_____

D Defining relative clauses (5 marks)

Complete the sentences with one of these words: *who, which, where.*

1 I like books _____ have a lot of pictures.

2 What do you think of the woman _____ played the part of Cleopatra?

3 That's the house _____ we stayed in May.

4 The police have arrested the thief _____ stole the furniture from the museum.

5 I have a car _____ looks like yours.

E Mixed forms (5 marks)

Complete the sentences with one of these: *for, too much, very, too many.*

1 You've put _____ sugar in this coffee. It's horrible!

2 He's always been _____ good at tennis.

3 What do you use this thing _____ ?

4 There are _____ people at this party.

5 There's _____ noise. I'm going home.

F Question tags (10 marks)

Add question tags to these sentences.

1 It isn't a difficult test, _____ ?

2 The questions are easy, _____ ?

3 We've done a lot of revision, _____ ?

4 Susan's got to mark this test later, _____ ?

5 You remembered everything, _____ ?

G Quantity: *some- any- no- every-words* (10 marks)

Complete the sentences with these words:
nothing, anyone, everything, something, anything.

1 I'm going out to a nightclub this evening but I haven't got _____ nice to wear.

2 There's _____ you can do to help at the moment, but thank you for offering.

3 Let's have _____ to eat. I'm hungry.

4 _____ that man says is wrong. How can I ever believe him?

5 Has _____ ever told you that you're mad?

VOCABULARY

H Crime (10 marks)

Wordsearch. Find ten words in the puzzle (across or down) connected with crime.

```
C  O  B  U  R  G  L  A  R  U  O  G
R  J  W  X  T  S  O  R  F  T  N  U
I  M  S  T  E  A  L  R  S  B  O  N
M  U  H  R  O  K  S  E  L  O  E  W
I  T  X  L  H  D  F  S  A  S  R  T
N  P  Q  M  U  R  S  T  N  Q  Z  H
A  R  O  B  T  O  B  A  P  O  F  I
L  V  O  C  Z  Q  D  L  R  U  H  E
X  T  H  D  K  I  N  K  I  L  L  F
N  E  V  I  D  E  N  C  E  Z  E  M
S  D  T  P  R  I  S  O  N  L  P  S
```

I Mixed adjectives (10 marks)

Complete the sentences with these words:
dangerous, tidy, relaxing, talkative, cheerful, lazy, expensive, shy, bad-tempered, sociable. Use each word once.

When I was at school I was very quiet and
(1) _____ and always kept my books neat and
(2) _____. Then, when I was about sixteen, I
became very (3) _____ : I never stopped talking.
·I also became very (4) _____ and often didn't do
my homework. At home I was difficult to get on
with. I was horrible and (5) _____ – a fairly

typical teenager, I suppose! However, with my
friends I was always (6) _____ and happy. Now
I'm in my mid-thirties and I'm not as (7) _____ as
I used to be, although I still love to see people
quite often. Now I enjoy more (8) _____ hobbies
like yoga, but in my twenties I used to love
(9) _____ sports like hang-gliding and deep-sea
diving. I've got two children now who cost me a
lot of money and those hobbies are too (10) ___.

J Mixed nouns (10 marks)

Complete the sentences with a noun. The first letter is done for you.

1 They were very angry. They were having a serious *a*_____ about money.

2 What's your date of *b*_____ ?

3 Cross the road at the *t*_____ lights.

4 I'm tired. I want a *b*_____ from work.

5 *C*_____ on passing your exam! Well done!

6 Have you seen the Picasso *e*_____ at the local art gallery?

7 My best subject at school is *l*_____ – I speak very good French.

8 Mozart was a great *c*_____ .

9 He's in the front *r*_____ of the cinema.

10 What's the exchange *r*_____ for yen?

WRITING

K Linking expressions (5 words)

Use each of these words once to complete the sentences: *also, however, although, too, but.*

1 _____ he confessed to killing his wife, he didn't go to prison.

2 Pat said, 'I can't live with you. You have a girlfriend and you have a wife _____!'

3 The policewoman had a recording of the man. He said he killed his wife, _____ the judge didn't send him to prison.

4 They talked about life and love. They _____ talked about his wife.

5 The killer loved the policewoman. _____, he didn't love his wife.

Test 4 Units 16-20

GRAMMAR

A The passive (10 marks)

Complete the sentences with the correct from of the verbs in brackets. Sometimes you will need the passive.

I remember the first time I went to teach in Greece. I (*meet*) (1)_____ at the airport by an English friend who (*drive*) (2)_____ me to her house. When we walked in, I (*greet*) (3)_____ in Greek by her husband, but I (*not know*) (4)_____ how to reply, so I just (*say*) (5)_____ 'Hello!' in English. They had three children who (*teach*) (6)_____ me a lot of Greek. Each day I (*take*) (7)_____ around the house and garden, things (*show*) (8)_____ to me and I (*tell*) (9)_____ how to say the words in Greek. Soon I (*can*) (10)_____ say enough in Greek to go shopping, catch buses and taxis, and generally enjoy being in a different country.

B *For* or *since*? (5 marks)

Complete these sentences with *for* or *since*.

1 I've been studying English _____ three years.

2 Have you seen Jane _____ last Friday?

3 What have you been doing _____ the last half hour?

4 I've been waiting for you _____ three o'clock.

5 We haven't seen each other _____ we were at school.

C Present Perfect Continuous (10 marks)

Write sentences using the Present Perfect Continuous.

1 How long / you / learn Spanish?
_____

2 She / work / in London for two years.
_____

3 You / wait / for a long time?
_____

4 I / read / this book all morning.
_____

5 How long / Susan / clean the car?
_____

D Reported sentences (10 marks)

Report these sentences using the verbs in brackets.

1 'Go to sleep now,' George's mother said to him. (tell)
_____

2 'Don't forget to brush your teeth,' she said to him. (ask)
_____

3 'Get up early,' she said to him. (tell)
_____

4 'Don't watch television,' she said to him. (tell)
_____

5 'Don't tell me what to do,' said George to his mother. (ask)
_____

E Verb patterns: *if, when, unless, as soon as* (10 marks)

Underline the correct word in italics and put the verb in brackets in the correct form.

1 *Unless / If* you don't buy me an ice-cream, I (be) _____ very angry.

2 *When / If* the film (finish) _____, we'll go for a pizza, shall we?

3 I'm going away for two days. I (phone) _____ you *as soon as / if* I get back.

4 *If / Unless* we (leave) _____ now, we'll be late for the wedding.

5 I hope you get that new job. *When / If* you (do) _____, I'll take you out for dinner.

© Longman Group Limited 1995 Photocopiable

F Verb patterns: verb + 2 objects
(10 marks)

Rewrite these sentences. Change the underlined words to *it, him, her or them*.

1 I've given the <u>information</u> to <u>the policewoman</u>.

_____

2 He made <u>the cake</u> for <u>John</u>.

_____

3 We've played <u>the CD</u> to <u>the children</u>.

_____

4 I've showed <u>the picture</u> to <u>the old lady</u>.

_____

5 The actor bought <u>the cake</u> for <u>his fans</u>.

_____

VOCABULARY

G Negatives (10 marks)

Make negatives of these words: *sense, honest, pleasant, kind, expensive*. Use *dis-, non-, un-* (x2) or *in-*. Then complete the sentences with one of the negatives.

1 I'm afraid he's _____ ; he was caught stealing money yesterday.

2 It's a lovely restaurant. The food's very good and it's _____ , too.

3 Don't talk _____ ! That isn't true.

4 That was very _____ of you to say that to her. She's nice when you get to know her.

5 There's a very _____ smell coming from the fridge. Some of the food is bad!

H *Do* or *make*? (10 marks)

Complete these sentences with the correct form of *do* or *make*.

1 Have you _____ your homework?

2 Children sometimes _____ a lot of noise.

3 Sarah _____ the ironing yesterday.

4 Henry has _____ coffee for us all.

5 Oh, dear! I've a _____ mistake.

I Sports (10 marks)

Wordsearch. Find ten words in the puzzle (across or down) connected with sports.

G	A	D	E	Q	B	B	O	O	T	S	P
L	C	B	L	O	P	Q	X	Z	L	M	N
O	X	R	A	F	P	I	T	C	H	A	L
V	B	R	A	C	K	E	T	G	K	E	O
E	Y	P	O	O	L	M	A	B	Y	P	R
S	P	S	O	B	A	R	F	E	D	F	C
O	I	L	P	H	T	R	A	C	K	L	O
C	G	N	J	M	L	O	T	L	R	I	U
R	I	N	G	Z	J	K	P	U	O	W	R
R	W	S	H	O	R	T	S	B	B	X	T

J Mixed vocabulary (5 marks)

Underline the correct words.

1 Can you *lend / borrow* me some money?
2 I'm tired. I'm going to *lie down / lie on*.
3 How long does this film *finish / last*?
4 Who has the *world champion / world record* for the marathon?
5 Pass me the paint brush. Let's *decorate / dust* the bedroom.

WRITING

K Punctuation (10 marks)

Punctuate these sentences.

1 You're very late he said

_____

2 He shouted at me stop

_____

3 Where are we I asked

_____

4 I want a coffee he told me

_____

5 Be a good girl her mother said

_____

Key

TEST 1   Units 1 - 5

(Total marks 100)

A Question forms

2 marks for each completely correct answer. 1 for correct choice of verb forms. (10 marks)

1 Have they got/Do they have?
2 What time/When does she go to...?
3 What do you do?/What is your job?
4 Did you go..?
5 Why are you wearing/buying ...?

B The present

2 marks for each completely correct answer. 1 for the correct choice of verb forms. (10 marks)

1 washes
2 's/is raining
3 are meeting/are going to meet
4 's/is speaking
5 don't/can't play

C The past

1 mark for each correct answer. Lose half a mark for incorrect spelling. (15 marks)

1 were you doing
2 was coming
3 ran
4 were carrying
5 did you see
6 were wearing
7 did you do
8 shouted
9 were looking
10 went
11 hit
12 happened
13 fell
14 ran
15 caught

D The future

2 marks for each completely correct answer. 1 for correct verb form. (10 marks)

1 'm going
2 'll come
3 'm going to be
4 'm playing/going to play
5 'll find

E Modals

1 mark for each correct answer. (5 marks)

1 have to
2 mustn't
3 don't have to
4 should
5 can

F Mixed verb forms

2 marks for each completely correct answer. 1 for the correct verb form. (20 marks)

1 arrived
2 always wears
3 Can/Could/Will/Would you open
4 went
5 don't usually like
6 were watching
7 'll stay
8 Did they enjoy
9 Are you coming/going to come
10 went

G Words and expressions

1 mark for each correct answer. (15 marks)

1 Portuguese
2 butcher's
3 suit
4 fit
5 niece
6 take after
7 ambitious
8 honest
9 give up
10 lose weight
11 throat
12 ride
13 on foot
14 dangerous
15 reliable

H Punctuation

Half a mark for each correct item. Please note a comma is also possible after *English*, but since this is optional we suggest no extra mark is given for it. (10 marks)

Kate and **N**ick **M**oss are both models. **T**hey are **E**nglish but **K**ate works a lot in the **U**nited **S**tates. **S**he is very famous there, **I** think. **H**ave you ever seen photos of her in magazines**? T**heir mother's got dark hair, a nice face and dark brown eyes.

I Linking words

1 mark for each correct item. (5 marks)

1 because
2 so
3 but
4 and
5 so

TEST 2   Units 6 - 10

(Total 100 marks)

A Quantity expressions

1 mark for each correct answer (10 marks)

1 any 2 some/ a few 3 a few/some 4 many 5 a
6 a little 7 some/a few 8 any 9 a lot 10 much

B Present Perfect and Past Simple

2 marks for completely correct answer. 1 mark for correct choice of verb form. (10 marks)

1 have seen 2 have arrived 3 called 4 met
5 hasn't rained

C Time expressions with the Present Perfect

2 marks for each completely correct answer. 1 mark for correct choice of time expression. (10 marks)

1 I've never been to Paris.
2 She's just left.
3 I haven't had breakfast yet.
4 Have you ever eaten them?
5 I've just had some.

D Opinions about the future

2 marks for each completely correct answer. 1 mark for correct choice of verb form. (10 marks)

1 will be
2 might go
3 won't forget
4 'll hurt/might hurt
5 might win

E First Conditional

1 mark for each answer. (10 marks)

1 work/'ll pass
2 'll leave/wins
3 'll have/continues
4 won't be/run
5 stays/'ll probably have

F -ing or to?

1 mark for each correct answer. (5 marks)

1 to change   4 learning
2 to meet   5 to see
3 taking

G -ing or -ed adjectives

1 mark for each correct answer. (5 marks)

1 interesting   4 depressing
2 boring   5 embarrassed
3 frightened

H Phrasal verbs

2 marks for each completely correct answer. 1 mark for correct choice of phrasal verb. (10 marks)

1 hang on   4 get on with
2 picked up   5 will give up/gives up
3 tried on

I Adjectives

1 mark for each correct answer. (5 marks)

1 cheap   4 difficult
2 mean   5 dirty
3 safe

J Mixed vocabulary

1 mark for each word. (15 marks)

```
T O W E L P C D B I L L
I A C B R E N S F Z W O
P B L A R A R T V W T E
G S A B F R I D G E S Q
C E N M U X N R Q P O P
Q N L A M B B A N Q A I
S G R I L L W O T A P L
M I F U Y V T N V T B O
U N Q A R C H I T E C T
L E V B T Y O O I T V Q
S E R V I C E N P Y B L
U R S A U C E P A N T U
```

House (bathroom/kitchen): towel, soap, tap, fridge, grill, saucepan
Restaurant/food: tip, bill, service, onion, pear, lamb
Jobs: engineer, architect, pilot

K The

1 mark for each correct answer. (5 marks)

1 I've always enjoyed listening to the country music.
2 I have finished reading the book I bought last week.
3 She doesn't like the weather in this country.
4 Many British people have the rabbits as pets.
5 Do you like watching the horror films?

L Adjectives and adverbs

1 mark for each correct answer. (5 marks)

1 good   4 hard
2 well   5 easily
3 fast

TEST 3 Units 11 - 15

(Total 100 marks)

A Making comparisons

3 marks for each correct answer. Lose 1 mark for spelling mistakes. Lose 1 mark for missing words. (15 marks)

1 are nicer than
2 is the highest
3 is better than
4 are not as good for your health as
5 as tall as

B Second Conditional

1 mark for each correct answer. (10 marks)

1 won/'d travel
2 'd stay/were/was
3 liked/'d learn
4 spoke/would/could communicate
5 'd keep/wanted

C Adjective word order

2 marks for each correct answer. Lose 1 mark if two adjectives are in the wrong place. (10 marks)

1 large grey leather   4 small brown wooden
2 short black cotton   5 tall white china
3 big round pink

D Defining relative clauses

1 mark for each correct answer. (5 marks)

1 which   4 who
2 who   5 which
3 where

E Mixed forms

1 mark for each correct answer. (5 marks)

1 too much   4 too many
2 very   5 too much
3 for

F Question tags

2 marks for each correct answer. Lose 1 mark for incorrect punctuation or spelling. (10 marks)

1 is it?   4 hasn't she?
2 aren't they? 5 didn't you?
3 haven't we?

G Quantity: some-, any-, no-, every- words

2 marks for each correct answer. (10 marks)

1 anything   4 Everything
2 nothing   5 anyone
3 something

H Crime

1 mark for each correct answer. (10 marks)

```
C O B U R G L A R U O G
R J W X T S O R F T N U
I M S T E A L R S B O N
M U H R O K S E L O E W
I T X L H D F S A S R T
N P Q M U R S T N Q Z H
A R O B T O B A P O F I
L V O C Z Q D L R U H E
X T H D K I N K I L L F
N E V I D E N C E Z E M
S D T P R I S O N L P S
```

burglar, criminal, arrest, steal, thief, rob, prison, evidence, gun, kill

I Mixed adjectives

1 mark for each correct answer. (10 marks)

1 shy	5 bad-tempered	8 relaxing
2 tidy	6 cheerful	9 dangerous
3 talkative	7 sociable	10 expensive
4 lazy		

J Mixed nouns

1 mark for each correct answer. (10 marks)

1 argument	5 Congratulations	8 composer
2 birth	6 exhibition	9 row
3 traffic	7 languages	10 rate
4 break		

K Linking expressions

1 mark for each correct answer. (5 marks)

1 Although   4 also
2 too   5 However
3 but

TEST 4 Units 16 - 20

(Total marks 100)

A The passive

1 mark for each correct answer. Lose half a mark for incorrect spelling. (10 marks)

1 was met	6 taught
2 drove	7 was taken
3 was greeted	8 were shown
4 didn't know	9 was told
5 said	10 could

B For or since?

1 mark for each correct answer. (5 marks)

1 for   3 for   5 since
2 since   4 since

C Present Perfect Continuous

2 marks for each correct answer. (10 marks)

1 How long have you been learning Spanish?
2 She's been working in London for two years.
3 Have you been waiting for a long time?
4 I've been reading this book all morning.
5 How long has Susan been cleaning the car?

D Reported sentences

2 marks for each correct anwer. (10 marks)

1 George's mother told him to go to sleep.
2 She asked him not to forget to brush his teeth.
3 She told him to get up early.
4 She told him not to watch television.
5 George asked his mother not to tell him what to do.

E Verb patterns: *if, when, as soon as, unless*

1 mark for each correct word underlined. 1 mark for each correct verb form. (10 marks)

1 If/'ll be   4 Unless/leave
2 When/finishes   5 If/do
3 'll phone/as soon as

F Verb patterns: verb + 2 objects

1 mark for each correct answer. (10 marks)

1 it/her   3 it/them   5 it/them
2 it/him   4 it/her

G Negatives

1 mark for a correct negative. 1 mark for choosing the correct sentence. (10 marks)

1 dishonest   3 nonsense   5 unpleasant
2 inexpensive   4 unkind

H *Do* or *make*?

One mark for the correct verb; one mark for the correct form. (10 marks)

1 done   3 did   5 made
2 make   4 made

I Sports (10 marks)

```
G A D E Q R B O O T S P
L C B L O P Q X Z L M N
O X R A F P I T C H A L
V B R A C K E T G K E O
E Y P O O L M A B Y P R
S P S O B A R F E D F C
O I L P H T R A C K L O
C G N J M L O T L R I U
R I N G Z J K P U O W R
R W S H O R T S B B X T
```

gloves, boots, pitch, track, racket, club, court, ring, shorts, pool

J Mixed vocabulary

1 mark for each correct answer. (5 marks)

1 lend   3 last   5 decorate
2 lie down   4 world record

K Punctuation

2 marks for each sentence. Take off half a mark for each mistake. (10 marks)

1 "You're very late," he said.
2 He shouted at me, "Stop." (or Stop!")
3 "Where are we?" I asked.
4 "I want a coffee," he told me.
5 "Be a good girl," her mother said.